THE MOTORCYCLE MOB

Angels today are more likely to wear suits than colors. They still value the grinning death's head, but keep it for funerals, runs, initiations, and laying heavies. Angels, like the undercover policemen who tail them, prefer street clothes to blend in with the surroundings. They've replaced their Harleys with Corvettes, Lincolns, and Cadillacs. The new mob shows class.

HELL'S ANGELS®

Call them the knights of the open road.
Call them something more sinister.

This is the book that calls them what they *are*, and tells it like it is.

HELL'S ANGELS

TAKING CARE OF BUSINESS

Yves Lavigne

BALLANTINE BOOKS • TORONTO

This book has been published with the assistance of the Canada Council and Ontario Arts Council under their block grant programs.

ISBN 0-345-36153-9

This edition published by arrangement with Deneau & Wayne Publishers Ltd.

Printed in Canada

First Ballantine Books Edition: June 1989

To two tiny souls who never had a chance:
July 16, December 3, 1986.
Fly high little guys.

A man may destroy everything within himself, love and hate and belief, and even doubt; but as long as he clings to life he cannot destroy fear; the fear, subtle, indestructible, and terrible, that pervades his being; that tinges his thoughts; that lurks in his heart; that watches on his lips the struggle of his last breath.

—JOSEPH CONRAD, *AN OUTPOST OF PROGRESS*

(Come in under the shadow of this red rock),
And I will show you something different from either
Your shadow at morning striding behind you
Or your shadow at evening rising to meet you
I will show you fear in a handful of dust.

—T.S. ELIOT, *THE WASTE LAND*

CONTENTS

ACKNOWLEDGMENTS

THE author wishes to thank the individuals and agencies that helped his investigation of the Hell's Angels Motorcycle Club. To name persons will jeopardize lives and investigations. Agencies that cooperated are the Broward County (Florida) Sheriff's Office, the US Bureau of Alcohol, Tobacco and Firearms, the US Drug Enforcement Administration, the US Federal Bureau of Investigation, the International Association of Chiefs of Police, the US Marshals Service, the Attorney-General's Office of California, the New York State Police, the Western States Information Network, the Florida Governor's Task Force on Organized Crime, the Pennsylvania Crime Commission, the Criminal Intelligence Service of Canada, the Sûreté du Québec, the Bureau de Recherches du Québec sur le Crime Organisé, the Ontario Provincial Police, Canada Customs, the Attorney-General's Office of British Columbia, the Royal Canadian Mounted Police, and several private investigators and researchers.

Special thanks to two people who taught me through a lifetime of example to work hardest when exhausted, to fight viciously against unbeatable odds, to come up swinging when knocked down, to ignore pain, to dare

intimidation, to speak freely, to challenge man's small-
ness, to respect the individual's quest for fulfilment, to
seek truth among lies, to find beauty in the commonplace, to hold on tight to my dreams, to love life and
plunge back in with bleeding wounds.

INTRODUCTION

THE Hell's Angels are the underside of the American dream—the American nightmare. The club turns 40 years old in name on March 17, 1988. It turned 40 in fact in the spring of 1987. The bikers who ride and plunder under the authority of the grinning, winged death's head have regaled and terrified the world over five decades with deeds of lust, violence and death. They are the gang out of which all outlaw motorcycle gangs grow, the primal ooze out of which the last link crawls, white trash on wheels.

The Hell's Angels, like other outlaw motorcycle gangs, reject society, its values, its laws. The Hell's Angels are predators. They take what they want, when they want it. They have, unfortunately, been romanticized since their birth as rugged individualists sorely misunderstood by a regimented society. Bleeding hearts and rednecks consider the Angels the last truly free men—those who dare break laws. It is a sorry myth bred in ignorance and man's willingness to smother in fantasy rather than chase his visions.

The myth must die.

The Hell's Angels Motorcycle Club, once an organization dedicated to bikes, booze and boobs, is now a multinational, multi-million dollar business that peddles drugs, pussy and death. Yesterday's rebels have become today's pushers, pimps and hit men. The Angels operate their criminal empires out of fortified clubhouses, not unlike the knights of old. They ride iron horses, fight holy wars with other gangs over the honor of club colors, loot and wench in their jealously guarded fiefdoms and rely in the end on the protection offered by the castle—the club.

The Hell's Angels are a way of life. They breathe death and drugs, prostitution, extortion, rape, intimidation and corruption, to name a few of their pastimes.

Fear helps the Angels in their quest for wealth. Violence is their guardian angel. Members and citizens alike live in terror of the club. The Hell's Angels' willingness and ability to take care of business helps them reign supreme among outlaw motorcycle gangs. They are the epitome, the extreme against which other gangs measure themselves. The Hell's Angels go farther faster and more determinedly than other bikers. They are better disciplined, better financed, better organized and better trained.

The Hell's Angels are both blessed and plagued by myths. Most inaccuracies about the club are created by the media and lazy law-enforcement officers who accept hearsay as fact and fill gaps in their knowledge with erroneous assumptions. Public literature and police intelligence reports are rife with useless crap about the club.

The bullshit might help cops boost their budgets, but it does nothing to combat the problem. Poor intelligence also endangers the lives of police officers.

The Hell's Angels are a formidable criminal organization. They are more cunning and better equipped than the police who track them. If they weren't so greedy and paranoid, if they weren't prone to killing their own members, if they didn't scare fellow Angels into becoming police informants, the Hell's Angels would rule the underworld. But the Hell's Angels have become victims of their own success. The sentimental notion of brotherhood that is supposed to bind the club has been eclipsed by fear and greed—the by-products of the drug business that is now the club's backbone.

Yet, the Hell's Angels may still become the over-lords of crime, surpassing even traditional organized crime families. Few organizations know how to take care of business as do the Hell's Angels.

PART

I

I

BORN TO BE WILD: A HISTORY OF THE HELL'S ANGELS

THEY tear out of war's wasteland into an America too slow for their feet and too fast for their minds. Their innocence lies smothered in the mud of Europe, the undergrowth of Asia, the creaking hulls that claw the ocean sands, the seared soil of Hiroshima. The land that receives them sucks at their heels like pungent earth on a fresh grave. Run, run, run. They chase life in the setting sun. They cling to youth where the earth shoves against the sea. In the darkest of night they howl through infinity on wheels of fire.

No man walks away from war unscathed. The worst wounds bleed through the eyes. A scream unhinged from the soul clatters through the light. Desperation feeds on death. Fury salvages the rest. A man tears into the wasteland looking for life.

Two generations cleanse the wicked wounds of war:

A literary fete flourishes in the decade of wanderlust that trails the armistice of 1918. Ernest Hemingway scribbles death and deceit in notebooks he optimistically brands with the mark of the rising sun. Wine and laughter flow in the bistros and high-ceiling flats of Paris. Every road leads to adventure or Spain. Every road leads home again.

A bankrupt nation prospers in 1945. Nuclear heat scorches soul and white-man's eyes as yellow man fries. Conquerors driven back into time. Barbaric hordes fester in the mind. Wait to be unleashed. Wildness, boredom, wanderlust. The many faces of Attila grate the Pacific mist . . . wait . . . for those born to be wild.

Pretenders court the beast.

Jack Kerouac cheats the icy Atlantic on a merchant ship. Takes to the road for a decade with poolhall-cool Denver Neal Cassady. Gets stoned. Screws. Sucks Allen Ginsberg's dick. Leaves baby driver in the rearview mirror. Returns to mama and writes the footloose bible. Throws up blood in The Galloping Gourmet's face. Dies with tuna on his breath. The fish gets him in the end.

Others answer the call. Leather aviator jackets. Trophy Nazi crosses. The warmth of Hitler's ashes on their cheeks. Follow the asphalt to Carmel and piss into the sea. Take to the road. Take the road. And stay. *They* are born to be wild.

California is a magnet for the footloose who buck the suburban fantasy as Amerika rebuilds on the corpse of Germany in 1945. They feast life with lust whetted by death and tempered with blood. The young who sacrifice youth to save democracy from Teutonic hordes and the yellow peril return home to exercise their choice. They create life on barren stretches of road at the continent's end. They wrap their legs around hulking, throbbing Harley-Davidsons, Indians and chase freedom in the sea-blown wind.

They work, ride, drink, ride, fight, ride. Youths without families form rag-tag groups. They hang around the garage. They roar around town. Hang around. Roar around. Life goes round. Up and down the coast: hang around, roar around. They create surrogate families: the Booze Fighters; the P.O.B.O.B.s—Pissed Off Bastards of Bloomington; the Market Street Commandos—for the intersection of Market and Leavenworth streets in San Francisco. They vent wild-eyed venom with fists, motorcycle chains and knives. Across the ocean, angry young men fight instead with words in ice-cold garrets.

Bikers terrorize California towns in national anonymity for two years. They chain-whip, gang bang and smash broken beer bottles into eye sockets. The wild ones roam highways unleashing hate with the flicker of a blade. Mindless forays into roadside surgery. Flayed flesh by the pound.

* * *

The rebels brand their hate into the nation's consciousness and forge forever the stench of terror that clings to motorcycle gangs when they take over the garlic capital of the world for three days in 1947. The Salinas Ramblers' Motorcycle Club and the Hollister Veterans' Memorial Park Association sponsor the 1947 Independence Day weekend Gipsy Tour in Hollister, south of Oakland. The American Motorcycle Association sanctions the annual racing and hill-climbing event. Bikers roar into town early on July 4. More than 4,000 motorcycles tear around the streets by nightfall. Those who sleep plop down in haystacks on the edge of town or crash on the courthouse lawn. Most bikers unleash 40 hours of drunken terror on the town.

The Booze Fighters and the P.O.B.O.B.s take over San Benito Street, Hollister's main drag. They drink, fight and piss with abandon. Bikers throttle their machines into bars and restaurants, run red lights and hold drag races in the streets. They throw thousands of beer bottles out hotel windows onto sidewalks and roads. The P.O.B.O.B.s demand that a jailed member be released from jail. The police refuse. The bikers rampage. The town's seven policemen are helpless. They call in 40 state highway patrolmen who threaten to use tear gas and drive the bikers out of town on July 6. Nearly 100 bikers are jailed and 50 persons injured during the three days. Police Commissioner Charles Krieger takes Hollister off the motorcycle racing map:

"It isn't going to happen here again. You can quote me on that."

He's right. More than 6,000 bikers converge on Riverside, California, during the Labor Day weekend two months later. The AMA and the California Highway Patrol sponsor the US championship 50-mile and 100-mile races that weekend. Drunken bikers decide to race down two blocks of city streets. William Gately, a 20-year-old local, crashes his motorcycle into a car Saturday night and walks away. Gloria Bigness, his 18-year-old girlfriend, dies on Sunday.

The American Motorcycle Association bars roving motorcycle gangs from membership for casting the sport into disrepute.

Riverside police are more optimistic than those in Hollister. They don't ban motorcycle races until after the Independence Day weekend of drinking, fist fights, flying beer bottles and firecrackers 11 months later. About 2,000 bikers and 3,500 pedestrians take over the town's main street on Saturday and Sunday nights after 100-mile dirt-track scrambles. One person dies in the melee. A US Forest Service fire truck hoses down the crowd while police arrest rioters.

Riverside Sheriff Carl F. Rayburn blames "a bunch of crazy kids" for the fighting. "They made their brag they would bring motorcycle racing into disrepute. The motorcycle boys are a bunch of good, clean sports. The trouble here was caused by a lot of riff-raff."

Rayburn labels the rebel bikers "outlaws" to differentiate them from law-abiding motorcyclists. The breed is christened; outlaw motorcycle gangs are born in an angry lawman's mouth. The bikers add another important word to the outlaw lexicon to further distance themselves from the straight world. The flyboys turned bikers call non-outlaws citizens—a variation on civilians. A member of the Missiles in Chicoutimi, Quebec, reflects in 1979 on the meaning of the label citizen:

> For us, it's like this: for us, a citizen, it doesn't mean someone we don't care nothing for or nothing like that. It means someone we can think of as a friend or someone like anyone here, but who . . . who doesn't think like us about bikes. For us, he's a citizen because, for us, there's this feeling we get on the bike, and for us, that's how we think. He's a citizen like any other. Like you could say we're different and use another word. I dunno. For us, that's our language. It's everywhere. . . . They can think like us or not and still be a citizen. If he don't have a patch on his back, for us, he's a citizen. 'Cause a biker is a biker and a citizen is a citizen. He can wear jeans and a leather jacket, cut-off sleeves and long hair and still not be a biker, 'cause a biker . . . he's like me.

Hollister and Riverside in 1947 and 1948 also give rise to another important biker tradition—the July 4th run. A jail term or hospitalization are the only legitimate excuses in most clubs to miss the run.

A wild generation crowds itself into the fringe of civilization reserved for nightmares in postwar America and defines itself with sporadic outbursts of fury. Gangs focus the hate.

Otto Friedli forges the most famous gang with disgruntled

P.O.B.O.B.s he assembles in 1947. The nameless gang forms its first chapter in San Bernardino on March 17, 1948. It adopts a name favored by World War II fighter-plane pilots later that year 12 miles west in Fontana—Hell's Angels. A seamstress sews their crest: a grinning, winged death's head wearing a leather aviator's helmet. The chapter name is shortened to Berdoo to fit on the bottom rocker on the back of the jacket. Dozens of seamstresses across the US produce the Hell's Angels colors for the club over the years. Ruby Clanton owns Clanton Monogram Service in Gastonia, North Carolina, in 1981. The 64-year-old woman sews colors for the Angels and the Outlaws in her house on Crescent Lane.

"Their money is as good as anybody else's," she says.

The clubs won't let Mrs. Clanton display the colors with those of other organizations, such as bowling leagues. And she deals only with presidents to prevent imposters from buying colors.

The bikers who choose the name Hell's Angels in 1948 are former pilots, bombardiers, navigators and gunners. They bring to earth a rebellious tradition bred in the cloudy battlefields of Europe, Africa and China. The club name goes farther back. Aviator Howard Hughes dumps his first wife Ella Rice for Hollywood in the middle of the flapper decade. The lanky 22-year-old Texan buys 87 planes for his first movie in 1927—a World War I flying epic with spectacular fight scenes that include a zeppelin raid over London. He calls the flick *Hell's Angels*. Hughes films the silent movie with Norwegian actress Greta Nissen in the lead role. He replaces her with Jean Harlow when talkies are introduced well into the filming and re-shoots the entire movie. Harlow makes them drool in the aisles when she slips into something more comfortable to seduce Ben Lyon. *Hell's Angels* makes money and fans.

Real-life aviators adopt the title of Hughes' movie as America sits back for the first years of World War II and watches Europe blast itself apart.

The transposition of American names in the Orient begins when an aggressive Japanese army attacks Chinese troops on the Marco Polo Bridge near Peking on July 7, 1937. Japan wants China and turns several years of land grabbing into all out war. It plans to isolate China from the coast and the world. The Japanese army takes Peking on July 28 and attacks

Shanghai. Nanking falls on December 12 and 80,000 Japanese soldiers kill 200,000 men and rape 20,000 women. Chiang Kai-shek flees with his army to Chungking from where he fights the Japanese and the provisional governments they set up in Peking and, later, Nanking.

Madame Chiang Kai-shek hires retired US General Claire L. Chennault in 1937 to set up an aviation school and airbases in China. Pilots call Chennault, the archetypal deeply tanned and wrinkled warrior, Old Leatherface.

"He looks as if he'd been holding his face out of a cockpit into a storm for years," one pilot says.

Chennault is a pioneer air tactician who argues the need for fighters as the US War Department states in the 1930s that bombers don't need protection. He is also a perfectionist barnstormer whose air show—three men on a flying trapeze—features a trick where three planes tied together with a string take off, perform intricate manoeuvres and land without snapping the cord.

Chennault suggests in 1941 that China use US volunteer pilots to fight the Japanese. The group is put together within months. The British lend the Chinese 100 Curtiss P-40 Warhawks. US army and navy reserve officers travel across the states and recruit pilots who must resign their commissions before they volunteer. Officially, the US pilots are recruited by the Central Aircraft Manufacturing Corporation, a subsidiary of International Aviation in New York City. One hundred pilots and 200 ground crew, including three doctors, one dentist, two female nurses and two medical orderlies sail to Burma on five ships. Three squadron leaders are paid $750 a month; seconds in command get $675 a month; pilots receive $600.

Chennault's American Volunteer Group—the Flying Tigers—trains in Burma and arrives in China in November 1941. The pilots paint white sharks' teeth in red mouths on the noses of their P-40s. They form three squadrons: the Panda Bears, Adam and Eve, the Hell's Angels. Dick Rossi, now 72, explains the origin of the names:

Panda Bears was chosen because it's typical of China. Hell's Angels goes back to World War I fighters; Adam and Eve was the first pursuit. Charlie Barnes drew up that insignia of Eve chasing

Adam with a red apple. But we didn't want red dots on our planes so we changed it to green.

The Flying Tigers go into action after the Japanese bomb Pearl Harbor on December 7. They decimate a squadron of Japanese bombers over Rangoon in December and force the Japanese to restrict their attacks to nighttime raids. The Japanese, who outnumber the Tigers 20 to one, lose 286 planes in seven months against six for the volunteers. The Hell's Angels protect Rangoon under the watchful eye of squadron commander Arvid Olsen—a footloose flyboy from San Bernardino.

The pilots are wild, cocky men between the ages of 20 and 26, with a few lying old-timers in the bunch. Chennault makes them expert fighters and a shortage of ammunition makes them cool-headed warriors. They become known as one-burst gunners—eight of 10 planes they shoot down are hit by the first burst of bullets.

The US enters the war and decides to absorb the free-wheeling Flying Tigers into the US Army Air Force's China Air Task Force, which later becomes the 14th Air Force. Only five Tigers enlist. About 80 return stateside to enlist in other branches of the service and 15 join the China National Air Corporation to fly supplies over the Himalayas. Dick Rossi flies more than 750 missions over the "hump." He explains why so few Flying Tigers stay with the US Army Air Force on July 4, 1942:

There were several reasons for not joining the 14th Air Force. They were operating on a shoestring budget and were short on supplies. The officious colonel who was recruiting started threatening the guys. They told him to shove it. We had a meeting and he told us he wanted no one to go home. If we did we'd end up buck privates. He was one of these people with no combat experience who feels he knows it all.

The pilots are too independent to put up with bureaucratic crap. They get flying jobs where they don't have to put up with tight-ass officers. Many of those who return to the US fly covert cross-Atlantic missions for the navy under guise of American Export Airline. The airline, whose front is American Export Steamship Lines, flies supplies into neutral Swit-

zerland. American Airlines buys the company after the war.
AA later sells it to Pan-American.

Arvid Olsen and some of his Hell's Angels take a different
route. They sign up with Major-General Orde Wingate to form
the 1st Commando Group that supplies the legendary Chindits
who fight a guerrilla war behind the lines in Burma. The
Chindits are named after the mythical beast Chinthe, which
lends its name to the Chindwin River. Olsen's group flies supplies and commandoes behind the lines in gliders to disrupt
communications and railroads. The Japanese foil the operation. They drag logs across the airstrip at night to wreck landing gliders. The rope between Olsen's glider and the tow plane
snaps one night. He crashes into the Irrawaddy River, but
manages to walk out. Wingate isn't as lucky. He dies when his
plane crashes in the jungle on March 24, 1944.

Pilots christen all planes and several groups of flyboys
adopt the name Hell's Angels during World War II. The US
303rd Bombardier Squadron in England is one of them. The
B-17s bomb Germany, refuel and take on bombs in North
Africa which they drop on Germany during the return flight.
The 303rd has a bomber called Hell's Angels. Its crew is wild.
The pilots come out of the cockpit half stewed. All they want
to do is drink and raise hell. No one wants to conform to
regulations. The name Hell's Angels seems to breed a tradition of nonconformity that makes heroes of wild youths on
many war fronts.

Olsen ends up in San Bernardino with former Hell's Angels
after the war. The West Coast draws flyboys like a shapely
pair of legs draws glances. The flyers exchange their wings
for wheels and form motorcycle gangs. Olsen tears around
with them, but doesn't join the gang that continues the tradition of the Hell's Angels.

The Hell's Angels work hard to create a scuzbag image.
They decorate their cutaways—later called colors—with Nazi
insignia to shock the squares. The racist connotation of wearing the swastika comes later. The original Angels just latch on
to the most revolting images they can find. Nothing is more
revolting than a Nazi in the late 1940s.

They try to cater to all senses and dump buckets of piss and
shit on prospects during lurid initiation ceremonies. The new

member lies on the floor and the woman with the cheesiest
twat sits on his face for an hour—after she's banged the boys.
Someone drips oil on his cutaway, which club rules forbid
washing. A woman bangs the club then squats over a prospect's colors and lets the sperm dribble out. The prospect in-
dulges the club's mascot—a dog. The Hell's Angels in their
early days stick their dicks into anything—a risky proposition
for your most prized possession.

The Hell's Angels are the first outlaw motorcycle gang of
note and set a trend that all gangs follow to this day. A biker
with a rural Quebec gang in 1979 embodies the spirit that
drives outlaw bikers since the beginning.

> Mebbe in the years to come, the next years, I think that, as for me,
> say I'm dead, I won't be a biker no more, but in the next years, so
> long as I'm alive, I'm gonna be a biker an' one day the world will
> change their mind, 'cause they'll know the difference between the
> clubs an' they'll see that some clubs, you know, trip out like I
> said, 40 years ago, eating on the go, raping women, beating peo-
> ple for nothing, old people on the streets to steal their money an'
> stuff like that.

Movies, in part, lend the Hell's Angels their name. Cinema
later gives them an ideal to strive for, a *raison d'être*, a dream
to chase in someone else's nightmare.

A young Hollywood director spreads shithead biker philosophy and helps the Hell's Angels' quest for notoriety when he
sparks an outlaw motorcycle gang cult with his 1954 film *The
Wild One*. Stanley Kramer is mesmerized by a *Harper's* magazine piece on the 1947 takeover of Hollister. He sees the
outlaw biker as America's last individualist—a motorized bo-
hemian hell-bent on living without the shackles of job and
family, who prefers to drink, fuck and fight his way through
life. Kramer helps make outlaw bikers—epitomized in real
life by the Hell's Angels—the symbol of rebellion for two
generations. Peter Fonda's *Easy Rider* entraps a third generation in 1969. Ironically, *Hell's Angels on Wheels* with Jack
Nicholson and legendary Hell's Angel Sonny Barger doesn't
have the same impact in 1967. The left-leaning media and
entertainment business, decades after Kramer, also sympathize
with cultists and fawn over weirdos like Charles Manson and
Jim Jones until they perform impromptu caesarian sections
and spike the communal Kool Aid.

Marlon Brando (the good biker) and Lee Marvin (the heavy biker) portray Kramer's wild young men who rebel against an unjust system that doesn't understand them. Actors like Brando and James Dean become idols by emulating punks—romantic portrayals that make heroes of misfits. Kramer and the movie makers who follow his lead spawn a self-perpetuating phenomenon where man begets myth and myth begets manhood. Outlaw bikers across the country vie to outdo each other imitating Brando's cool toughness.

The Wild One is such a hit with the brass-knuckle set that Frank Sadilek, president of the Hell's Angels San Francisco chapter—formed on August 1, 1954—drives to Hollywood to buy the blue-and-yellow striped T-shirt that Marvin wears in the movie. Sadilek is a powerful president whose reign from 1955 to 1962 boosts the club's notoriety and embellishes its tradition. He is elected president one year after the Market Street Commandos, hyped up by *The Wild One*, become the Frisco chapter of the Hell's Angels.

The paternalistic press tolerates the youthful rebelliousness of the Hell's Angels. The Associated Press wire service leads off with a romantic touch in its June 2, 1957, report on the bikers disrupting races at Angels Camp, California:

> Daredevil elements among 3,700 touring motorcyclists brought the lawlessness of the gold rush back to this sleepy mother lode town of 1,250 Saturday night, roaring at breakneck speed along the main street and littering the curbs with beer cans and bottles.

A 19-year-old warehouseman joins the Hell's Angels and forms the club's third chapter in Oakland on April 1, 1957. He has the date tattooed on his right shoulder. The green tattoo on his left arm—a snake coiled around a dagger—is the symbol of the US infantry. Ralph Hubert (Sonny) Barger Jr. drops out of 10th grade and joins the army in 1955. He completes basic training and advanced infantry training in 13 months before his honorable discharge for being too young. He's proud of the infantry's motto: "Death before dishonor." Barger also clings to his working-class roots in Modesto, California, where he is born in 1938. His mother abandons him. His grandmother and railway-worker father raise him in Oakland.

The intense, sinewy Barger is five foot ten and weighs 145

pounds. He is self-assured and charismatic. He is elected club president in 1958 when Otto Friedli is sentenced to jail. Barger moves the club's mother chapter north from Berdoo to Oakland. Friedli is an unknown in the ever shifting world of the Hell's Angels decades later, while Barger is accorded the status of a god.

Barger continues the Angel tradition of life on the lam. He leads the oil-stained greaseballs on weekend romps of terror as they drink and fight through the underside of the American dream. Sonny Barger makes his public debut as club president in 1958 when he gets his skull bashed in a riot quelled by five carloads of policemen. Rumbles. Shootouts. Boys just wanna have fun.

The American Motorcycle Association tries after the Hollister and Riverside debacles to put some distance between its members and outlaw bikers who give motorcyclists a bad name. Successive AMA presidents impress on the public that only one percent of motorcyclists are outlaws.

George (Baby Huey) Wethern, former vice-president of the Hell's Angels Oakland chapter, describes in his 1978 book, *A Wayward Angel*, how the club and outlaw bikers use the AMA statement to bind the brotherhood.

In early 1960, Ralph (Sonny Barger) and I putted across the Bay Bridge to the home of Frisco president Frank Sadilek. The Hell's Angels statewide leadership, including representatives from Southern California, was sprawled around the room tilting gallon jugs of red wine. Interspersed were leaders of clubs like the Gypsy Jokers, Road Rats, Galloping Gooses, Satan's Slaves, a North Beach club called the Presidents and the Mofos, a funky outfit that looked more like winos than bikers. (The Mofos was a contraction for 'motherfuckers.')

It was a historic gathering, sort of like the Yalta conference. Clubs that had traded stompings and chain whippings for years were parleying over a mutual problem—police harassment.... And we kicked around a hostile statement from the American Motorcycle Association, the Elks Club of biking. To draw a distinction between its members and us renegades, the AMA had characterized ninety-nine percent of the country's motorcyclists as clean-living folks enjoying pure sport. But it condemned the other one percent as antisocial barbarians who'd be scum riding horses or surfboards too.

The Angels and our friends, rather than being insulted, decided to exploit the glowing tribute. We voted to ally under a 'one percenter' patch. As a supplement to regular colors, it would identify the wearer as a righteous outlaw. The patch also could help avoid counterproductive infighting, because an Angel, Mofo or any one percenter would be banded against a common enemy.

Everyone knew the patch was a deliberately provocative gesture, but we wanted to draw deep lines between ourselves and the pretenders and weekenders who only played with motorcycles.

Buoyed by the alliance and wobbly from wine, the outlaws dispersed to all corners of the state to inform their troops and to order patches. Sonny and I mounted our Harleys, zonked yet obsessed with outdoing the rest. A little patch may have been adequate for the other one percenters, but not for us. A trans-bay ride took us to Rich's tattoo parlor in downtown Oakland. After a briefing, Rich's needle made biker history. Although I was too drunk to know it until the next morning, Sonny and I had the first of the famous one percenter tattoos—a symbol that likely will survive as long as outlaw gangs.

Soon our Oakland brothers were lining up for theirs. We were beginning to believe our own mystique. As we stacked a few rules and rituals on the simple foundation of motorcycle riding, we thought we were building a little army. But in fact, it was a rough blueprint of a secret society.

Outlaw bikers take the one-percenter patch seriously. Ray Lindsay, a six-foot-two, 220-pound outlaw who can bench press 405 pounds, applies for Hell's Angels membership in September 1984, from his cell in Ulster County Prison in New York State. He has the one percent tattoo on his back, his chest, both arms and on his dick.

Barger doesn't harbor Robin Hood delusions as he leads the Angels into ritual bloodlettings. He is asked if he considers himself a thug.

A thug? Probably a hoodlum. I don't know about a thug. See, the one thing that the police and everybody fail to say when they charge us with these so-called, uh, what do we call it, heinous crimes against society . . . they refuse to admit that there is more than one society here. You know? There's the lower class element, I guess you would call it, or the criminal society or the people on the fringes of it. And then there's what you would call normal society.

And the majority of people that have been hurt by Hell's Angels, you know—the majority of people involved in any crime that was against them by a Hell's Angel—has been somebody in the same element that we're in. What I'm saying is we don't go out and attack society. The only citizens that ever get hurt by us come to us looking for trouble.

Barger works as a machine operator from 1960 to 1965. He loses the job for taking too much time off. His main income until 1973, he says, comes from advising two film companies that make movies about Hell's Angels. Barger stars with Jack Nicholson in *Hell's Angels on Wheels* in 1967, the same year Hunter Thompson immortalizes him in his book, *Hell's Angels, The Strange and Terrible Saga of the Outlaw Motorcycle Gangs*.

Barger's foresight, drive and cunning shapes the Hell's Angels into the fearsome gang it is today. Sonny Barger does for the Hell's Angels what Lee Iacocca does for Chrysler Corp.—he converts a sloppy, rudderless organization into a lean, mean, no bullshit company. He trims idiot cavemen from chapter rosters and embarks on an expansionist course that swells the club from six chapters in 1965 to 67 in 1987. The assimilation of other motorcycle gangs by the Hell's Angels in the 1970s and 1980s differs only in bloodshed from the corporate takeovers that shake Wall Street. Taking over a club is a business transaction. The target club buries its corporate colors and takes on those of the new parent company. It contributes to the head-office treasury and in return receives expert advice and support when needed. Takeovers get sloppy when the sought-after club seeks shark repellent and allies with other gangs to fight off the suitor. But most gangs willingly join the world's most feared outlaw bikers.

The Hell's Angels, because of their military background, are rabid patriots. Barger describes Hell's Angels loyalty as the US sinks into Vietnam in 1964:

"Our oath is allegiance to the United States of America. If there should be trouble we would jump to enlist and fight. More than 90 percent of our members are veterans. We don't want no slackers."

Barger reiterates his position one year later in a telegram to President Lyndon B. Johnson that he reads at a press conference on Friday, November 19, 1965:

Dear Mr. President:

  On behalf of myself and my associates I volunteer a group of
loyal americans for behind the lines duty in Viet Nam. We feel that
a crack group of trained gòrrillas [sic] would demoralize the Viet
Cong and advance the cause of freedom. We are available for
training and duty immediately.

                          Sincerely
                          RALPH BARGER JR.
                          Oakland, California
                          President of Hell's Angels

  The Hell's Angels, despite their outrageous behavior,
spend 16 years in near anonymity as they tear strips off California ass and plug pussy. Two hysterical teenage twats make
them world-famous during the Labor Day run in Monterey on
September 6, 1964. The 14- and 15-year-old girls tear into the
Monterey cop shop and scream rape. The cry shrinks every
righteous dick in the bunch. The cops tear out to the run site,
block the highway, arrest 46 Angels and finally nail the four
largest, hairiest and freakiest bikers with the rape—Terry
the Tramp, (Mouldy) Marvin Gilbert, Mother Miles and Fillmore
(Crazy) Cross.

  Newspapers report how the beasts drag the sweet young
things away from their dates on the beach and hump them in
the dunes. The story spreads along the coast like a dose in a
fern bar. Not as much attention is paid to a September 25th
letter from the Monterey County district attorney, who requests the charges be dropped because a doctor finds no evidence of rape, one girl refuses to testify and the other is
deemed unreliable by a lie-detector test.

  The false charges, ironically, force the club into the rank
underworld of large-scale speed manufacturing and drug trafficking. The Hell's Angels do anything for kicks in the early
1960s. Little white pills stretch their lives into the desperate
crash of dawn. But the Angels, like all greaseballs, prefer
booze to drugs. They deal a little weed and speed, but only to
skim a bit for themselves.

  The Angels are a financially unstable club in the early
1960s. The guys who work have menial jobs that pay for rent,
gas, oil and booze. Legal costs incurred after the Monterey
rape charges leave the Angels hard up for cash. The Hell's
Angels are on the brink of extermination. One hefty push by
the police can topple them. They need money to survive.

Some members decide to sell speed to recoup losses—a one-shot deal. An Angel contacts a chemist and gets the formula to manufacture methamphetamine. Easy money hooks them and a bid to top up club coffers turns into an international enterprise.

The Angels are virtually unknown outside California in early 1965. Thomas C. Lynch, the state's attorney general, becomes an unwitting partner in the largest publicity coup of the decade with his annual report on crime in early March. The report lists 18 incidents of violence that involve Hell's Angels. An intelligent reader would notice that only two—bar fights—occur after the alleged Monterey rape in September 1964. Everything else is old news, including the alleged rape. The *New York Times* California correspondent rewrites the institutional news like a good, albeit inaccurate, stenographer on March 16. The hyped report and subsequent matchers by *Time* and *Newsweek* turboboost the Hell's Angels to national stardom. An irreversible myth is born.

Time and *Newsweek* blur the line between reality and fiction when they compare the Angel takeover of Porterville in 1963 to a similar debacle depicted in *The Wild One*. The comparison starts a nonsensical chicken-egg debate in which turdbrain pseudo-intellectuals say the film causes bikers to take over towns. The ignorant draw smug satisfaction from constipated logic.

The Hell's Angels, with four chapters and a group of homeless nomads in California, and one chapter in Auckland, New Zealand, become the official US nightmare early in 1965. The stigma boosts membership at a time when the club is in its worst shape ever. Another chapter is added to the club roster within months—the Nomad chapter chartered on June 1, 1965. The legend grows with every press, television and radio interview. The Angels begin to understand power.

The Hell's Angels and hippies are bound to meet sooner or later in the mid-1960s. Hunter S. Thompson makes it sooner. Thompson hangs out with the Angels three days a week in 1965. His socially acute antennae tell him the phenomenon is ripe for a book. And, what the fuck, Thompson also likes action and drugs—an appetite that later earns him the honorary title "doctor."

Thompson is the future of journalism in 1965. He's crapped out his share of hack stories and flexes his brain to push back the envelope that restricts his mind. He heads to San Francisco to expand an April 1965 piece that appears in *The Nation*. The Hell's Angels are badass punks, but not heavy-duty drug dealers or killers. They prefer breaking heads and breaking in engines and women. They also have broken the publicity barrier and soar on a wave of notoriety. The *New York Times*, *Life*, the *Saturday Evening Post* and *True, The Man's Magazine*, blow the minds of eastern straights with sordid, inaccurate tales of rape and carnage in the far west.

Thompson puts back beer with Oregon wildman Ken Kesey in a San Francisco bar one summer day in 1965. Kesey's novel, *Sometimes a Great Notion*, is one year old. The author becomes famous for an earlier novel—*One Flew Over the Cuckoo's Nest*—but his 1964 book remains his generation's best tribute to individualism. Kesey is a pioneer in drugs and mind expansion in the 1960s. He trips around with his Merry Pranksters, bodies decked out in day-glow, minds stretched out on LSD. The legendary Neal Cassady, stud extraordinaire and literature's muscleman manic, chauffeurs the weirdos around in a hippie colored bus with a destination sign that reads "Furthur." Cassady is a natural speed freak who blasts through life on a timetable that ends sometime during a cold Mexican night three years later, when he passes out and dies of exposure while he counts railway ties on a desolate stretch between two towns on February 4, 1968. The Holy Goof succumbs to goofballs.

Thompson takes Kesey to the Box Shop garage after they finish their beer and introduces him to some Angels. Kesey invites the club to his place in La Honda for a bash on Saturday, August 7. Forty Angels led by Sonny Barger are greeted by a sign that reads: "THE MERRY PRANKSTERS WELCOME THE HELL'S ANGELS." The hippies have just spread their legs and the Hell's Angels' dicks begin to drip. The freaked-out pranksters ply the Angels with LSD and usher them into the world's largest mass consumer market for illicit drugs—the Haight-Ashbury community. The Angels meet the new left intelligencia—like poet Allen Ginsberg and acid guru Richard Alpert—who help them gain acceptance among the hippies.

The honeymoon between left and right lasts two months.

The first clash between the hippies and the Angels—a warning the dinks fail to heed—occurs on October 16, 1965, when police stop thousands of anti-war marchers en route to the Oakland Army Terminal from the Berkeley campus, then stand aside while the Hell's Angels tear into the crowd and bash heads. One Angel snaps a policeman's leg with a kick.

Barger announces that a larger contingent of Angels will disrupt the November 20th anti-Vietnam march. Kesey, Ginsberg, Pranksters, and left-wing intelligencia meet with the Angels at Barger's house and try to persuade the club to respect their exercise in democracy. Barger sneers at the Commies.

But Barger is already thinking business in 1965. He balances the worth of bashing a few lefties against the negative effect on the club balance sheet. The Angels don't want to alienate potential customers. The Oakland president calls a press conference on November 19 and hands out a self-serving press release that illustrates his finely honed ability to take care of business—regardless of the cost in personal and club neo-fascist pride. Sonny Barger does not let ideology stand in the way of making money.

> Although we have stated our intention to counterdemonstrate at this despicable, un-American activity, we believe that in the interest of public safety and the protection of the good name of Oakland, we should not justify the V.D.C. [Vietnam Day Committee] by our presence . . . because our patriotic concern for what these people are doing to our great nation may provoke us to violent acts . . . any physical encounter would only produce sympathy for this mob of traitors.

The Hell's Angels spawn imitators from the day they adopt their name in 1948. Every incidence of violence sends more bikers tearing around the streets with fake Hell's Angels colors. The Angels realize after the media attention they get in 1965 that their name is worth money. The club incorporates and issues 500 shares in California in 1966 for the "promotion and advancement of motorcycle driving, motorcycle clubs, motorcycle highway safety and all phases of motorcycles and motorcycle driving." The Hell's Angels emblem—the flying death's head—receives Patent No. 926-590 from the United States Patent Office on January 4, 1972.

* * *

Hunter Thompson contributes to the momentum of the Hell's Angels myth with publication in 1967 of his book on the bikers as he knows them in 1965. Mush-brain pseudo-intellectuals who like to surround themselves with folk heroes court Sonny Barger. The Angels become tokens in the battle of one-upmanship among the ponderous left. They are careful, however, not to invite more than a few Angels at a time—with colors—to their parties. The relationship is typical of the 60s—both sides use each other.

The love affair comes to a brutal end 50 miles east of San Francisco on December 6, 1969 at the Altamont Speedway in Livermore. The city's other claim to fame is Sharon Marie Gruhlke, who wins the Maid of Livermore beauty pageant at 19 and captures Sonny Barger's heart. The Rolling Stones hire the Hell's Angels for $500 in beer to protect them from a crowd of 300,000. The English Hell's Angels act as security at the July 5, 1969 free Stones concert in Hyde Park that attracts 250,000 fans. That concert is uneventful. Altamont isn't. Barger describes the reaction as his column of choppers arrives at Altamont early in the day:

> It was out of sight. They got up and moved real nice. Some people offered us drinks on the way down. . . . One broad jumped up and said something pertaining to a four-letter word about an Angel and that Angel asked his old lady if she was going to let them talk about the Angels like that. She jumped off the bike and smacked the other broad . . . got back on and proceeded down. No problem.

The Angels bash heads from the moment they park their bikes in front of the stage. They take any request by the announcer for the crowd to calm down as a cue to charge in with chopped-down pool cues. The Stones take the stage after sunset. David and Albert Maysles' documentary of the last leg of the Stones' tour—*Gimme Shelter*—records a macabre slaughter within spitting distance of the band.

An Angel near the stage is offended by the pairing of a black man and a white woman as Jagger raunches out "Sympathy for the Devil." Angel Alan David Passaro punches 18-year-old Meredith (Murdock) Hunter, who is trapped by a wall of flesh. The Hell's Angels creed requires members to help when a brother gets into a fight. Other Angels charge in. Hunter pulls a gun. Passaro knifes him. Meaty fists hack at Hunter's head with blades and expose his brain. Hunter falls to his knees. Patty Bredehoft, his girlfriend, tries to get help. Angels stop her.

"Don't touch him. He's going to die anyway. Let him die. He's going to die."

Jagger stops singing. The music dies. The Prince of Darkness pleads to the crowd.

"Brothers, sisters, come now. We can cool out. Everybody be cool. Come now."

Jagger looks over to where the Angels kill Hunter.

"How are we doing over there? Everybody all right? Can we still collect ourselves? I don't know what happened. . . . Everybody just cool down. Okay? I think we're cool. We can groove. We always have something funny happen when we start that number."

Angels kick, stomp and stab Hunter as he lies on the ground. He rolls over.

"I wasn't going to shoot you."

An Angel thumps Hunter with a garbage can, kicks his head, then does a headstand beside the body and walks away.

Media coverage of the Hell's Angels in the mid-1960s spreads notoriety of the California phenomenon eastward. Many motorcycle clubs write the Angels and ask for a charter. California doesn't want whimps on its roster. One man on the East Coast is driven enough by his desire to become a Hell's Angel that the club gives him a chance late in 1966. Donald (Skeets) Picard, president of the local motorcycle club in Lowell, Massachusetts, negotiates a bold deal with the Oakland chapter. He offers to take his entire club to California to prospect. Picard leads a cavalcade of 30 bikers across the country. The West Coast Angels are rough on them. Distance will weaken their control over an eastern chapter and they want to ensure the new Angels won't give the club a bad name.

Picard's bikers meet every Hell's Angel in the world during their six-month stay in California and learn about being Angels from the men who shape the club. Picard's gang becomes a Hell's Angel chapter on April 17, 1967. Only half the prospects make the grade. Picard and the Lowell chapter are held in the highest esteem by other eastern Angels to this day. They are considered real Hell's Angels, not a bunch of bikers who get their colors by mail. No other motorcycle club has had the balls to ride to California to prospect and no eastern chapter is closer to the West Coast Angels. Picard is now retired after spending 10 years in jail. He is one of the few members to leave the club who will always be considered a Hell's Angel.

The fate of the second East Coast chapter remains a sore point with most oldtime Hell's Angels. The Buffalo, New York, Road Vultures negotiate long distance for a charter in 1968. Sonny Barger and West Coast Angels come east to party with the Lowell chapter. They stop in Buffalo on the way home and give the Vultures their charter. Most chapter members are arrested in the early 1970s, causing the chapter to violate the club's standing rule that six members are needed on the road to retain a charter. The Hell's Angels don't like to use the word "dissolve." The Buffalo chapter is "frozen" by Oakland. The club still owns the Ogden Street clubhouse, which is registered in Rochester. Buffalo Angels join the Rochester chapter and most East Coast Angels want the chapter reopened.

The third Hell's Angels chapter on the East Coast produces some of the club's most powerful men. It also is the focus of a minor dispute that gives rise to an all-out war with the Outlaws in 1974. The Aliens Motorcycle Club is a badass New York City biker gang with chapters in Queens, the Bronx, Staten Island and Manhattan in the 1960s. A California boy and Hell's Angels hang-around called Sandy Frazier Alexander joins the club in 1967 when he moves to New York. It doesn't take him long to realize the Aliens are not true outlaw bikers. They commit crimes for the mob, not for themselves. They're gophers on wheels.

Alexander is a tough motherfucker and ultra-right Cuban nationalist who hates Fidel Castro. Alexander's family, which prospers under dictator Fulgencio Batista, flees to the United States when Alexander is seven to escape the impending Communist rule. Alexander enlists in the US Marine Corps at 18 and learns to kill with his hands in the reconnaissance unit.

New York sweats electric day-glow decadence in 1967 in anticipation of the summer of love. The Electric Circus disco short-circuits optic nerves with strobe lights and baffles the ears with onslaughts of sound. A young actor from California called Sandy Alexander works there as a clown and trapeze artist doing somersaults above the bar.

William (Wild Bill) Medeiros hits the Big Apple after he is discharged from the US Marine Corps in 1967. He pals around with the clown at the Electric Circus. Medeiros joins the Aliens too. Alexander decides after a few months the club is too wimpy for him. His brute charisma convinces 13 Aliens to break away and form a Nomad chapter. They rent a basement apartment at 77 East Third Street in 1968. The rebels realize in 1969 that even a Nomad Alien isn't a real biker. Alexander heads off to California to ask the Angels for a charter. Fellow Alien Peter A. (Greased Lightning) Rogers (who uses the alias Courtney) allegedly rapes Alexander's wife Collette while he is away and runs south. Alexander searches in vain for the alleged rapist and puts out the word on the street he wants Rogers alive.

Every gang that prospects for the Hell's Angels has to wear prospect colors without the grinning death's head. Alexander's hardcore bikers agree to prospect, but refuse to part with their Alien colors until they get Angel colors. The West Coast Angels show up at an East Coast run in Laconia, New Hampshire, in 1969. They are offended by the Aliens' red on white patches. The Angels won't allow other clubs to use the color combination. The Aliens don't back down when threatened and only serious negotiations prevent a rumble. Alexander's Aliens become the Hell's Angels Manhattan chapter in New York City on December 5, 1969. Rochester joins the club the same day. The Hell's Angels are well entrenched on the East Coast as they roar into the 1970s.

Sandy Alexander flourishes as a leader and Wild Bill Medeiros gets swept up in his rise to power. Alexander wants his Manhattan chapter members to epitomize Angeldom. He demands unquestioning loyalty. Prospects must murder to earn their colors. Wild Bill Medeiros, as security officer, keeps files at home on club enemies, complete with maps locating clubhouses, places of employment and interior diagrams of houses. Prospects leaf through the files and pick five potential hits. They must return to the club with a newspaper clipping to prove the target is dead. Medeiros files the clipping.

Sandy Alexander's power and influence rivals that of Sonny Barger by the mid-1970s. John (Pirate) Miller is a member of the Grateful Dead Motorcycle Club in Bridgeport, Connecticut, when it becomes a Hell's Angels chapter on February 17, 1975. Only 15 of 100 Grateful Dead are deemed man enough to be Angels. Miller transfers to the Manhattan chapter in 1980 where he becomes assistant sergeant-at-arms. He comments on Alexander's power:

"They refer to Sandy Alexander and Sonny Barger as Hell's Angels in stereo."

Alexander, like most Angels, is violently against injected drugs such as heroin. The Manhattan clubhouse at 77 East Third Street sits between First and Second Avenue on the Lower East Side. This section of Manhattan is plagued by junkies—except for the block on which the Angels live. The club won't allow heroin on the street and protects everyone on the block. The Angel heroin extermination program includes ripping off junkies, flushing their junk down toilets and smashing their hypes. They also take their cash, often as much as $4,000 in stolen money stuffed in pockets and shoes. The Angels boast they are more successful than federal authorities at getting heroin off the streets.

Alexander imposes on his chapter a tight structure he adapts from the marine corps. He requires members to work under a buddy system so one Angel can continue the business if his partner is arrested. This way, the club reaps the benefits without having to know where the money comes from.

Sandy Alexander is a powerhouse in the 1970s and early 1980s. His power fades with his arrest on May 2, 1985, and members find out he is screwing the club. Alexander owns half of the Manhattan clubhouse; members own the other half. At least that's what they think. Alexander secretly registers the ownership in his name before the arrest. The Angels don't attend his court hearings, except for the one at which he is sentenced. Alexander is serving a 16-year prison sentence for drug offences. His world caves in with the clang of prison doors. The club worries he's so despondent he'll roll over. They consider killing him, but decide not to. Alexander is finished with the Hell's Angels. He has no influence and can't demand anything of the men he molded into his vision of Hell's Angels.

Brendan Manning replaces Alexander as president of the

Manhattan chapter. Manning is well-liked on the West Coast and wears an Oakland headband. He is growing in stature and power and is the future of the Hell's Angels on the East Coast.

The Hell's Angels grow like a dick in a tight twat in the early 1970s with Alexander and Barger at their peaks. Although the myth of the loveable rebels dies with Altamont, a 1972 trial reveals how opportunistic and untrustworthy the Angels are all along. They deal with anyone to save their asses. Barger and three other Angels are acquitted on December 29, 1972, in the murder of 29-year-old Texas cocaine courier Servio Winston Agero, who allegedly sells them $80,000 in useless coke. Barger says he's in bed with girlfriend Sharon Gruhlke when Agero is shot while asleep, dumped into a bathtub and burned inside his torched house. The trial embarrasses police when Barger reveals the Hell's Angels' deal with Oakland Police Sergeant Ted Hilliard from 1967 to 1972. Hilliard fears left-wing terrorists like the Weather Underground and the Black Panthers are arming themselves. The Angels agree to buy all weapons and explosives on the black market for the police if they turn a blind eye to club activities.

"Mr. Barger would load them in the back of my car—automatic rifles and dynamite," says Hilliard, who denies giving the Hell's Angels protection.

Barger also offers to deliver the bagged body of a leftist for every Angel released from jail. Hilliard won't deal.

The cops finally put Barger on ice in 1973 when he is sentenced to 10 years for possession of heroin for sale and possession of marijuana and other drugs. He is paroled from Folsom Prison on November 3, 1977, after his lawyers convince the California Supreme Court the sentence is aimed at his link to the Hell's Angels rather than at the crime.

The Hell's Angels keep a low profile while they wheel and deal in the 1970s. They show, while Sonny Barger is jailed, that the club can function without a leader. They get down to business while their market gets down and boogies. The Angels build their reputation for violence by emulating Brando in *The Wild One*. They build up their business, war fund and treasury by imitating Brando in *The Godfather*.

Policemen are slow to realize just how involved the Hell's

Angels are in drug trafficking. When they do find out, they flub their first major attempts to ice the club.

The US Government decides to take on the Hell's Angels in June 1979. It charges 32 people, including most of the Oakland chapter and Sonny Barger's wife Marie, with violating the Racketeer-Influenced and Corrupt Organizations (RICO) statute. The case is known as The United States of America vs. Ralph Barger Jr., et al. The indictment—the most comprehensive case ever compiled against the club—alleges that the Hell's Angels deal in drugs, weapons and death.

"The cornerstone of this illegal drug enterprise was the large-scale manufacture and mass distribution of methamphetamine, also known as speed and crank," US Attorney G. William Hunter says.

"The club's bylaws clearly spell out that members will engage in distribution of drugs of a specified quantity and quality in order to remain members," Jerome Jenson, regional director of the US Drug Enforcement Administration, says.

The government is cocky and "federal sources" tell newspapers the case against the club is "airtight."

Barger's bail is set at $1 million. The government tries to protect against fuck ups. Bulletproof plexiglass is installed between the audience and participants. People entering the 17th-floor courtroom are checked twice for weapons. A sign outside the door reads: "NO BELT BUCKLES OVER TWO INCHES: NO EXCEPTIONS." Twelve jurors and six alternates are chosen so the case isn't aborted by juror illness. They are given folders with photographs of the accused. Blank space is left on each page for jurors to make notes on them. US District Judge Samuel (Hanging Sam) Conti presides. Would-be presidential assassin Sara Jane Moore and Black Panther David Hilliard know his sting.

A 41-year-old Barger draws first blood on the trial's opening day. Conti orders a photograph taken of the defendants sitting together. Barger places a binder over his face.

"Take that down," Conti says. He threatens to have the president of the Oakland chapter put in a holding cell.

Barger lowers the binder, but looks away from the camera.

"Face forward," Conti barks.

"I don't want my picture taken," Barger says softly.

FLASH.

"Well, you've just gotten your picture taken," Conti says. "Great. Take it home with you."

Barger is 10 years older than the 31-year-old Hell's Angels Motorcycle Club in 1979.

"I never thought I'd live to be 40," he says. "To me, when I was 20 years old, 40 years old was just an age that, you know, when you got that old you should have been dead."

His first wife, Elsie, doesn't make it. She dies at 24 after an illegal abortion in 1967. Barger remembers her with a tattoo on his right arm shaped like a tombstone cross lettered with the word *BARGER*.

Sonny Barger leads the Hell's Angels through their wildest and toughest times as club chapters become involved in multimillion dollar operations and embark on a course of success that any corporate executive would envy.

"I can tell you why they want to get rid of the Hell's Angels," Barger says in San Francisco county jail in 1979.

First of all, we're a virtual army. We're all across the country, and now we're in foreign countries also. And they have no idea how many of us there are. We have money, many allies that are outlaw bikers that are not Hell's Angels, that would probably do anything we asked them to, if something happened. Like a revolution. Or anything like that.

They know we're basically the most probably well-armed people in the United States. We've never took a political stance on anything other than that one time against the V.D.C. [at the Oakland-Berkeley border in October 1965] and at that time I thought we were right, but I've done 180 degrees on that since . . . and I think that scares the authorities—this untold number of people that really have no fear of dying for what they believe in. And they're armed. And they won't commit themselves to one side or the other. And I think that's where it lies.

The government has been against the Hell's Angels since the club started, Barger says.

They tried to paint us as rowdies, you know, we're sort of against society, or whatever, just drink beer and tough guys that didn't get along with anybody. And when that didn't work, it changed to marijuana-smoking-crazed, you know. And when that didn't work, then it became drug dealing.... They needed something to go after that's visible. And we're a highly visible group.

While the government fears and hates the Hell's Angels, Barger feels the public loves the wild ones.

I just don't know what it is [he says]. I think we probably stand for what the majority of people would like to be. But they just, you know, maybe not what they would like to be, but maybe they have a vision that at least once they'd like to just get on a motorcycle and roar down the street and somebody would sneer at them and they'd punch them in the nose.

Four months into the trial of 18 Hell's Angels, Judge Conti harshly criticizes prosecutors on January 22, 1980, for their poor witnesses and threatens to throw the case out of court.

"It's a big waste of time to listen to witnesses like this. If this was solely the evidence, I would grant an acquittal."

The 57-year-old judge faints twice in court from exhaustion on February 15. The jury begins deliberations on June 15 after eight months of testimony by more than 100 prosecution witnesses who accuse the Angels of threatening and murdering to protect a lucrative speed, heroin, LSD and cocaine business. The defence argues that individual Angels commit crimes without club support or endorsement. Barger tells the court he uses and sells heroin and other drugs during the 1960s. Such matters are his "personal affairs," not those of the club.

He sways the jury.

Judge Conti declares a mistrial on July 2, 1980, after the jury announces it can't reach verdicts on 32 of 44 counts against 18 defendants. The government's multi-million dollar attempt to prove the Hell's Angels Motorcycle Club is a rough and tumble Mafia fails. Undaunted prosecutors prepare for a retrial.

Sonny Barger's bail is dropped to $100,000 on August 1 and he is a free man after spending 14 months in jail. The government drops charges against Barger and his wife on August 6 "in the interest of justice." Prosecuting attorneys "restructure" their case against 11 Hell's Angels and are back in court on October 3. A federal district judge declares a mistrial on February 24, 1981, when the jury fails to reach a verdict. The government dismisses all charges the next day. Jurors in both trials are bothered by attempts to convict an organization. They also are disturbed that prosecution witnesses are granted immunity for serious crimes in return for testimony. One former Hell's Angel is given $54,000 and immunity for six murders.

"They let these people off, people who committed more crimes than the people they were trying. I felt I just couldn't believe them," William Aylward, a 44-year-old juror from San Jose who votes for acquittal, says.

Government lawyers estimate the cost of trying to convict the club at $4 million to $7 million. Defence lawyers peg the price tag at $10 million to $20 million.

The myth of Sonny Barger that starts with massive media coverage in 1965 is bolstered by trial evidence and testimony during the next decade and a half and peaks with the nation's young blood wearing "Free Sonny Barger" T-shirts during the 1979–1980 RICO trial. The portrait that emerges of the rebel hero flatters an outlaw, but frightens the lawful.

James Crew, Barger's lawyer in the 1972 murder trial: "He lands on his feet when he's in a tight spot."

A former cellmate: "Ralph's philosophy is when somebody is doing something wrong to you, it's not for you to judge. Kill him first, and let God be the judge."

Anonymous man: "If Sonny ever asks for a favor, you do it. That's all. You can drop out, but if the club ever feels it needs you, they can call on you. If you screw up, they'll kill you. That's just an accepted method of conduct."

An anonymous person close to the club: "Barger was the one who could harness and direct Angel power. He had a sophistication that no other Angel leader had. He was the first one who saw the whole picture and how he could use the Angels to make a million."

A policeman: "Barger could put his hands on an armory that could outfit a Central American army. He had everything from Viet Cong machine guns to American-made pistols and hand grenades. He had parts of weapons that hadn't even been released by army ordnance yet. The troops didn't even have them."

* * *

Nature deals Sonny Barger his toughest blow. Barger steps down as Oakland president—he also relinquishes the position while jailed in the 1970s—to have his cancerous larynx removed in May 1983. But even the shadow of death doesn't keep the man down. The convalescing biker comes across a depressed patient in a wheelchair as he walks the hospital grounds. He pushes the man up a hill, jumps onto the wheelchair and bombs down with him.

Barger is back on the road for the Angels' Memorial Day run to Bass Lake one week after his release from hospital. His wife Sharon accompanies him on a motorcycle he gives her on Valentine's Day. Angels who talk with Barger at Bass Lake must put their ears to the blowhole in his throat or read his written comments on a notepad.

Michael (Irish) O'Farrell, whose favorite dish is macaroni and cheese, fills in as Oakland president while Barger recovers. O'Farrell lives in a part of town the club dubs Madness Mountain because of all the Angels who live in the area. His wife Teddy brings up their son Eddie in the best Angel tradition. Black children chase him home from school one day. Teddy pushes him out and watches his first fight.

"It was hard."

Membership in outlaw motorcycle gangs swell in the late 1960s and early 1970s with a second wave of disgruntled warriors—soldiers from the Vietnam War bring to the gangs much needed explosives and weapons skills as well as military contacts who arm the clubs.

The Hell's Angels understand they must expand to solidify their grip on the drug market at home and abroad. Sometimes a member steps down from his chapter to organize a chapter in another state or province. Sometimes the club assimilates existing outlaw motorcycle gangs. Every chapter has a story.

Several Hell's Angels leave the US and settle in Rio de Janeiro, Brazil, in the early 1970s. The boys decide to fly the colors and form a bootleg chapter. It receives an official charter on June 16, 1984. The Windsor, England, chapter is also a bootleg club started by local rockers before it is officially sanctioned on December 22, 1985.

Sandy Alexander's erratic behavior causes dissent in the

Manhattan chapter's fanatic fringe in 1984. Herbert Reynolds (Burt or One-Armed Burt) Kittel convinces members like pro boxer John (The Baptist) LoFranco to form a Hell's Angels Nomad chapter in New York City on November 11, 1984. The seven-member chapter headed by Kittel includes Angels from the Mid-State chapter. More members from this chapter join the Nomads after the May 2, 1985, FBI arrests decimate the Troy and Binghamton chapters that make it up. The Bridgeport chapter is frozen later that year when every member is jailed.

The Original Jokers in Winston-Salem, North Carolina, are a much sought after club in the 1970s. The Lexington Outlaws and the Durham Hell's Angels woo the club. Jokers president Joe C. Smith sends the Outlaws his club colors with a note: "Cram the colors; the Jokers aren't wearing any colors but our own." The Jokers become Angels on June 6, 1979. Half of them don't make the grade.

Hell's Angel James Lewis (Oats) Oldfield leaves New York in 1975 to organize a chapter in Charleston, South Carolina. Oldfield, a member of the Filthy Few, has the Hell's Angels death head tattooed on his left bicep and FTW (Fuck the World) on his right bicep over a skull and motorcycle. He is an experienced and shrewd biker. He watches from afar as police drive a disbanded Third Reich out of Fayetteville in 1974. Its members, including former Green Beret Artie Ray Cherry, party with the Tribulators in Charleston. Oldfield convinces them to become the only Big Four outlaw motorcycle gang in South Carolina on February 7, 1976.

Japanese bikers—rabid red-dot nationals—bug the ass off Oakland Angels for a charter in 1983 and 1984. Bikers from Tokyo and Yokahama fly to Oakland to plead their case. They win some West Coast support, but hyper-patriotic East Coast Angels are adamant: No goddamn fucking slants in the club. The yellow cocksuckers bombed the shit out of Pearl Harbor. Many Angels also feel the Japanese culture is not conducive to Angelhood. It's common for two non-faggot men to walk arm in arm there. Can you imagine two fucking Angels doing that? The subject is a hot topic at the 1984 USA run. A compromise is reached: East and West Coast representatives visit Japan in April 1985 to assess the little fuckers. They have authority to vote the bikers in.

The East sends the right men: Charles Alfred (Chuck) Zito from New York, who is Sylvester Stallone's bodyguard; One-Armed Burt Kittel; and Oats Oldfield. Kittel is a mean motherfucker. He loses an eye and an arm when a bomb he makes in his clubhouse apartment in 1975 blows up. His prosthesis has two attachments which he alternates, depending on the occasion: a pincer and a hook. The Angels aren't impressed by the Oriental bikers. Thumbs down Japan. The US Government makes the trip more exciting for Zito and Oldfield. It issues warrants for their arrest in conjunction with the May 2, 1985, FBI raids. They surrender at the US Embassy and are deported.

The Hell's Angels' most aggressive expansion takes place in Canada. It begins with the conquest of Quebec when the club takes over the Popeyes in the country's second largest province on December 5, 1977.

The Hell's Angels aren't satisfied with control of Quebec. They want all of Canada. Montreal Angels criss-cross the country in 1980 when the two-year-old war with the Outlaws cools temporarily. They party with gangs and build alliances. The Angels eye British Columbia. Control of the westernmost province creates a drug and weapons pipeline north from California to British Columbia and across Canada to Quebec. The Satan's Angels monopolize British Columbia's drug traffic. They also terrorize smaller gangs. The club's bylaw #3 reads: "No member will disgrace the club by being yellow." The Satan's Angels cruise the British Columbia coast and make forays into Oregon to strip colors off other bikers like scalps. They embarrass the L'il Devils in Vancouver, the Devil's Escorts in Kamloops and the Gypsy Jokers in Oregon. They hang stolen colors on the clubhouse wall next to the coats of arms of the Vancouver City Police and the Royal Canadian Mounted Police.

"Some guys join the Kinsmen Club," Angel Ronald Doxey, a 34-year-old truck dispatcher, says in 1981. "I like to ride Harley-Davidsons."

The minutes of a 1966 Satan's Angels meeting record Doxey's contribution:

"Doxey farted and cleared the room, the rotten pig."

* * *

Outlaw motorcycle gangs around the world continue to work as bodyguards at rock concerts in the early 1970s despite the debacle at Altamont. Officials at the Bath Festival of Blues and Progressive Music in Shepton Mallet, England, during the last weekend of June 1970 keep the crowd of 150,000 under control with an announcement that leather-jacketed Hell's Angels are handling security. A voice warns over the loudspeakers that the Angels will take care of trouble-makers as the bikers wave bottles, staves, hammers and motorcycle chains on stage.

The Satan's Angels flex their muscles in May 1970 at the Strawberry Mountain Fair 40 miles from Vancouver. Altamont ends the love affair between hippies and bikers. The Satan's Angels bash heads when they feel they need to. Yippies threaten to extort the concert's promoters with weapons cached nearby. The bikers promise to perform open-air lobotomies and the radicals back off. Hippies screwing in a field threaten to destroy a helicopter that keeps landing nearby. The Angels help the flyboy.

Satan's Angels David James Black, 34, and Rick Ciarniello, the club's 32-year-old treasurer, describe their club in the fall of 1977. Black is one of the club's most powerful members after the sudden and unexplained departure of 33-year-old president William Arthur Cross.

"There are definite spirits and we identify with that particular one which has been called Satan," Black says. "It's an upside down world. Our virtues are other's vices. You could say we're Satanists."

> We're used to violence. It's an accepted medium. There are times when a situation can become ugly, but for the most part we just like having a good time. There's nothing else this country has to offer high-spirit kids. So bike clubs are just one avenue that a person can express those high spirits. Violence just goes right along with it. . . . This is a better way of life. It's breaking away from the mainstream. It's doing what you want to do.

Ciarniello adds: "I don't think even an atomic war can stop us. There is a subculture growing and it's based around us. And we're not going to do anything to stop it."

* * *

The Satan's Angels keep a low profile despite their notoriety. They lead an easy life and watch with concern as eastern bikers visit British Columbia. The club amalgamates associate gangs to bolster its strength eight months after the Hell's Angels take over the Popeyes in Quebec. The 101 Knights in Nanaimo and the Gypsy Wheelers in White Rock become Satan's Angels chapters. The club wants all its members on the street, not in jail, and punishes gangs that bring down police heat on bikers.

Two Victoria policemen visit the Bounty Hunter Motorcycle Club clubhouse in an abandoned motel on June 18, 1980, to arrest a member on a traffic warrant. They wait outside while the man gets his belongings. Ten Satan's Angels ride up, park near the cruiser and walk into the clubhouse. The arrested man walks out a few minutes later with a cut lip and bruises. He refuses to tell the policemen why he's bleeding, but accepts a ride to the hospital. The Satan's Angels are frustrated by the attention the Hunters are drawing to bikers that spring. They beat everyone in the clubhouse and strip the club of its colors.

The Satan's Angels don't like competition. A group of restless Vancouver men move 60 miles east to Mission in the early 1970s to form a motorcycle club. Their leader is Charles Donald (Chuck the Duck) Drager, a laborer with Pacific Grain out to shake off 15 years of nine-to-five and a broken marriage. The bikers tear around on Harleys and Indians, bang young pussy, do acid and fight at the Bellevue Hotel. They motor to runs in Washington State and link up with the Ghost Riders. Drager's nameless motorcycle gang adopts their colors—a motorcycle wheel partially shrouded in a white cloud.

The Satan's Angels rumble with the Ghost Riders in 1979 over use of a campground during runs. The Angels order the Riders to stop wearing their colors in BC. Drager leads his pack in December that year to Lethbridge, Alberta, where they are the only outlaws in town. Many Ghost Riders resent losing face. Drager slows down at 40. Most of his gang works steady. He works as a laborer, buys and sells used cars, and speculates in real estate and the stock market. Drager renovates a run-down house and decides to settle down. The Ghost Riders lobby against laws requiring bikers to wear helmets and attract the attention of more powerful gangs in Calgary and Edmonton, which take exception to the American offshoot.

Drager motors back from Medicine Hat at night on his three-wheeler with his 20-year-old girlfriend in October 1980. A tire blows at 65 miles per hour. Drager leans back to grab his girlfriend and balance the bike. It jackknifes. The girl dies. Drager leaves half his face on the asphalt. He hands in his colors.

Drager finds a duck's head on the hood of his car around Halloween. He writes it off as a prank. Drager's stereo blares on the morning of March 4, 1981. Ghost Rider Steven Haudenschild rings the doorbell at 9:45. Drager lets him in. Haudenschild puts four .22-calibre bullets into Drager's head. He pulls a knife and starts to cut the 41-year-old biker's head off. The woman in the downstairs apartment feels a draft and walks up. Haudenschild runs off without his trophy. The gang that flees British Columbia's Satan's Angels to survive disperses in Lethbridge.

Police in British Columbia use the Satan's Angels' fearsome reputation to manipulate migrant fruit pickers in the Okanagan Valley town of Osoyoos in June 1980. Young Quebeckers invade the valley every year to party and make enough money to get back home. The farmers appreciate the cheap labor. Town rednecks hate the French-Canadians they call frogs.

Rain keeps the pickers out of the orchards and in town. They pitch tents in a local campsite. Six locals storm the site Thursday night, June 26, swinging bats and chains at men and women. One man tries to protect two women. The locals knock him out and throw him into the lake. They rip apart tents, dent cars, smash windows and throw backpacks into the fire. The Royal Canadian Mounted Police don't charge anyone, but say they will keep an eye on the situation.

The Satan's Angels plan a run near Osoyoos during the last weekend of June. The RCMP warn the fruit pickers to leave town. They pitch their tents in orchards.

"We heard a rumor that the bikers were coming to clean up our French problem for us," Sergeant Lou Turcott says.

The 70 Satan's Angels who party peacefully don't realize that the RCMP are boosting their reputation.

The Hell's Angels want the gang that controls British Columbia. They take every opportunity to party with the Satan's Angels. Hell's Angels from Quebec and Boston, Massachusetts, attend the 1981 Labor Day run in Coronation, Alberta, sponsored by Edmonton's Rebels Motorcycle Club. They luck into the worst shakedown of a run ever by Canadian police.

The Labor Day run to the Brownfield campsite 20 miles north of Coronation starts in 1973. It's a quiet bash that fills the beerhall coffers in the farming town of 1,389 people. Bikers politely use the telephones of nearby residents and five of them accept a grandmother's offer of hot chocolate in her trailer. They also leave the campsite clean.

The 1980 party on the banks of the Battle River gets a little rowdy. The boys shoot at stars. Two out-of-town girls are gang banged. One loses count at 17. The Mounties seize on the 1980 ruckus to flex muscle in 1981. Superintendent Phillip J. Helfrich in Red Deer wants to stage a large-scale crime prevention exercise. What better way than to stop and skin search 150 bikers lusting for beer, steak and pussy.

Police invade Coronation on Saturday, September 5—160 horsemen and 40 Edmonton policemen, three nosy German shepherds, 40 cruisers, two buses and a helicopter. The Mounties bring along a video crew for posterity. The Rebels host the bash. They roar up Highway 12 and pull into Coronation at 5 p.m.—55 choppers, motor homes and pickup trucks. They tank up their beer bellies at the Frontier Hotel and head out to Brownfield. Camouflaged Mounties watch from the bushes. The cops stop the bikers along the highway. Those at the back of the pack whip around and roar back. Pursuit cars and a helicopter head them off. Police hand out 112 traffic tickets, seize six bikes with altered serial numbers and five shotguns. They charge nine men for possession of cocaine and marijuana and 12 others with liquor offences. Four bikers are caught with restricted weapons.

One Rebel dekes around the cops cross-country and stops the remaining bikers in Coronation. About 180 cops sit on the highway in the middle of nowhere—and wait. Five Mounties pace nervously in town while the group of bikers grows. The Grim Reapers arrive from Calgary. The Hell's Angels from Quebec and Boston drink with them at the Coronation Hotel. The Satan's Angels motor in from Calgary where they had their motorcycles trucked from British Columbia because of bad weather. Some Angels pull up in a rented Lincoln.

Corporal J. Ross McKay from the Red Deer detachment asks the bikers to continue to the campsite through the police stop. The bikers refuse to submit to bum checks. McKay negotiates with the Satan's Angels road captain. The cops can't force the bikers to go to the campsite. They also can't lose face by letting them through untouched. The bikers mill around Main Street at midnight and watch the two men talk. They compromise—the bikers agree to a pat search. The cops get to grab Angel ass, but not until morning. The bikers crash at the local drive-in with 50 cases of beer from the Coronation Hotel after the owner offers the site for $2 a head. He throws in *Superman II*, *Clash of the Titans* and *The Dogs of War*. People might not want bikers, but they don't mind their money.

"We go a thousand miles out of our way to be in the middle of nowhere, where we won't bother anyone and they're all here waiting for us," a Satan's Angel says.

"The police chiefs are printing slander in the papers, telling everyone we're into organized crime," says another. "Why on earth would we come out here dressed in our colors and meet in the middle of a field to discuss organized crime?"

The Satan's Angels negotiate with the Hell's Angels Oakland chapter and three chapters—Vancouver, White Rock and Nanaimo—don the death's head on July 23, 1983. Vancouver's East End chapter is formed on December 22 that year. The club wipes out all outlaw motorcycle gangs except two: the 15-member Tribesmen in Nanaimo and Squamish, and the 15-member Highwaymen in Cranbrook. Both gangs are associates of the new Hell's Angels and Tribesmen members prospect for the club.

The Hell's Angels East End chapter is a hard core group of bikers that wants to eliminate most of the Angels in the province's three other chapters. The Montreal chapter, which oversees the club's Canadian operations, agrees that more than half of the Angels in British Columbia are weekend bikers the gang can do without.

The Hell's Angels add two more chapters in eastern Canada the next year to solidify their grip on the country.

A dozen Hell's Angels from the Montreal chapter thunder in formation along a rural road near Saint-Pie-de-Guire on

September 8, 1984, toward the Drummondville cemetery. The Angels want to pay respect to Yves (Le Boss) Buteau, the chapter president who is gunned down outside Le Petit Bourg bar a year earlier. A priest who rushes to see the Pope on his cross-Canada tour runs a stop sign and crashes into the pack. Bikes pile up. Prospect Daniel Matthieu dies. Angel Wolodu-myr (Walter or Nugget) Stadnick is severely burned and loses several fingers. Stadnick is the only anglophone Angel in Quebec. He doesn't like the treatment he gets at a Quebec hospital because he doesn't understand French. The Montreal chapter pays for his transfer to the burn unit at St. Joseph's Hospital in Hamilton, Ontario.

Stadnick is a former Wild One from the steel city. His parents and friends live there. He is the Hell's Angels' most important foothold in Hamilton—a link they hope will lead to the formation of the club's first Ontario chapter. But the Out-laws and Satan's Choice control Hamilton. They don't like Angels. The club asks the Hamilton-Wentworth Regional Po-lice to provide paid duty officers to protect Stadnick at night. Paid duty is supplementary work police officers do to inflate their paychecks. The most common paid duty job is security at concerts. The force considers refusing, but realizes it will look bad if Stadnick is killed. The Montreal chapter pays for months of police protection.

The 13th Tribe motorcycle club from Halifax prospects for the Hell's Angels in 1984. Members fly to Hamilton to protect Stadnick in hospital during visiting hours. The task earns them their colors. The 13th Tribe becomes the Hell's Angels Hali-fax chapter on December 5, 1984, the same day the Gitans in Sherbrooke become the third Angel chapter in Quebec.

The Hell's Angels are the second most powerful criminal organization in Quebec after traditional organized crime. Their power grows daily as hundreds of Italian, Irish and French-Canadian mobsters move their operations to the US, especially Florida.

The Hell's Angels now spread their wings from coast to coast in Canada. They have 80 members in British Columbia, 60 in Quebec and eight in Halifax. Many of the eastern members are in jail for crimes that range from murder to pros-titution. But history shows the club always bounces back, probably because police tend to slack off after they jail a few

HELLS ANGELS

PITTSFIELD-LEE
TROY
LOWELL
SALEM
ROCHESTER
BINGHAMTON
BRIDGEPORT
NEW YORK CITY

MINNEAPOLIS

SONOMA CO
SACRAMENTO
RICHMOND
VALLEJO
OAKLAND
SAN FRANCISCO
DALY CITY
SAN JOSE
MONTEREY
VENTURA
SAN FERNANDO
SAN BERNARDINO
SAN DIEGO

OMAHA

CLEVELAND
AKRON

RICHMOND

WINSTON SALEM
WINSTON SALEM
CHARLOTTE
DURHAM

CHARLESTON

⊙ MOTHER CHAPTER

HELLS ANGELS WORLD CHAPTERS

CANADA
HALIFAX
MONTREAL
SHERBROOKE
VANCOUVER

WHITE ROCK
EAST END
NANAIMO

GREAT BRITAIN
LONDON
WEST COAST
ESSEX
KENT
WESSEX
SOUTH COAST
TYNE & WEAR

NETHERLANDS
AMSTERDAM
HAARLEM

WEST GERMANY
HAMBURG
STUTTGART

DENMARK COPENHAGEN

SWITZERLAND
ZURICH

AUSTRIA VORARLBERG

FRANCE
PARIS

UNITED STATES
CHAPTERS
THROUGHOUT
USA

AUSTRALIA
MELBOURNE
SYDNEY
WESTE
MONARO

NEW ZEALAND
AUCKLAND

BRAZIL
RIO DE JANEIRO

members. The Angels, on the other hand, work harder to reorganize the club and keep its businesses going. Fighting the Hell's Angels is like trying to rid yourself of a dose of the clap—you can use copious amounts of penicillin but you won't shake it unless you also stop fucking the bitch who gives it to you. Police can jail all the Angels they want, but if they don't cut off the club's income there will always be another Angel to wear the colors.

The number of Hell's Angels fluctuates constantly as members die or are jailed. The club today has about 1,000 members worldwide in 67 chapters in 13 countries on four continents.

Hell's Angels chapters and date of charter:

Berdoo (San Bernardino), California 03–17–48
Frisco (San Francisco), California 08–01–54
Oakland, California 04–01–57
Auckland, New Zealand 07–01–61
Richmond, California 02–14–62
Nomads (Vallejo), California 06–01–65
Daly City, California 02–19–66
Dago (San Diego), California 05–03–66
Omaha, Nebraska 10–27–66
Lowell, Massachusetts 04–17–67
Cleveland, Ohio 12–16–67
Buffalo, New York ("frozen" in early 1970s)   68
San Jose, California 07–01–69
London, England 07–30–69
Salem, Massachusetts 07–17–69
West Coast, England 08–17–69
New York City, New York 12–05–69
Rochester, New York 12–05–69
Zurich, Switzerland 12–20–70
Sonoma County, California 01–21–72
Hamburg, West Germany 03–16–73
Binghamton, New York 06–12–73
Durham, North Carolina 07–24–73
Sacramento, California 08–09–73
West Coast, England 08–17–74
Bridgeport, Connecticut 02–17–75
Melbourne, Australia 08–23–75
Sydney, Australia 08–23–75
Vorarlberg, Austria 11–19–75
Charleston, South Carolina 02–07–76

Essex, England 08–15–76
Kent, England 12–04–76
Wessex, England 01–29–77
South Coast, England 02–26–77
Montreal (Sorel), Quebec 12–05–77
San Fernando Valley, California 01–01–78
Ventura, California 05–06–78
West Sydney, Australia 06–02–78
Troy, New York 08–23–78
Charlotte, North Carolina 10–19–78
Amsterdam, Holland 10–28–78
Akron, Ohio 03–01–79
Tyne and Wear, England 06–02–79
Winston-Salem, North Carolina 06–06–79
North (Laval), Quebec (Dissolved 03–24–85) 09–14–79
Haarlem, Holland 01–19–80
Nomads, Australia 08–14–80
Copenhagen, Denmark 12–31–80
Monterey, California 04–04–81
Paris, France 04–18–81
Stuttgart, West Germany 12–04–81
Frankfurt, West Germany .... —
Berkshire County, Massachusetts 04–21–82
Mid-State, N.Y. (merges Troy and Binghamton) 08–18–82
Minneapolis, Minnesota 09–18–82
Fairbanks, Alaska 12–18–82
Anchorage, Alaska 12–18–82
Mat-Su (Manranuska-Susitna), Alaska 12–18–82
White Rock, British Columbia 07–23–83
Vancouver, British Columbia 07–23–83
Nanaimo, British Columbia 07–23–83
Adelaide, Australia 10–01–83
East End, British Columbia 12–22–83
Vallejo-Martinez, California 02–11–84
Rio de Janeiro, Brazil 06–16–84
Nomads (New York City), New York 11–11–84
Halifax, Nova Scotia 12–05–84
Sherbrooke, Quebec 12–05–84
Windsor, England 12–22–84
Paducah, Kentucky .... 05– –85

2

HELL'S ANGELS: THE CLUB

The police call it a gang. . . . We call it a club.
—Ralph Hubert (Sonny) Barger Jr., 1983.

THE Hell's Angels Motorcycle Club is the prototype for every outlaw motorcycle gang in the world. The Angels are what they claim to be: the meanest and greatest gang of mother-fucking white trash on wheels. Nearly every biker wants to be an Angel. Men even tattoo their dicks to get into the club. Women who want to understand the pain caused by tattoo needles inserted into a penis should smother lighted cigarets with their twats.

The Hell's Angels are guided by a simple philosophy: Fuck the world. An Angel does what he wants, regardless of the consequences. No one tells him he can't rape, sell drugs or murder. The club doesn't care as long as it doesn't interfere with taking care of business, as it does in Quebec's North chapter in the mid-1980s. The Angels have their own uniform and code of conduct to show disrespect for society's rules. Anything that shocks or disgusts raises an Angel's status and image in the club. So the boys tongue kiss in public and engage in flying tackle embraces to snap the minds of straights. Angels consider anything outrageous a show of class.

The Hell's Angels are white supremacists. They don't allow colored members, although they'll bang black pussy. Angel chapters in the southern US are allied with the Ku Klux Klan. Durham Angels and Lexington Outlaws fight for one year to control Joe Smith's Original Jokers in North Carolina. The Angels win and the Winston-Salem chapter is formed on June 6, 1979. Members of the new Hell's Angels chapter work as bodyguards for Joe Grady's White Knights of Liberty —the KKK. The Angels protect the Klan even when the sheeted scuz shoot up Angel Carl Gordon's garage on April 9, 1980, and leave a slug in his ass. They mistakenly believe the Angel has stolen one of their guns.

A serious problem exists with one of four British Columbia Hell's Angels chapters. The Satan's Angels, as they are called before they don the death's head in July 1983, are a tough bunch of seasoned outlaws. One of their most loyal and proven members is black. The Satan's Angels refuse to conform to the Hell's Angels' white only policy when they bury their colors. Hell's Angels from Oakland and Cleveland threaten to kill the black Angel if he crosses the border into the US. Racism overrides brotherhood in the club. The black Angel can't attend USA runs or world runs with his brothers. Black punks in the US have their own outlaw motorcycle gangs, such as the Wheels of Soul in New Jersey, which has white members.

Many Hell's Angels have the words "White Power" tattooed on their bodies along with the white power fist. By the time they've finished tattooing themselves, these multi-colored bozos look like ambulatory rainbows with a pot of shit at either end. The Angels are racist, but not Nazis, although they wear swastikas. Howie Weisbrod, a Jewish Angel in the Manhattan, and later, the San Francisco chapter, says he'd never belong to a gang of neo-Nazis.

The Hell's Angels might not like blacks, but use them when it's convenient. An Angel in Charlotte, North Carolina, bases his motorcycle theft ring out of a house in the city's black neighborhood in 1979. The police don't think of looking for him there.

The ex-servicemen and handful of teenage rebels who form the Hell's Angels in 1948 give the club a military structure that Sonny Barger refines in his Oakland chapter in the late 1960s and early 1970s. The publication of Mario Puzo's *The Godfather* in 1969, along with the movie, influences the Hell's Angels greatly. Barger grasps the worth of a well-oiled machine and converts his chapter into a business school model of efficiency. Other chapters imitate Barger's hard-nosed business tactics.

The Hell's Angels, unlike the other major outlaw motorcycle gangs—the Outlaws, Pagans and Bandidos—do not have a national president and national officers who give the club direction. Sonny Barger, despite decades of press clippings and police intelligence reports that label him as club president and maximum leader, is nothing more than a highly-respected member. Barger is an *éminence grise* who may be consulted on touchy club business, but who will be told to fuck off if he tries to order a chapter around. Different chapter or faction presidents may influence the gang at one time or another because of their power or connections. But no one man guides the club. William (Wild Bill) Medeiros, former security officer for the Manhattan chapter in New York City, explains:

> We're considered the #1 outlaw biker club in the world. Outlaws don't conform to rules and regulations. We don't want to be over-governed. We don't want one person leading us.

The Hell's Angels Motorcycle Club is divided into East and West Coast factions, with Omaha, Nebraska, as a dividing line. Each faction has a president, vice-president, recording secretary and treasurer elected once a year. The president of the West Coast faction oversees chapters on the US and Canadian west coasts, including Alaska, and those in Australia and New Zealand. All other chapters, including those in Brazil and Europe answer to the East Coast president.

East Coast Officers' Meetings (ECOMS) and West Coast Officers' Meetings (WCOMS) are held every three months in different chapters' areas. The faction officers and the president or vice-president from every chapter in the faction discuss only official club business at the quarterly meetings: how to financially assist a chapter; should a new chapter be admitted; how individual chapters perform; how many new patches should be ordered; should the club issue a press release on the latest arrests of members. Drug deals and other crimes are not discussed. Each faction has a treasury to which chapters contribute. The money is used for national club business: to defray a chapter's legal costs, to send members on fact finding missions to Japan or Europe, or to buy confidential police reports on the gang.

Every member also contributes to his chapter's treasury at business meetings called "church" held at least once a month, but more often weekly. The club operates on a policy of strict financial accountability. Every chapter clears the books on the first Wednesday of the new year and starts fresh. Members are given until April 1st to catch up on late payments so the books can be balanced. The tardy are stripped of their colors and forced to prospect again. Disgruntled members can also nominate candidates to replace chapter officers at the first meeting of the year.

The East and West Coast factions hold a scheduled US annual meeting where presidents discuss Hell's Angels activities, policy and financing, including bail and lawyers' fees. They don't discuss criminal activity. The meeting takes place hours before the Hell's Angels' annual USA run that East and West Coast factions host alternately. The host faction president presides over the meeting at a hotel near the run site. The USA run is held in conjunction with the world run every second year and chapters around the globe must send members.

A special presidents' meeting is called during occasional emergencies. Leaders across the continent, or even around the world, are called and told to show up at a particular hotel in a certain city within days. Such a meeting is held in Milford, Connecticut, in the fall of 1984 where the influx of Hell's Angels colors surprises guests at the Holiday Inn.

Hell's Angels chapters are organized like little armies.

The chapter president is either elected or self-appointed because of his wealth and power. He rules with an iron hand and has final say in all club business. He can overrule any decision voted on by members. He rides at the front of the pack next to the center line and beside the road captain on runs. Members form two columns behind them and do not pass or stray unless they have mechanical difficulties.

The chapter vice-president is usually an heir apparent hand-picked by the president to fill in in his absence. He rides two abreast with other full-color members behind the president and road captain.

The secretary-treasurer keeps minutes of all club meetings,

collects dues and pays fines. He pays club bills and arranges bond for arrested members. He has the list of members' addresses and telephone numbers and keeps books on club business.

The sergeant-at-arms is usually the toughest and meanest club member. He is the president's bodyguard and the chapter's enforcer and executioner. He may stash the club's arsenal. He keeps everyone in line during meetings and outings. He rides next to the curb behind the full-color members and ahead of prospects and associates or honorary members. Some chapters have an enforcer who rides at the rear of the pack.

The road captain is the club's logistician and security chief during runs. He maps out routes and alternative roads to avoid roadblocks, and plans refuelling, food and maintenance stops. He carries the club's money to bail out jailed members and lets police know ahead of time what the club will do in their jurisdictions. He rides next to the president beside the curb. Larger chapters have an assistant road captain who rides at the back of the pack with an enforcer, if a chapter has one.

A prospect must be nominated by a club member in good standing after his stint as a hang-around allows him to meet all the members. The gopher does all the joe jobs around the clubhouse and on runs. Most members want prospects to free them for more profitable business. Canadian chapters do not accept prospects during the winter because you can't ride a motorcycle in the snow. A prospect, or striker, doesn't have colors. He wears an armband or a sleeveless vest with a rocker that indicates he is a prospect. The prospect is turfed out if he doesn't garner 100 percent club support during three votes taken to admit him as a full-fledged member. He must commit a crime before being admitted to prove he has the right stuff and is not a police officer. Many chapters require that he murder to receive his colors. Becoming a prospect is difficult. Chapters have size limits to ensure the president can control members. Large chapters are divided so that a police bust doesn't cripple the gang's business in an area. Probationary members ride behind full-color members on a run.

Honorary members retire from the club in good standing. They keep their colors, but don't pay dues. They can party with the club and must attend funerals. Some honorary members have never been Angels, but have helped the club as associates. These include lawyers, bail bondsmen, motorcycle-shop owners and auto-wrecking yard owners. They ride behind probationary members on runs.

Women are not allowed to join the club, but associate with members. Old ladies belong exclusively to a member and cannot be fucked or abused by anyone else. They can wear their old man's colors and can have their own denim vest with rockers that say "Property of so and so." Mamas, or sheep, are community twats. Members can do anything they want with them.

The Hell's Angels keep tight rein on members. An Angel who moves to an area covered by another chapter has to shift his membership to that chapter. Only members of the Nomad chapters in Vallejo, California, and New York City are allowed to float from chapter to chapter—a deference to tradition. The original Nomad chapter members are recruited from the now-defunct Nomad Motorcycle Gang. The New York City Nomad chapter is formed of members from other East Coast chapters.

Owning a motorcycle alone won't get a man into the Hell's Angels, as it will garner membership in the American Motorcycle Association, although you need a Harley to become an Angel. A man is severely tested for jam, criminal instincts, toughness and an ability to take care of business before he is allowed into the Hell's Angels.

William (Wild Bill) Medeiros, former security officer for the Manhattan chapter, conducts the first mud check on an applecunt—a man who applies to prospect—in his clubhouse. He smashes the guy in the face.

"I would learn a couple of things. Does the guy have the balls to fight me? If he fights, may the better man win. If he runs, I don't want him in the club."

Clarence (Addie) Crouch, former vice-president and founder of the Hell's Angels Cleveland chapter explains the process of trying to get into the club.

Someone that comes around the club and wants to join the club must have a good motorcycle—Harley-Davidson, be white, and be 21 or older. When he first comes around the club, there is a lot of mud checking. He has to fight a lot of people. A lot of people jump on him. They jump on him in twos, threes. Then after a period of time, which depends on the person, it may be three months, it may be one year or two years, he can become a hang-around. We will have a vote and it has to be a 100 percent vote that he is allowed to be a hang-around. And a hang-around is allowed to come into the clubhouse and hang around the outside of the clubhouse. They do that to keep everybody else away because a lot of people believe that the Hell's Angels are giants and they have got everything together.

They keep everybody at arm's length away from us, so that they do not really understand that we are just people or whatever, keep them in awe. And then he becomes a hang-around and he can come into the clubhouse and he can do flunky work. And he hangs around for no set period of time. Then he becomes a prospect. And he can be brought up for prospect three times. If he's voted down three different times, well, then they run him off. They beat him up, take his motorcycle, and run him away. The same way if he is a hang-around, if he does not go through the mud check or whatever, they beat him up, take his motorcycle, whatever, take his old lady, and run him off.

Then, as a prospect, he is just a general flunky. He does the moving, does everything, cleaning bikes, working on bikes. He is on 24-hour call. There is always a watch at the clubhouse. He stands watch upstairs. He is armed with—there are carbines, shotguns. There are twilight scopes. There are scanners, everything. They have a security room at the top of the clubhouse, and he sits there at night from 12 o'clock until daylight. That is the rule there. Some places it is all night and they change prospects.

Then in one instance where a prospect was down in a bar and got into a fight, and the guy took a shot at him and shot him through the side right here, he was ordered to either get this guy or do something to him or lose his patch. Because he was losing face, the club would be losing face if he did not do something to this guy. And being a prospect can carry on. Some people are prospects for five years. Some people six months, I think was the shortest period I ever heard, but normally it is one-and-a-half to two years. They have to go on all the runs. At the runs they build the fire, they carry all the firewood. They work 24 hours a day. They are just flunkies until they get their patch.

They are voted on—100 percent—and then they are pulled into the clubhouse and told that they have been voted on, now they are a member, and then their sponsor will explain to them that they have to come up with so much money for a bond fund, which is $500. Then they will have to . . . roll their bones. They have to kill someone. . . . He has to roll his bones within six months. . . . The person he kills is someone that the intelligence will set up with security. . . . If they renege on that, then they are killed. . . . He knows too much.

Phillip (Lightfoot) Kramer, an outlaw biker who loses a leg and right eye going over the high side, asks to prospect for the Hell's Angels Hudson Valley prospect chapter in Troy, New York, in 1978. The chapter, made up of former Breed members, gets its Hell's Angels charter in August that year. Angels in Cleveland are adamant that Kramer should not be allowed into the club because of his participation in the 1971 rumble in their city between Angels and the Breed. Sandy Alexander likes Kramer and talks to the vicious Cleveland Angels who want him dead. Alexander is at the peak of his power and the Cleveland chapter settles for the murder of Breed biker Savage Pamanonda as a token concession to allow Kramer to prospect. Pamanonda's body is found at an abandoned radar station on a Vermont mountain that the Hell's Angels frequent after frightening off the Breed. Kramer prospects for Alexander's Manhattan chapter and gets his patch along with Herbert (Burt or One-Armed Burt) Kittel in May 1979. The Hell's Angels' death head grins from the centre of Kramer's glass eye.

A Hell's Angel has nine days after he is given his patch to get the club tattoo—the club name, the winged death's head, the bottom rocker and the date he is made a member. Most members have that tattoo on their arm. A member must have the tattoo covered when he is kicked out of the club. Most of the time, the club does it for him with hot spoons. A member who leaves honorably can keep the tattoo, but must have the date he leaves tattooed in.

The Hell's Angels don't tolerate ego trippers who imitate them.

There have been incidences where people with tattoos—phoney Hell's Angels tattoos—have had them cut off their arms, had the whole tattoo just removed by knife [Addie Crouch says]. That has happened a couple of times. I think once in Omaha, once out in Los Angeles, Cleveland....A lot of people just more or less canned it and showed it around, showed it off. I know one guy, he kept one for a couple of years. It was considered quite a trophy.

A man accepted into the Hell's Angels is initiated into the club with his new colors, called originals. They can never be washed. Angel initiations, before the club hangs up the bucket of shit, are as raunchy as those of wanna-be motorcycle gangs. Even the most jerked off Times Square pervert can't imagine anything that hasn't been done during an Angel initiation.

The Hell's Angels no longer piss, shit or puke on new members and their colors to initiate them into the club. They feel they are above that. That's why you don't see many Angels with dirty colors. If an Angels' colors are soiled, then the guy's been around for a long time. Charles Alfred (Chuck) Zito, one of the toughest members of the Manhattan chapter, sports immaculate colors.

The wealthy and sophisticated Angels feel they are above degrading themselves. They feel it is more important to conduct a thorough background investigation on a prospective member rather than abuse him. At worst, the new member might have to go down on the foulest smelling mama in the clubhouse while everyone cheers him on. More often, he is just hugged.

Nothing is more precious to a Hell's Angel than his colors —not his motorcycle, his money, his old lady, or his dick. The colors represent the member's commitment to the club and the outlaw lifestyle. The colors are the club—the flag around which every member rallies. Touching an Angel's colors is like grabbing your grandmother's tits; to desecrate them means death. Angels beat people who pat them on the back. The Hell's Angels, as the first outlaw motorcycle club of note, set a code that all other clubs follow. To steal an Angel's colors or to drag them on the ground is a killing offence. A club stripped of its colors can't have another set made. An Angel who loses his colors can be thrown out of the club. Angels can beat a member they don't like if he shows up at a party without his colors. Bounties are sometimes paid to members who bring in rival biker's colors, like scalps.

Several Angels who visit Memphis, Tennessee, in the early 1970s to set up a chapter are severely beaten by club-wielding policemen. They threaten to sue for infringement of their civil rights. But the policemen have also stripped them of their colors, without which the Angels can't return to Cleveland. They drop the threat in return for the colors.

The Hell's Angels colors are a winged, grinning death's head that sports an aviator's leather helmet over which the

club's name, in red and white, arcs across the shoulders of the
sleeveless vest on a rocker. The letters *MC*, for motorcycle
club, sit underneath the tip of the skull's wings. Every chapter
has its name on the bottom rocker underneath the skull in the
club's early days. California chapters put the state name on
the bottom rocker in 1966 to hinder police identification. The
winged skull glares from all kinds of Angel paraphernalia in
Sonny Barger's house, including stained-glass windows.

The skull is a six-inch patch worn on the back of leather
jackets in 1948. Military tradition gives way in warm weather
to sleeveless Levis called cutaways that are easily tucked away
to hide from police. The Hell's Angels' Betsy Ross is a Fontana seamstress whose identity is lost in the exhaust of time.
The patch is enlarged in 1960, when the Angels start talking
about brotherhood and the need for solidarity. The feeling
spreads across the continent and everyone wants to become an
Angel. Those who don't make the grade start imitating the
club. That's why the Hell's Angels patent their death's head
emblem. Patent violations rarely get before a judge. The
Hell's Angels like to settle out of court.

The West Coast Hell's Angels wage a war of pride with the
Mongols in 1977. The Mongols dare wear the word California
on the bottom rocker of their colors—in red and white to
imitate the redoubtable Angels. The Angels warn them that no
one wears colors that slightly resemble the Angels' trademark.
Even the state name. The Mongols tell them to fuck off.

Two Mongols, Raymond (Jingles) Smith and Emerson (Red Beard) Morris, hugged tightly by their old ladies, throb south on Interstate 15 near Escondido, California, on September 5, 1977. The Mongols return to San Diego from their Labor Day run. A car pulls up. Hell's Angels hit men James (Brett) Eaton and Guy Castiglione, vice-president of the San Diego chapter, open up with submachine guns. Harleys and bodies tumble, mesh and skid on the asphalt. The bikers die. One old lady is slightly injured. The other is paralyzed from the waist down by a bullet lodged near her spine. The hit is organized by Thomas (Crunch) Renzulli, president of the San Diego chapter, and Angels Larry Gaskins and David Harbridge. Smith and Morris do not rest in peace. A Rambler pulls up in front of the heavily guarded funeral home and a man delivers red and white carnations—the Hell's Angels colors. He walks away. The Rambler explodes to injure three Mongol guards.

Smith and Morris are not the first Mongols to pay the price of defying the Angels. Allyn Bishop is blown away with a shotgun while he wears the bottom rocker on July 29. The hit man uses a $200 throw-away car bought by the Angels' sergeant-at-arms. The violence continues. An incendiary bomb explodes when Luis Gutierrez, president of the Mongols San Fernando Valley chapter, opens the door of his van in his driveway on September 30. The co-owner of the Frame-Up Motorcycle Shop and his helper are killed by an explosion in late October. The Mongols retaliate, albeit a bit late. They gun down Hell's Angel Raymond (Godfather) Piltz at the Lemon Grove biker bar in 1982.

The Hell's Angels are the underworld's Boy Scouts. They strive to win merit badges—embroidered cloth, tattoos or pins—mostly for sexual athletics. Badges must be earned in front of Angel witnesses to make sure no one cheats. The Angels have taken sexual braggadocio out of the locker room and into the living room.

The Angels phase out sexual badges after 21 years when Sonny Barger recommends in 1969 that the club clean up its act to improve its image and lower its profile. Few Angels plaster their colors with wings for sexual conquests anymore. In fact, Angels wear suits more often than their colors now. The lack of wings doesn't mean Angels have stopped going down in front of the boys. Once a muff diver, always a muff diver.

The symbols the Hell's Angels add to their attire over the years are more ad hoc than planned. Doodads are usually adopted to mark events. Montreal Angels charged with the murder of five members of the North chapter wear a finely sculpted, winged death's head made of gold in their left ear lobes during the inquest and trial.

Frank Sadilek, legendary president of the Hell's Angels San Francisco chapter from 1955 to 1962, sets the trend among outlaw bikers when he introduces the gold earring, the clip-on nose ring and the purple-dyed beard. He sports the blue-and-yellow striped T-shirt Lee Marvin wears in *The Wild One* until it falls to pieces.

Angels also decorate themselves ornately with tattoos. An Angel's tattoos record his history with the club, starting with the date he becomes a member. His sexual propensities and exploits are graphically detailed. His murders are inked in. Members who kill for the club graduate to the ranks of the Filthy Few and those words are tattooed on the inside of the forearm. Club hit men have Nazi SS lightning bolts tattooed underneath the words Filthy Few. Some Angels represent every rival Outlaw biker with a tattoo of a skull—black eyes for a man, red eyes for a woman. Prolific killers usually forgo the skulls.

Most Angels sport tattoos or wear patches that identify them as members of one group or another within the club. An Angel becomes a member of the Dirty Thirty when he reaches that age. A member of the Foul Five earns five sexual wings and survives five days and nights of debauchery.

Most insignia are dreamed up when the bikers are cranked up or drunk on a run. The Evil Force is the brainchild of Vincent (Big Vinnie) Girolamo, sergeant-at-arms of the Manhattan chapter. Girolamo and five other New York Angels on a run in North Carolina consider themselves the baddest of the bad and devise a tattoo to prove it: a backwards *F* that leans at 45 degrees against an *E* that leans 45 degrees towards it. The tattoo and patch are given to members of the Manhattan chapter who have killed an Outlaw. The words *Evil Force* are written all over the clubhouse. Sandy Alexander has the insignia on his apartment door.

Big Vinnie Girolamo, Burt Kittel, William (Flash) Starkey

and another Manhattan Angel create another tattoo that means fuck all. They hide it on the underside of the arm next to the armpit. The tattoo is half an inch high and two-and-a-half inches long. It starts with two Nazi SS lightning bolts followed by the numbers 0001, 0002, 0003 or 0004, and two more lightning bolts. The boys number themselves for the hell of it.

Big Vinnie Girolamo likes slogans. The funeral parlor card handed out at his burial says he died for what he believed in. It adds his motto: "Hell's Angels. 'When in Doubt, Knock 'em Out.' "

The Rumble Squad patch is worn by two Hell's Angels only: James (Gorilla) Harwood from the Troy, New York, chapter and Charles Alfred (Chuck) Zito from the Manhattan chapter. They attend a biker run in Laconia, New Hampshire, several weeks after the May 1984 run to Myrtle Beach, South Carolina. The Pagans show up in Laconia. The clubs barely tolerate each other. A group of Hell's Angels stands in the parking lot of a downtown Laconia motel. Six Pagans pull up at an intersection and yell obscenities at the Angels. Gorilla Harwood and Chuck Zito charge them. Zito, a karate expert, drop-kicks three Pagans off their choppers. Harwood mashes two faces with a kickstand. They beat the six Pagans severely. Other Pagans don't dare intervene. The two victorious Angels call themselves the Rumble Squad afterwards and have a patch made for their colors.

The most dangerous patch worn by a Hell's Angel, as far as police are concerned, is a red on white piece of cloth that reads "DEGUELLO"—no quarter. Mexican General Antonio Lopez de Santa Anna's regimental band plays the Moorish march "Deguello" as his troops march on the Alamo under orders to massacre all defenders of the old mission, including Jim Bowie and Davey Crockett. The patch is the Angels' red badge of courage. It is worn by Angels who violently resist arrest and dates to the early 1960s. About 15 members of the Lowell, Massachusetts, chapter wear it for a 20-minute bloody rumble outside their clubhouse in the late 1960s with 20 police officers.

These are some of the tattoos and patches worn by Hell's Angels:

A.F.F.A.—Angels Forever, Forever Angels.

A.F.F.L.—(Angels) Alcohol Forever, Forever Loaded.

D.F.F.L.—Dope Forever, Forever Loaded.

B.T.B.F.—Bikers Together, Bikers Forever.

P.P.D.S.C.E.M.F.O.B.B.T.—Pill Popping, Dope Smoking, Cunt Eating, Mother Fucker, Outlaw Biker, Brother Trash.

The white-power fist—The biker believes the Nazi ideology that whites are the superior race.

1%—All outlaw bikers wear the 1% inside a diamond shape as a tattoo or patch to indicate they are proud to be the 1% of motorcyclists who live outside the law.

13—The 13th letter of the alphabet, *M*, which stands for marijuana is embroidered in red on a white square.

22—For having done time.

*—Between the thumb and forefinger for times in prison.

24—For having downed 24 beers in less than eight hours.

69—For having engaged in mutual oral sex witnessed by club members.

666—The mark of Satan.

S—Speed.

MC—Motorcycle Club.

An upside-down license plate—Stolen from a policeman or rival biker.

F.T.W.—Fuck The World. One Montreal Angel has "FTW" tattooed on his penis.

WINGS:

The wings worn by Hell's Angels to denote sexual adventures are perverse adaptations of the wings worn by the pilots who first form the club in 1948. They can be cloth patches sewn to colors, or metal wings that are pinned on.

Golden wings—For participating in a gang bang involving more than 15 men.

White wings—For licking a virgin or white pussy.

Red wings—For licking a bleeding white pussy.

Black wings—For licking a black pussy.

Black on red wings—For licking a bleeding black pussy.

Yellow wings—For licking Asian pussy.

Green wings—For licking a pussy full of creepy crawlies.

Purple wings—For licking a dead pussy.

Brown wings—For licking a woman's asshole.

Blue and yellow wings—For fucking a policewoman.

Eightball—For buggering a man in front of Angels.

CROSSES (worn as an earring, patch or pin):

White cross—For digging open a grave, stealing something from
    the corpse and wearing it on the colors.
Red cross—For blowing a man in front of Angels.

The Hell's Angels brag about their vagabond lifestyle, their
freedom from society's laws and their liberty to pursue happi-
ness in whatever form they like it. Yet, they submit themselves to club rules that demand death or expulsion for failure
to comply. Angel law is merciless.

The word of mouth constitution of the Hell's Angels Motorcycle Club applies to members worldwide. It restricts
membership to males at least 21 years old who own Harley-
Davidson motorcycles and stand up for what the club believes.
The club doesn't believe in blacks.

"When you're a member of the number one motorcycle
club in the country, you don't have to prove much," Sonny
Barger says in 1982.

"In prospective members, we don't look for the 'baddest'
guys around, but for guys who believe in our lifestyle and
who'll stand up for it and be a man."

The first patch-pulling offence in the Hell's Angels rules is
a ban on needle-injected drugs. A junkie's first loyalty is to
the needle, not the club. The Angels can't risk being sold out.
An Angel can also lose his patch if he pulls a gun at a club
meeting, hits another biker, steals from a club member—
drugs, money, bikes or even his woman—or reneges on a
drug deal made with another member. Even a long-standing
member is beaten and fined for breaking a rule. He might
even have to prospect again.

The Angels also have an unwritten code that deals with
taking care of business. Some chapters are brazen enough to
include parts of this code in their bylaws. The code requires
that an Angel fight back when attacked—a matter of pride.
The Angels believe in retribution: not an eye for an eye, but
life for an insult. Oakland bylaw No. 10: "When an Angel
punches a non-Angel, all other Angels will participate." An
Angel always helps an Angel, right or wrong, because he is a

brother. The Angels enforce their code of honor strictly to instill fear and make it easier to take care of business. The code requires complete loyalty to the club and silence under threat of death.

Chapters draft bylaws to supplement the rules. Northern chapters, for example, don't require members to ride their motorcycles at least once a month as some southern chapters do.

The secretary of the Hell's Angels Mid-State New York chapter—which merges the Troy and Binghamton chapters on August 18, 1982—records birthdays and anniversaries. Members, for example, are awarded a gold belt buckle after 10 years of riding with the club. The secretary keeps in touch with other chapters and keeps the chapter informed of club news. He also keeps the chapter's handwritten bylaws in a lined notebook. The first page reads:

(1) All members may have in their possession for their own persnal [sic] patch 1 complete Hell's Angels patch.
(2) All members and prospects must attend one meeting a week as designated by the time and place set at previous meeting.
(3) All members and prospects are required to pay weekly dues of $20.00 a week with a back balance of no more than $60. Patch will be suspended for non payment of dues over maximum set.
(4) All members and prospects will wear their patch to meetings.
(5) All members and prospects will ride to meetings during April 1 and Nov. 1st.—Excuses will be discussed at meeting and fines levied if appropriate.
(6) All members and prospects are to fill out data sheets and have their photos taken for personal information sheets to be kept by sec.
(7) No member or prospect shall burn or rip off a business associate that would reflect on the honesty and the. . . .

The Mid-State chapter won't let members steal motorcycles within one mile of the clubhouse, or start a motorcycle or screw a tart younger than 17 in the building. A member who breaches a rule is fined: $5 if he doesn't wear colors to church, if he rides unsafely or is a goofball on runs, if he leaves tools lying around the clubhouse, if he leaves the lights on, if he doesn't take out the garbage, if he goes one week without riding a motorcycle and if he fails to call in every 48 hours when out of town. He must pay $100 if he loses any-thing with the winged death's head on it, if he doesn't have a motorcycle on the road by April 1, if he leaves drugs in the clubhouse or if he fires a gun there.

Bylaws and rules differ among chapters. These are rules in some California chapters:

(1) No dope burns.
(2) On California runs, weapons will be shot only between 0600 and 1600. Penalty for violation: patch pulled.
(3) No spiking the club's booze with dope.
(4) No throwing live ammunition into bonfires on runs.
(5) No messing with another member's wife.
(6) You can't pull the patch of another chapter's member.
(7) No snuffing a member with his patch on. (You can only snuff a member of your own chapter.)
(8) No using dope during a meeting.
(9) At least two officers from each chapter must attend a Califor-nia meeting every two months.

Hell's Angels are expert motorcycle riders. They do with a bike what a whore does with her twat. And the feeling is just as good. The price to pay is going over the high side. In surfer's language, wiping out. Ronald (Big Cheese) Cheese-man, president of the Hell's Angels Mid-State chapter, com-pares an accident to being violently beaten:

> You know . . . after ya hit somebody or kick somebody in the face, sometimes . . . the bones around the eye socket get broken and their eye falls out on their cheek? Well, basically that's what hap-pened. One eye fell out.

Although a Hell's Angel must own a Harley-Davidson mo-torcycle, usually with an engine with more than 1200cc dis-placement—the classic 74—the motorcycle is almost an anachronism in today's gang. Angels are more likely to drive Corvettes, Porsches, Jaguars, Cadillacs or Lincolns. A chop-per makes an Angel too obvious to conduct drug deals. So the bike, like the runs on which it is used, is a piece of nostalgia. But the Angels can't forsake it. You can't claim to be a biker if you don't ride one. The Hell's Angels in San Diego worry about the trend away from motorcycles and pass a bylaw in the mid-1970s that requires members to ride their hogs once a month or pay a $25 fine.

The motorcycle is crucial to the Hell's Angels' image as free-wheeling vagabonds of violence and vice. Every two-bit pimp and foreign-exchange student drives a Jaguar or a Porsche; only a biker is tough enough to ride a chopped Harley. A chopper, although it looks sleek and graceful, is a bitch of a machine to handle. A Harley 80 (which replaces the 74 in 1979) off the assembly line weighs 700 pounds. Hell's Angels bylaw No. 11 forbids members from wearing colors while they ride a garbage wagon. The Angels use machine shop aerobics to trim 200 pounds of ugly metal off the bike to make it a full-fledged outlaw hog. They replace the front end with extended forks that make the bike more difficult to handle, especially if you have to wrestle with ape hangers. They substitute a thin 21-incher for the fat front wheel and sometimes forget to reinstall the front brakes. They remove the rear shocks to hardtail the bike. They replace the long-haul gas tank with a lacquered teardrop that barely gets them 60 miles down the highway. They bolt on a low-slung saddle that transmits every bump to the spine. Riding a chopper hard takes its toll. Many older Angels now ride the comfortable garbage wagons they once sneered at.

Some Hell's Angels prefer to steal their expensive Harleys, although they can easily afford to buy them. Angels are not foiled by anti-theft devices such as fuel cut-off valves, hidden ignition switches or kill buttons. They can take an ignition lock number to a dealer who cuts new keys to replace their "lost" set. Or they just lift the bike into a pickup truck or van. The bolder ones leave a forged driver's licence with a dealer as security while they test drive a motorcycle they don't plan to return.

Angels ensure police and irate owners won't recognize stolen bikes. They are magicians at converting stolen motorcycles into legitimate property. The easiest way to make a stolen bike disappear is to cannibalize it for parts. Many Angels own motorcycle shops where bikes are stripped down. Junkyards sell frames with legitimate serial numbers that can be used to register a rebuilt bike. Replacing handle bars, gas tank and fenders drastically changes a motorcycle's appearance.

Changing a motorcycle's vehicle identification number (VIN) allows it to be registered without wasting time stripping it down. VINS are stamped on the frame and the engine. There are several ways to change them: grind the numbers off and restamp new numbers, or leave the space empty; stamp over the VIN; place a piece of metal with another number over the VIN; grind off or drill out one or more numbers, fill the hole with lead or some other metal, grind the surface smooth and restamp.

The Harley-Davidson Motorcycle Co. Inc. of Milwaukee standardizes its VINS in 1970 to foil thefts. Harleys are registered by easily altered engine numbers before 1970. That year, Harley starts stamping identical numbers on the right frame down tube and the right front side of the engine of its 1200 cc and 900 cc motorcycles. It also registers its bikes by the more difficult to change frame number.

The Hell's Angels are nervy enough to use the stolen bikes, once registered, to defraud insurance companies. An Angel falsely reports his motorcycle stolen, usually in the fall in cold climates, and collects insurance money. He rebuilds the bike and puts it back on the road.

One Hell's Angels rip-off scheme starts in 1974 when an Outlaw steals 25,000 blank motor-vehicle registration titles in Wisconsin. A Charleston, South Carolina, Angel pays $300 apiece for some of the titles. The club uses them to register stolen motorcycles after they alter serial numbers with Harley-Davidson dies made in Durham, North Carolina. They also transfer their motorcycle ownerships to friends who report the bikes stolen. The motorcycles are then given new serial numbers and registrations before being resold. The Angels take their scheme one step further. They forge Wisconsin titles to insure motorcycles they don't have, then report them stolen to collect insurance money. Then the Angels decide to save money and have a Fayetteville printer counterfeit 150 blank titles.

The Hell's Angels steal anything that rolls. The Manhattan chapter sets up a factory to convert stolen vehicles in the early 1970s on a rural property near Monticello and Middletown in upstate New York. They steal expensive motor homes, Corvettes and other sporty cars, motorcycles and boats. They change their vehicle identification numbers and equip them with new licence plates they stamp from tin pie plates. The vehicle is out of the shop in 30 minutes. Motor homes are driven west. Corvettes go south.

The Hell's Angels dump stolen motorcycle parts at swap meets they sponsor across the US. The club takes part of the gate since it organizes the meets and provides security. The Troy and Rochester chapters are involved in New York State meets. The Lowell and Salem chapters organize meets in Massachusetts and the Charleston chapter organizes meets in the Carolinas.

The Hell's Angels are involved in every aspect of motorcycling. The club controls the 18,000 member Modified Motorcycle Association and chapters around the world lead the lobby against laws that require motorcycle riders to wear helmets.

Much of the Hell's Angels jargon revolves around the motorcycle. Flying the colors means to ride a motorcycle while wearing colors. An Angels' bible is a Harley-Davidson motorcycle manual used at weddings or torn up at divorces. The bikers have a variety of names for foreign motorcycles: beezers—B.S.A.s; trump or trumpet—a Triumph; Jap scrap —obvious. A knucklehead is a Harley engine made before 1948 with large nuts above the cylinders on the right side of the engine.

3

HELL'S ANGELS: THE BUSINESS

Any indicia of membership in the HAMC is indicative of a readiness, willingness and ability to engage in illegal activity.

—FBI agent Kevin P. Bonner.

This is the best crank in the world. We make it ourselves.

—Gary Kautzman, president of the San Francisco chapter drops a shoebox of methamphetamine on a table in his office on May 1, 1982.

THE Hell's Angels Motorcycle Club is well suited to operate as a criminal organization, whether it's selling crank or corpses. Angels are committed to live outside the law. They are a close-knit group sworn to secrecy under threat of death. The club's 67 chapters in 13 countries on four continents form a reliable international pipeline for contraband and a dependable communication network. Chapters hide fugitive Angels and provide them with false identification and a cover. Members have disappeared for years in this counterfeit underground. The Hell's Angels maintain safe houses in northern New York State for Canadian members on the lam. The Charleston, South Carolina, chapter has three safe houses in the middle-class suburb of Woodside Manor north of the city in 1980. The club also has an abundance of manpower, even after major busts. Every Angel has about 10 associates—men and women—who help him commit crimes. These associates have their own networks of friends.

The Hell's Angels Motorcycle Club is organized to insulate its leadership from prosecution. The club is hierarchically structured and well disciplined so it can function even after the arrest of members. It enforces its code of silence with death and camouflages orders through layers of bosses who protect themselves with graft and corruption. The Hell's Angels organization chart resembles that of traditional organized crime, with which the club slowly aligns itself during the 1970s and 1980s. The club's East Coast and West Coast officers carry out the same duties that traditional organized crime's Commission does when they regulate and oversee club business such as the creation of new chapters. The chapter president is equivalent to the family boss. The secretary-treasurer is sometimes the most logical member and offers advice like a *consigliere*; a lawyer who is a club associate also may act in this capacity. The vice-president is like a Mafia underboss. The sergeant-at-arms and road captain are like *caporegima*, or lieutenants. And members are soldiers.

The Hell's Angels and traditional organized crime operate the same way. They control the area where they commit crimes. They corrupt police and public officials to insulate themselves from prosecution. They use associates and fronts to manipulate and influence people.

Drug trafficking is the Hell's Angels' main source of income. But the club is involved in countless other crimes. Angels are opportunistic and flexible. If a new member shows safecracking talents, a chapter suddenly finds itself involved in a new enterprise. Angels fiddle with these crimes in their spare time: arson, assault, blackmail, bombing, burglary, corruption, extortion, forgery of government documents, gambling, gun running, insurance fraud, international white slavery, kidnapping, truck hijacking, loan-sharking, motorcycle and automobile theft, murder, pornography, prostitution, rape, robbery and weapons thefts from military bases. Members of the Manhattan chapter in New York are fond of holding up jewelry stores and running guns. Traditional organized crime families commit the same crimes.

An example: John J. Polizzio, a 38-year-old vice-president of the Westport Bank and Trust Company in Fairfield, Connecticut, is charged with arson offences in February 1986.

Police say he pays Hell's Angels members to burn down a house in March 1985, after which the owners collect $110,000 from an insurance company.

The Angels learn the merit of keeping a low profile when they work for traditional organized crime families. Angels set the trend in outlaw motorcycle gang fashions and cultivate the grub look for more than two decades to instill fear. The mob teaches them that conspicuousness is a weakness in the drug business. Angels today are more likely to wear suits than colors. They still value the grinning death's head, but keep it for funerals, runs, initiations and laying heavies. Angels, like the undercover policemen who tail them, prefer street clothes to blend in with the surroundings. They've replaced their Harleys with Corvettes, Lincolns and Cadillacs. The new mob shows class.

The Hell's Angels Motorcycle Club incorporates in California in 1966 to curb imitators spawned by 18 years of kicking ass. The articles of incorporation describe the Angels as a club dedicated to the promotion and advancement of motorcycle driving, motorcycle clubs, motorcycle highway safety and all phases of motorcycling and motorcycle driving.

This is not a lie in 1966. But after 19 more years, FBI agent Kevin P. Bonner has this to say about the Hell's Angels following a 26-month undercover investigation that ends on May 2, 1985:

"The HAMC is an organization which lives for or lives on drugs."

The Hell's Angels beat and piss on people during the first half of the club's life in a pathetic grab for recognition. They spend the second half of their existence trying to dismantle the anti-social image and cultivate an inconspicuous conspicuousness. It's a tricky balancing act the Angels call "Taking Care of Business." It means the Hell's Angels are just as bad as ever, but you'd never know unless you're part of the underworld they crawl around in. The Angels walk around for nearly two decades with hands in their pants groping their balls. Now they've got one hand on the billfold and the other in someone else's back pocket.

The transformation begins around San Francisco Bay in 1967; the alchemist's stone is lycergic acid diethylamide. The Hell's Angels are everything the flower children aren't in the mid-1960s: they spell peace with an *ie* and the only beads they have are on gun barrels. The spoiled generation rebels by giving away free love, spurns all-American red meat for veggies, and fries its brains with the most unnatural chemicals. It also latches on—hoping the rebellious image rubs off—to the only true counter culture around: the Hell's Angels. The bikers don't understand why the flower children take to them. They stink, they're crude and they hate wimpy, long-haired faggots. But the love generation spreads its legs and the Angels fuck the flakes more ways than one.

The hippies dub the Hell's Angels the "People's Police" and turn them on to a wider variety of drugs than they've known. It's a symbiotic relationship—the hippies provide love and drugs, the Angels lend muscle. The Angels waste no time becoming parasites. They quickly grasp that a handful of pushers make a fortune selling acid to the psychedelic fur brains. The smell of money brings out the shark in several ambitious Angels, including George (Baby Huey) Wethern, vice-president of the Oakland chapter. Wethern tracks down the acid king, legendary underground chemist Augustus Owsley Stanley III. He taps the source and corners the LSD market in California. He twists arms and enlarges nostrils with the cold barrel of a .45-calibre handgun to drive out competition. Wethern has the club's biggest gun collection.

Owsley is a 25-year-old job hopper when he signs up at the University of California at Berkeley in 1963. He adds "dropout" to his resumé within one semester. All he gets out of university is a 24-year-old chemistry major girlfriend called Melissa who knows how to make acid. Sexual chemistry leads to his famous Purple Owsley and other highly marketable pieces of chalk soaked with the stuff of dreams. Owsley reportedly makes $1 million selling his shit before acid is outlawed in April 1966. Novelist Ken Kesey and psychologist Timothy (TURN ON, TUNE IN, DROP OUT) Leary are among his best promoters as they garner followings of snug-assed tighties with talk of multi-colored mind- and snatch-expanding experiences.

The late 1960s give North Americans a chance to re-assess their values then quickly forget they doubted them. The era gives the Hell's Angels and other outlaw motorcycle gangs a drug subculture that fattens their coffers. Americans now spend more than $80 billion a year on illegal drugs. Canadians

spend $10 billion, a frighteningly high figure when you con-
sider the US population is 10 times that of Canada.

Wealth makes the club tone down its hell raising and work
toward a better public image to fend off police attention that
hurts profits. Men reconciled to a brawling working-class life
unexpectedly find themselves in mortgage-free homes with
three cars. They've traded the chip on their shoulder for a
buck in the pocket. The Hell's Angels could disappear forever
into suburbia if not for the rivalry for drug trafficking territory.

But every wop, spic and fairie chases the American dream
with a nose full of white powder and an M-60 machine gun
tucked under his arm. The Hell's Angels' flirtation with anonymity is at best sporadic. Sidewalk assassinations and car
bombings replace the parking-lot rumbles. Profit replaces
pussy as the Angels' reason for being in a netherworld where
the existential question is answered with a dry bed and a wet
snatch.

The transformation of the Hell's Angels from a motorcycle
gang to an international drug trafficking network is a master-
piece of business ingenuity greased with sweat and blood. The
Angels decide early to concentrate their efforts on LSD, PCP
and methamphetamine. They make the drugs in clandestine
laboratories and control the distribution network from whole-
salers to street-level pushers. It's a secure system, tough for
any cop to crack. The self-contained network also eliminates
competition. More importantly, complete control allows gang
leaders to maximize profits—they cut pure speed with baby
laxative, vitamin B or PCP before it goes to the next rung on
the distribution ladder. The drug is dilated at every level,
earning the seller a larger profit.

The Hell's Angels promise their crank is the world's best.
It's true. But they don't say anything about its purity. The only
Angel regulation about diluted drugs is that you don't sell
them to a fellow Angel. It's also club law that you don't sell
shit to anyone. Burns hurt business.

"Selling somethin' bad would be putting my patch on the
line. That's against the rules," says James (Gorilla) Harwood,
former vice-president of the Hell's Angels Troy, New York,
chapter and security officer for the club's East Coast chapters.
Harwood explains what happens to an Angel who sells bad
dope.

The guy lost his patch for a year. Plus, he had to pay back all the money that he made off it. The Hell's Angels, we're in business to make money. But it gets around when we're scum, scumbags like that.

The Hell's Angels strive for quality control, but not all crank cookers are equal.

"I'm a dope dealer. I know my business," says Ronald (Big Cheese) Cheeseman, former president of the Hell's Angels Binghamton, New York, chapter and head of the club's Mid-State chapter on July 14, 1983.

Cheeseman is one of the club's biggest methamphetamine producers on the East Coast. He has a moveable lab he alternates between Binghamton and a house on a dirt road in Montrose, Pennsylvania, where he keeps tanks of ether in the chicken coop and $15,000 of glassware in the kitchen. He also deals in cocaine smuggled to Florida in a Dominican Republic diplomatic pouch. He ships his speed across to Canada in cookie boxes.

Cheeseman's crank is not as good as that made in California.

"The methamphetamine that came from Binghamton was brown and smelled like perfume and it had a real violent taste," Harwood says. "Plus, it wouldn't get you high. It was sort of like a club joke."

Oakland Angels get lucky in the early 1970s. They recruit a Richmond, California, oil-company chemist to cook methamphetamine full time. He teaches members in many chapters how to make the drug. The Hell's Angels become the country's top crank producers and control 75 percent of the California market. Four Angels make $6 million selling crank at the wholesale level between 1976 and 1979. The Angels send technicians to chapters around the world to teach them how to produce Angel crank. A New York college chemist teaches four Manhattan chapter Angels—Sandy, Ted, Mike the Bike and Howie—how to make base drugs to produce methamphetamine.

The Hell's Angels corner the methamphetamine market through control of chemists. The club owns or controls most speed labs in California and British Columbia. They let associates run the labs to distance themselves from prosecution. Former Hell's Angels hit man James (Brett) Eaton says the club takes over methamphetamine laboratories two ways:

"They find someone already making speed and say: 'O.K., now you make it for us.' "

Sometimes they are more subtle. They pay a chemist $25,000 for five pounds of crank and front him $25,000 for the next shipment.

"Now the guy owes the club."

One Hell's Angels' lab in central Ohio can produce $14 million of speed a month. It supplies druggies from Ohio to California and in West Virginia, New York and New Jersey. The lab in North Carolina is staffed by a New York–trained chemist in the late 1970s and produces most of the speed sold by the southern and Omaha, Nebraska, chapters.

The Hell's Angels buy and steal the chemicals they need to make methamphetamine. Sergey (Sir Gay) Walton, president of the Oakland chapter in January 1977, steals enough laboratory glassware and chemicals during a break-in at a chemical company to set up several labs. He is helped by Angel Kenny Owen, president of the Vallejo chapter, and drug dealer Henry Crabtree. Owen uses the name of D&H Speed Engineering to order 40 pounds of chemicals needed to make speed from a Portland firm.

Two employees of the Loomis Scientific Co. of Santa Cruz travel to Florida and Arizona in 1984 to buy monomethylamine and phenylacetic acid which the company sells to the Hell's Angels in Oakland for their methamphetamine laboratories. The company is charged in January 1985 with providing chemicals to the club.

Crabtree isn't around to see how the club's drug business has expanded. He finds it too monolithic in 1978 and breaks off his dealings with the Angels one year later to work for himself.

> I got kind of tired of all the killings. The game of hustling is fun when you're down in the small rackets. When you get in the big rackets, it ain't fun. The hustling part of it I enjoyed. I still would. The killing part, no.

An Angel pays the white supremacist Aryan Brotherhood to ice Crabtree. They miss.

The drug business makes killers of the Hell's Angels. They lean on debtors for a while then cut their losses. Carl Billham,

24, is a drug-dealing associate of the club from Summerville, South Carolina. Four men jump him outside the can at the Nashville East Club in Charleston at 2:30 a.m. on October 12, 1979. He dies five days later from a knife wound to the gut. Police issue a warrant for the arrest of Hell's Angel and former Green Beret Artie Ray Cherry. Federal police raid Cherry's home on unrelated weapons charges on October 18. He avoids arrest when he produces a driver's licence that identifies him as Vincent Mark Guinta. He disappears before local police arrive to serve the murder warrant.

Jerry David Guy, an associate of the Hell's Angels in Durham and Winston-Salem, North Carolina, owes the club money in late 1980. The 37-year-old man and Pamela Merrell Boaz, 22, are found in an abandoned tobacco shed on November 6—stiffed.

The Winston-Salem Angels shoot Richard Hill, a 17-year-old associate who owes them money, twice in the head in August 1981. They tie a cinder block to his waist and dump him into 52 feet of water in a quarry outside the city. The Hell's Angels must own stock in concrete block companies. The Angels are too hurried or impatient to pour fresh cement overshoes like the Mafia does. It shows in the quality of their work. How many Mafia stiffs float to the surface? Jimmy Hoffa may have disappeared between two sesame seed buns, but he could also harbor in his fleshless bones a den of crayfish, a handful of minnows and a few leeches.

The Hell's Angels make and sell drugs that push body and mind beyond their limits and give users a terrifying glimpse at human circuitry gone awry. Some never look back.

Methamphetamine kicks the central nervous system into action the same way adrenaline does. That's why it's called uppers, speed and crank. The yellowish-white powder is snorted or mixed with water and injected. It sends blood pressure through the ceiling, decreases appetite, increases alertness and energy and keeps the sandman at bay. Users are generally speedy and aggressive. Heavy amphetamine users get run down from lack of sleep and food. They suffer amphetamine psychosis, which is similar to paranoid schizophrenia, and get violent. They usually need barbiturates, alcohol and opiates to calm down. As a last resort, they kill themselves.

The basic components of methamphetamine are phenyl ac-
etone, a controlled substance that can be made in a simple
four-step process with chemicals bought from supply companies, and N-methyl formamide. The base chemicals are
cooked for about six hours to create granular white methamphetamine.

PCP, or phencyclidine, is developed as an intravenous anes-
thetic for humans, but bombs out in 1965 when it causes con-
vulsions during surgery, delirium and hallucinations. Shrinks
consider using it to treat flakes, but back off. Veterinarians
now knock out monkeys with it. PCP hits the street illegally as
the peace pill in the 1960s. The white crystal powder is also
called angel dust and horse tranquilizer. It is snorted, injected
or eaten, but is most often smoked with marijuana or parsley
—a mixture called killer weed.

PCP short-circuits the body's electrical system in the name
of fun. It fucks up a person's ability to handle information
from the brain and the outside world. It distorts time, space,
hearing and sight. It zaps memory and logic. Panic and violence take hold. Sometimes, a dusty old door creaks open and
a nasty mental problem squirts out—artificial schizophrenia at
its best.

PCP is made with two chemicals in a five-step process. One
of the base chemicals is bromobenzene, a motor oil additive
more commonly used to make plastics. PCP is as dangerous to
make as it is to ingest. The cooking produces hydrogen cya-
nide gas, which is used in gas chambers. The gas also explodes if it comes into contact with water, another by-product
of the process.

LSD, or lysergic acid diethylamide, starts life as a fungus
called ergot that rots rye and other grains. LSD is made from
the alkaloid lysergic acid that is squished out of ergot. The
white, odorless drug is sold as little colored pills or as drips on
blotter paper. Enterprising packagers print groovy messages
like "LOVE" on their product. Others stamp Mickey Mouse or
Donald Duck faces on the tabs. Acid makes you see things
that aren't there. It disintegrates the boundaries between ob-
jects and turns the world into an ambulatory Dali painting. It
makes you tingle and leaves a weird taste in the back of your
brain. Timothy Leary and the hippies say it expands the mind.

Cocaine is the nostril cleanser of choice among athletes,
movie stars, uptown cuties, honky-tonk angels, juke-joint

johnnies, hookers, yuppies and whatever groovin' Americans of African descent call themselves these days. Coke is mostly snorted, but can be injected. The more adventurous sprinkle it on their gums, swirl it around their assholes or smear it on their snatches. Cocaine is like a desperate one o'clock Romeo —any hole will do. The white crystal powder makes you feel like wow, everything is so clear, I'm so strong, I'm so smart, let's boogie. It can dissolve nose membranes, cause hallucinations, stop breathing, fry the brain, inhibit pissing and prevent hard-ons.

The smiling Peruvian and Bolivian Indians in *National Geographic* photographs that show tits without uproar decades before *Playboy* magazine, chew the leaves of the Erythroxylon coca bush. Inca high priests and nobles drink a coke concoction—the original, original taste—to seek religious truth. Today, starving peasants chew the leaves to stave fatigue and hunger.

Sigmund Freud, whose sexual hang-ups society has willingly imposed on itself for 100 years, boasts in papers published in the 1880s that cocaine cures depression, alcoholism and morphine addiction. The man who brings us sublimation doesn't recognize substitution. The Coca Cola Company subliminally seduces taste buds through the brain when it laces its original-taste coke with coke in 1902—"I'll have a coke and a straw, please." The company removes all cocaine from the drink in 1903.

Traditional organized crime and outlaw motorcycle gangs argue they commit victimless crimes—that they cater to society's vices and customers come to them willingly. Angel cocaine dealer Gorilla Harwood rejects that argument when he walks into his house and finds his daughter imitating her father and his friends.

"My daughter was taking a straw and a mirror and putting it up the noses of her stuffed animals."

Speed kills, cocaine slaughters. Montreal Hell's Angel Noël Mailloux demonstrates that. Mailloux is a former Wild One from Hamilton, Ontario. He joins the Angels in Quebec with Walter Stadnick and both men spend a lot of time in their home town, which is controlled by enemy Outlaws and Satan's Choice. Mailloux is a heavy cocaine user. He dusts his nostrils with $21,000 of the white powder from December 25,

1982, to February 18, 1983. Mailloux is, at the best of times, paranoid. He sees Outlaws behind every stare and death in every glare. He carries a knife and a .357 Magnum revolver. He checks his car for bombs.

Mailloux, like other Hell's Angels, has an affinity for strippers. The 30-year-old biker spends the first two weeks of February 1983 at his girlfriend Connie Augustin's house, where he snorts coke and talks about an Outlaw who might kill him. The 24-year-old stripper works local clubs to support her four-year-old son, Stewart Hawley.

Mailloux and Augustin start a coke binge on Valentine's day. They get coke from Mario D'Alimonte, the bouncer at a downtown Hamilton hotel, on February 17. He comments on how wired they look for lack of sleep. Mailloux talks to D'Alimonte over the telephone later in the day. He hangs up and convinces Augustin the bouncer's coke is bad. He also suspects he's an Outlaw associate. The conversation frightens D'Alimonte so much he takes precautions that night.

"I loaded a couple of guns up—shotguns."

D'Alimonte spends a fearful night. Mailloux and Augustin live paranoia to its grisly end. Cindy Lee Thompson, an 18-year-old stripper, visits Augustin's house. Mailloux convinces them that D'Alimonte has set them up for an Outlaw hit. They turn off the lights and wait in the dark. Mailloux sits on the boy's stool with his loaded revolver.

Augustin decides after midnight that Mailloux is getting too weird. She gets her son and Thompson in the front seat of her car and tries to escape. Mailloux jumps into the back seat, puts the gun to Augustin's head and orders her to drive. Augustin leaps out at the first red light. She hopes Mailloux will chase her and give Thompson and her son a chance to escape. The Angel pulls the trigger as she opens the door. A bullet tears through her arm and right breast. She keeps running. He shoots the baby and the stripper in the head and takes off after Augustin.

"He's going to kill me," Augustin screams as she tears down the Hamilton Mountain suburban street. She runs up to John Perrins' car and grabs the door handle. The 25-year-old steelworker watches Mailloux fire two shots at her and speeds away.

"I thought maybe they were out partying and decided to make a scene and acted out this little scene."

Perrins stops and watches Augustin run to the car of his 26-year-old workmate Kevin Pomeroy. Mailloux catches up to her before she can get into the car and shoots the driver in the arm and chin.

"I felt a burning sensation in my chin. He didn't say anything. He looked like he had something on his mind and he didn't care whether he shot me or not."

Pomeroy drives away and Mailloux turns to Augustin.

"I looked up and he was looking at me. . . . He pulled the trigger, but there was no bullets left in the gun."

Augustin dashes off. Another driver stops for her. Mailloux disappears into the darkness. Hamilton-Wentworth Regional Police Sergeant Charles Bamlett spots the Angel in a nearby field and approaches cautiously. Mailloux crouches and holds the gun in both hands. Bamlett is 100 feet away.

"He was squeezing the trigger. I could hear it going click, click, click, and he was saying: 'Bang, bang, bang.' "

The East Coast and West Coast factions of the Hell's Angels each have a methamphetamine board of directors made up of officers from each chapter. The board meets regularly to assess how much crank the club has and how to split it up. It controls drug sales by ensuring chapters don't tread on each other's territory. It also issues customer lists. Angels can't sell to anyone not on the list. The rule is good for business and security.

Every chapter holds at least one monthly business meeting called "church." Club matters are discussed openly, but drug deals are negotiated on paper, with sign language or on a blackboard during an innocuous conversation. Some members are so worried about police bugs they discuss deals outside the clubhouse only.

Each Angel gives part of his drug profits to the chapter as weekly dues—usually $20. The chapter then pays into the club's national treasury. The Hell's Angels also keep a multi-million dollar defence fund to which members and chapters are occasionally asked to contribute, especially after a major bust. Some of the dues money is used to support the families and businesses of jailed members. The club also has a TCB fund for security/intelligence officers and hit men. Sandy Alexander thanks two potential drug buyers on December 29, 1983, for what they are doing for the Hell's Angels, as a large part of money members make through dealing goes to the club.

All Hell's Angels are assessed a $250 fee at the 1981 USA run to help defray the legal cost of the Omaha chapter's RICO trial.

In the Barger trial [1979–1980, says Clarence (Addie) Crouch, former vice-president of the Cleveland chapter] each person was assessed I think it was $100 the first time. But then once they got to selling the T-shirts and the bumper stickers and all that, it was a full-page ad taken out in a motorcycle magazine called *Easyrider* [sic] did not cost us anything, and all the moneys from that went into that fund there, which caused a lot of trouble in the club, because they wanted a counting of how much money it was, but Oakland would not tell them, which I assume—from what I have gathered from a lot of hearsay and talk and everything that it was quite a lot of money. They were taking bags each day from the post office to Oakland.

T-shirts and posters sold through ads in *Easyriders* are now commonplace. Those on sale to raise money for four Montreal chapter Angels on trial for the liquidation of the North chapter on March 24, 1985, read: "FREE EAST COAST CANADA," and show a pair of hands breaking manacles.

Chapters and members are leery to flaunt their wealth for fear they will be leaned on by less successful Angels.

"They do not let each other know in case something comes up," Addie Crouch says.

"One charter is not assessed more than another charter, so everybody kind of plays it poor . . . every member places a low profile on his money, because money always puts everybody out on front street."

Some Hell's Angels are millionaires. Crouch names one in New York, one in Cleveland and one in Oakland.

They are there to back any play that is really heavy, any kind of really heavy trials that come down or anything. They always feel that they can fall back on them.

They made most of their money from drugs. They have got fronts. [One] owns [a] restaurant out in Oakland. And [one] owns a little bar there in Cleveland, a couple of bars. And [one] just— he stays way back—New York don't flaunt their money at all.

Angels register property in the names of parents or girl-friends to hide their wealth. They are high rollers despite the crude image they like to project at times. A member of the Manhattan chapter spends $400,000 a year on good times. He rents a yacht in New Jersey for a week to party. He periodically stays in the penthouse suite at the Plaza Hotel with one of his many sweeties and fucks his brains out for three days. He rents cars, as do many Angels, and doesn't hesitate when hungry to walk into the poshest restaurant and order the most expensive items on the menu. Angels know life is short. They enjoy it while they can.

Several Angels in Quebec and British Columbia are also millionaires. Michael (Sky) Langlois, president of the Hell's Angels in Canada, owns a 1981 Harley, a car and an airplane. He receives $400 a week from 112628 Canada Inc.—the Montreal chapter's registered name—in 1985.

Rick Ciarniello, 41-year-old Hell's Angels president in British Columbia, and owner of a blue Lincoln with vanity plates that read "ANGELS," denies in 1985 that members are wealthy.

> What a fairy tale. You're gonna have one helluva time finding any millionaire bikers. There's no such thing. The truth is, we are a group of people who like motorcycles. It's so simple that anybody can grasp it.

The lower British Columbia mainland has a rapidly expanding drug market within easy reach of the California drug network. BC Angels make most of their money selling cocaine. The four Angel chapters in BC control all outlaw motorcycle gang activity in the province as well as 40 registered companies.

The BC Angels own a campground called Angel Acres in Nanaimo. The heavily wooded property has a large in-ground swimming pool, trailers and a bandshell. Angels and prospects guard the chained-off roadway into the property, part of which is off limits to anyone but Angels. The BC Hell's Angels host more than 3,000 bikers from across North America at their anniversary party on August 2, 3, 4, 1986. The Para-Dice Riders from Toronto make the event a mandatory

one-month run for the club's 39 members during the gang's
25th year. It is unusual for any Toronto gang to show such
support for either the Angels or Outlaws.

The Hell's Angels Motorcycle Club imposes strict accountability on drug dealers. Even Angels who brag about being
high-school dropouts keep books to record customers, drug
deals, debts and profits. Many chapters, such as the Lynn-
Salem, Massachusetts, and the Sorel, Quebec, chapters, keep
their records on computer floppy disks, which are easily hidden and transported. Computers also allow the transmission of
information between chapters over telephone lines using
modems. Volumes of information can be transmitted in minutes and none of it can be easily listened to by prying ears.

The club treats the business seriously, as the North chapter
in Quebec finds out. James (Gorilla) Harwood has a brush
with discipline in 1982. The Manhattan chapter tries to collect
$100,000 it fronts Harwood in methamphetamine. He doesn't
deny receiving the drugs, but hasn't kept records. New York
has. Troy, New York, Angels dig Harwood's grave and dust it
with lime. Murders within the club don't have to be sanctioned by East or West Coast presidents, but these officers are
sometimes consulted for their greater grasp of the implications
of the killing. Troy Angels pay a courtesy call on Sandy Alexander to inform him they plan to do in Harwood. They ask for
his opinion, not his sanction. They want him to assess the
repercussions. Alexander tells them not to kill. The Angels
pull Harwood's patch for 10 months instead so they can get
the money back.

The Angels, like thousands of businessmen, use courier
services to get drugs to customers overnight. Gary Kautzman,
president of the San Francisco chapter, ships drugs east
through United Parcel Service in May 1982. He pays a UPS
employee for seven years to ensure the shipments aren't
ripped off. Manhattan vice-president Howard Weisbrod sends
drugs via air-freight services such as Federal Express and
Emery in 1984.

The Angels also ship their crank from California to New
York by train, usually in a suitcase carried by a prospect. No
one bothers train passengers or their luggage. Harwood sends
drugs to Canadian chapters by rail in the late 1970s and 1980s
and once transports cocaine in his daughter's luggage. An

Angel called Pee Wee plans to haul crank from Oakland to Alaska in toolboxes in early March 1985. He buys so much he uses a trunk instead.

Angels who carry drugs in their cars continually worry they'll be caught. Phillip Utley, vice-president of the Durham, North Carolina, chapter and prospect Ronnie Blackwell deliver drugs to Baltimore, Maryland, in February 1985. They hide the drugs in the car's emission control system. Harwood delivers drugs from Staten Island, New York, to Baltimore on March 22, 1985. He hides them in the car's door panel. A Quebec Angel flies drugs to an airstrip near Salem, Massachusetts. Canadian Angels exchange speed with US members for LSD, heroin and cocaine.

The earth-bound Hell's Angels also take to water with an ever-expanding fleet of smuggling boats. But being an expert motorcyclist doesn't qualify one to sail. Richard Snyder, a member of the Monterey chapter, scrambles to safety as his boat sinks off Hawaii in March 1985 with 15 tons of marijuana in the hull.

The Hell's Angels are continually on guard for narcs and use the latest technology to check their clubhouses for bugs. They also use less sophisticated techniques to foil electronic eavesdroppers. They crank up radios, televisions or record players to drown out conversations when they conduct drug deals at home. They also unplug telephones to foil equipment that can eavesdrop on conversations held in a room with a phone in it. Angels refuse to talk business in cars for fear they are bugged.

Angels use complex codes when they deal over the telephone. But they hop a plane to discuss transactions in person when business is too important to trust even their phone codes. Angels use their telephones so often many members have speed dialers that allow them to ring their regular contacts with one touch of a button. Sandy Alexander, president of the Manhattan chapter in 1985, has one. So do chapter vice-president Howard Weisbrod and Harwood. Gorilla screams into the telephone one day just in case he is being bugged:

"Any cops raid this house, I'm shooting the first that comes through the door."

Technology alleviates some of the fear of using telephones.

Mobile cellular phones are a boon to bikers and mobsters. Few police forces have the technical ability to tap the radio frequencies on 99 channels that cellular phones operate on. A person who travels through a large city could be automatically switched through 15 channels in 10 minutes. Police don't have the technology to follow such rapid switches. The equipment to track a cellular telephone call costs $100,000. And you need one of these for every caller you chase. Police need complete conversations to build solid cases against drug dealers. The problem is compounded in 1987 by the introduction of call incrypters that transform cellular telephone conversations into jibberish for third parties that listen in.

Angels operate on the premise they are being followed and continually try to thwart surveillance—real or imagined. James (Oats) Oldfield, president of the Charleston, South Carolina, chapter in April 1985, drives past a motel where he is supposed to meet someone and doubles back through parking lots. He takes a circuitous route on the way home and sits in a parking lot for 30 minutes before he continues.

Angels rarely carry drugs when they deal. They bury them and tell buyers where to pick them up. Business is so brisk bikers wear pagers on their belts that alert them with an inaudible buzz when a customer calls. The pagers also display the incoming number digitally.

The club is a professional, sophisticated organization run on business school principles. Few chapters blow their profits on parties, drugs and booze anymore. The price paid by the North chapter in Quebec in March 1985 is a lesson for all Angels. Chapters invest part of their money in legitimate businesses as fronts to launder illegal earnings. The club sends Andy, its East Coast treasurer, to an Ohio college to learn accounting in the early 1980s.

Angels own amusement arcades, auto salvage and wrecking yards, bars and clubs, entertainment companies, food producing and catering companies, massage parlors, motorcycle shops, real estate, restaurants, construction firms, antique stores, firearm shops, vending machine companies, tattoo parlors, billiard parlors and trailer parks, private security firms, auto and truck paint shops, investment firms, apartment buildings, resort hotels, trucking firms, ice cream shops, tow truck companies and many luxurious homes.

Sergey (Sir Gay) Walton, former president of the Hell's Angels Oakland chapter, says the club has a "buy out, burn out, bomb out" program to launder profits from its methamphetamine business. Front men buy failing businesses to legitimize the cash. Companies that won't sell are burned or bombed. The club also launders money through real estate.

"You try to sidestep the IRS, you get yourself money managers," says former Hell's Angels hit man James (Brett) Eaton. "Money is power. It buys policemen, judges."

Legitimate club businesses also provide jobs for Angels who need a job unrelated to crime to be released from jail on parole.

Douglas Chester (Dutch) Schultz, the 32-year-old president of the Hell's Angels San Diego chapter, owns the Rich Man Poor Man Limousine Service in 1985. He has 14 cars and a bus in the lot and a .45-calibre assault rifle in the office. At times he also has more than 50 pounds of methamphetamine under car seats. He sells the stuff out of his office at 4252 40th Street. The limousine service is profitable. Schultz owns a 1964 Bentley, a 1970 Mercedes Benz, a Rolls Royce, a 30-foot limousine, four Lincolns and a Cadillac.

Manuel Rubio, the most enterprising Hell's Angel, owns a motorcycle in 1973. He invests $200,000 in an Oakland, California, body shop. He opens a motorcycle shop. He sells both and invests in Siesta Catering in San Leandro in 1976. The industrial catering company prospers and buys out competing firms after they are coincidentally bombed or burned out. He sells the company for $6 million in 1980 before he begins a jail term. His partners, John Thomas (Johnny Angel) Palomar and club associate Jacob (Jake) Sanchez Jr. go into the catering business in Sacramento, California.

"Can you imagine having the Hell's Angels cater your wedding?" asks an FBI agent.

Not all Hell's Angels are rapists, drug traffickers and murderers. Many enjoy motorcycling and club camaraderie. They also run legitimate businesses. Charlie Magoo Productions is a thriving six-year-old Oakland, California, company that stages country music concerts in 1983. James (Fu) Griffin runs the company with his wife Corrie. The couple meet in the anthropology library at the University of California in Berkeley in 1976. She is Griffin's Spanish tutor. He is out on parole after he spends eight years in jail on a narcotics conviction.

* * *

The Hell's Angels deny repeatedly the club is a criminal organization. US Marshal Budd Johnson, a drug investigator in San Diego, says this after a 1984 bust of the club:

"The Hell's Angels today are the new Mafia. The Angels are 25 years ahead of other gangs. They went from a looseknit bunch of guys to an organized crime family."

Sonny Barger's reaction:

> The government is waging a smear campaign against us. It is a Hollywood image and a government image, but it is not the truth. A lot of Hell's Angels have gone to prison for individual things, just like policemen.

The US President's Commission on Organized Crime reports in April 1986 that Hell's Angels in the San Francisco Bay area buy property in the Sierra Foothills with illegal drug profits.

> It's all hype [Barger says]. It's a big fucking joke. If they did, and the government has proof of that, why aren't they all in jail? The whole thing is, all these agencies are going around and making accusation after accusation. That's how they get their money. If they make enough accusations, then Congress will give them the money. We're always expanding. Lots of people don't like to live in the cities. We're no different from anyone else. The Hell's Angels are not involved in anything but motorcycling.

Matthew F. Zanoskar, a member of the Hell's Angels Cleveland chapter, writes to newspapers following coverage of Angel court trials. He sends a copy of one letter to Angel Luc (Sam) Michaud, imprisoned in Montreal's Parthenais jail during his trial for the murder of five North chapter Angels. Zanoskar signs the copy with bold strokes: "They left out 3 of my most damaging paragraphs. Love & respect. Matt SS [lightning bolts]." Here is a condensed version of that edited letter:

> I have never tried to put a pretty face on anything other than a woman I once woke up with.
>   Show with 'evidence' to me, Matt Zanoskar, and to your

readers that Hell's Angels Motorcycle Club, 'as a club,' was involved in drug sales, rapes and killings. . . .

Yes, we have had problems in the past finding a minister to bury our dead, but the true outrage arises when baptism is denied our children! Tell me about moral ethics.

You call me Mafia! First you must strap a spud wrench belt to yourself and climb a red iron column with me to the truss. Then walk with me, ever so carefully, to the apex, just below where the eagle stands, earn my wage as you stand alone, and then look me in the eye and call me Mafia.

Flexibility and adaptability are among the Hell's Angels' most formidable assets. The Angels convert their most psychotic members into hit men when the battle for drug trafficking turf gets violent in the early 1970s. Some Angels knock off the competition for a thrill. Others kill brother Angels when financial success breeds paranoia and fear of rats in the pack.

A biker's colors scare off most of the competition. But there's always some asshole who thinks he can screw the club. Harwood sports the Filthy Few tattoo. He is just as mean before he joins the Angels. The drug dealer is a member of the Breed in 1974 when he lays a heavy on a band promoter who sells drugs on his turf in Albany, New York. He meets the man at a junkyard. The dealer wants to show Harwood something in the trunk of the car. He pulls a shotgun on the biker. Harwood—300 pounds of tattoos—breaks it in half and beats the dealer. He also likes to shred rival bikers' chests with the nails in his leather wristband. He helps murder four members and two old ladies of the rival Invaders on January 7, 1981, in a fight for the methamphetamine market in Richmond, Virginia. The victims, including club president Steve Smith, are shot between the eyes.

Harwood, like his brother Angels, knows that subtlety is the thinking man's muscle. He flexes it when necessary. He pays a judge to put in a few good words for some buddies at a hearing.

"It wasn't bribing him," Harwood says. "We paid him. That wasn't a bribe."

Harwood, with 33 convictions that include rape and sodomy, is so well versed in law he lectures Baltimore bikers on how to beat Title 18, United States Code, Section 1962,

Racketeer-Influenced and Corrupt Organizations (RICO) statute.

The Angels don't always beat the rap.

Jail is sometimes a worse fate than death on the job. Many
Angels, despite precautions, get nailed selling drugs, pussy
and fear. They also get caught when they rape. Investigations
reveal that the rapists, in their perversity, like to roll a woman
over after they plug her and shove it up her ass. Hell's Angels
rack up quite a few sodomy convictions.

Angels don't like jail cells. The club has bondsmen and
lawyers on call 24 hours a day to ensure members don't spend
too much time behind bars. The club once posts $3-million
bail for 11 California members who are picked up in a chauffeur-driven limousine.

Imprisoned Angels don't rely on the club's mystique for
protection. They ally themselves quickly with other outlaw
bikers or white-power groups. The most notable of these in
the southwest and western US is the Aryan Brotherhood. The
Angels use the racists for an occasional hit.

The club ensures jailed members don't feel forgotten. They
write, visit and deliver all the necessary drugs. Angels rent a
plane on Sonny Barger's birthday in 1974 and drop leaflets on
Folsom Prison that wish him happy birthday. Tom (The Bomb)
Alexanian worries in his jail cell where he serves a sentence
for the murder of Angel Digger Hansen. His wife tells him
some guy is on her case. Alexanian writes to inform Gorilla
Harwood, who convinces the dork to stop bugging the lady.

Drug dealing makes the Hell's Angels wealthy and powerful. It also undermines the principles on which the club is
founded. Money replaces brotherhood as the bond between
Angels. Colors, an Angel's most sacred possession, are occasionally sold for services or narcotics connections, not for loyalty to the club. Chapter leaders are often the richest Angels.
Much of their wealth comes from members who watch their
money get sucked to the top of the pyramid. Jealousy sneaks
into the brotherhood. Members are loyal to the man who will
make them rich. Competition for the best drugs, the best
deals, the best customers, the best turf gnaws away at the
club. Angels see enemies in friends. They kill. Those who

fear they are next rat when arrested. More busts. More paranoia. The Hell's Angels Motorcycle Club, like traditional organized crime, becomes an organization from which you don't retire. Greed succeeds where years of police work fail.

William (Wild Bill) Medeiros leaves the club because he feels drug dealing undermines the brotherhood.

> The more you get into the business part, the more you're going to screw your brother. When we got into big business we cut each others' throats. Years ago, we'd know a guy before he joined. People now ask what will the guy do for the club? What will he bring in? Before, if a guy was down and out, we'd give him money.

John (The Baptist) LoFranco has an insight into the club's weakness while in jail. The pro boxer starts his career as a Hell's Angel with the Manhattan chapter. He moves to the Mid-State chapter, then to the floating Nomads chapter in 1984. He ends up behind bars one year later when an Angel fingers him as operator of a moveable drug lab with Big Cheese Cheeseman. A reflective LoFranco writes this letter which is read at the 1985 annual Sturgis, South Dakota, classic motorcycle run:

> It's time for our true colors to come out. Please don't let others be able to say, "They're just like the Breed, Pagans or Outlaws—when the going gets tough, they rat on one another or they don't help each other." It's time to show others and ourselves there is a difference between Hell's Angels and all the others.
>
> I remember when I first came around. Hell's Angels didn't talk to hang-arounds or prospects about drugs. If anything, Hell's Angels would check you out to see what you had. Somehow we stopped communicating. How else could this happen? We have forgotten our basics.
>
> We must go back to basics, so we can see just how much a person or persons want what we have. I don't mean drugs or money, either. I mean what a Hell's Angel has when everything else is gone. His pride.

LoFranco's letter stirs the Angels. The club is grateful to lawmen for the May 2, 1985, FBI bust of more than 100 Angels and associates. "Thanks for cleaning out our deadwood," they say. The Hell's Angels rebuild, as they always do after a raid. Forty years of police arrests seem to strengthen, not weaken the club. It's almost as if regular busts are part of the natural selection process to weed out the weak in the out-law motorcycle world.

4

PUSSY GALORE

First priority of any club member is his feelings and respect for his colors and the club. They rate equal loyalty, and it has been said members would give their life for either one.

Second priority is the biker's motorcycle.

The third priority is either his dog or old lady, depending on which one he owns. If he owns both we must keep in mind that there are very few cases known that members have bought, sold, traded or given away dogs, as the women are.

—US Marshals Service outlaw motorcycle gang manual.

Hey, come on. Give us biker chicks a chance. We want to see more dudes with their pants down, taking leaks.

—Sweet Betty, Mount Olive, Illinois, in an April 1979 letter to *Easyriders* magazine.

MAN slips into the world from between a woman's legs and spends the rest of his life trying to get back in. The Hell's Angels, despite their braggadocio, are no different from other men—they put their dicks in one inch at a time. Selling drugs in the mid-1960s teaches the Angels the basics of supply-demand. When they learn men pay to rent the empty space between a woman's legs, they put their holes to work. In the violent, profit-oriented fringe inhabited by the Hell's Angels, that's all a woman is—a hole. More respectful Angels call her property.

Women take up with the Hell's Angels for the same reasons flies are attracted to shit: some are hungry, some need a warm place to stay, others feel safe in the crowd. While the Angels abduct and rape many women, most attach themselves voluntarily to the club and everything it stands for—drugs, alcohol, parties, fast bikes and cars, cheap thrills and sex. Horny bitches want endless cock every way it comes. Rebellious teenagers who strike back at their parents numb their minds with drugs and screw their brains out on the clubhouse floor. Bored clerks take a walk on the wild side with macho men who lead dangerous, exciting lives. Dumb dames become somebodies when they attach themselves to respected and feared Angels. Shiftless girls like the freedom from responsibility. The unloved and homeless confuse sex with affection and cherish the arms that hold them. Every notch in an Angel's dick is a plug for their self-esteem.

The Hell's Angels are master seducers, if knocking over a tart rates anything. An Angel, like any other man, picks up a bar fly or a hitch-hiker and shows her a good time. She's attracted to the violence and virility his colors symbolize. She's impressed by his business sense if he's wearing a three-piece suit. If the Angel likes what he sees, he keeps her as personal property. If he couldn't care less, he takes her to the clubhouse to meet the boys.

There are three kinds of women in the macho world of the Hell's Angels: old ladies, sweeties and mamas or sheep. An old lady is the property of one Angel and can't be used or abused by other club members. Once in Oakland, though, loud-mouthed Jan is taken into a member's basement, stripped, lashed to a post and peppered with BBs. Old ladies, like children, should be seen and not heard. Angel women have no rights, but an old lady gets to wear a jacket or vest that says "Property of so-and-so." She might also have a property belt.

The US Marshals Service sensationalizes the position of women in the Angel hierarchy.

"If a guy holding a gun tells me to hand over the colors or

he'll kill my wife, then he gets them," William (Wild Bill) Medeiros, former security officer for the Manhattan chapter in New York City, says, "What'd ya think I'm crazy? We're human. I love my wife."

Sweeties are flames Angels fuck on the sly. Any Angel worth his dick has up to 10 sweeties ready to milk his gonads on short notice.

A mama is the sexual equivalent of the public well—anyone can dip into her, at any time, as often as he wants. Mamas like fucking bikers and have more mileage put on them during a week in an Angel clubhouse or on a run than most married women rack up in a lifetime. Women have been known to pull the train for as many as 200 bikers in three days. The only tight pussy in an Angel clubhouse is drunk. A mama's jacket reads: "Property of Hell's Angels." She's the one with stretch marks around her mouth.

"For a sex-starved teenager like I was in those early days, joining a motorcycle gang was like a wet dream," says one biker, not an Angel, who aptly describes the role of women in his world.

> I'd never seen so many willing women in my life. Most of the clubhouses were real holes. There was no furniture left, it had all been smashed up. But there were always a couple of filthy squashed mattresses and at any time of the day or night there would always be at least one woman on her back giving it away.
>
> In every club there would be two or three chicks who were off limits—other guys' wives or old ladies—but most of the girls belonged to whoever wanted them at the time. And they were kept pretty busy. On some nights, you could have 15 guys lining up for one girl with quite a few coming back for seconds. Some of the girls may have got more than they bargained for, but most of them seemed pretty eager and willing to me. They got a kick out of belonging to the gang. It was their way of saying thank you. Like us, they were just out to have a good time.

Outlaw bikers and those who think like them are so numerous that several magazines cater to their tastes. *BIKER Lifestyle* is one of them. A full-page color advertisement that solicits subscriptions to the magazine shows four hulking, tattooed bikers and three women—one with white cotton panties and a red plastic top, one with a string bikini that hides less than her full-body tattoos, and one with cute black-and-white checkered tights and a see-through black lace top. The clip-out subscription label contains two checkoff boxes, the contents of which hint at what you can expect from the magazine. They read:

"I can't find your fuckin' rag anywhere, so here's $24.00, send me the next 12 issues of your leg-wetting rag."

"I'm really sick, and want *BIKER Lifestyle* all the time, so send me the next two years (24 copies). I'm sending $36.66."

An explicit full-page color advertisement in *Iron Horse* magazine announces:

The year's most exciting adult videotape movie! Scooter Trash, starring six *Iron Horse* covergirls. The first adult video made fer our breed. Real partyin! Real bikers! Real leg-wettin' action. Directed by Wolfman. Featuring Fatbob, Strut, Dynamite, Ron Jeremy, Buddy Hatton, Ricky Di Rico.

The six covergirls who appear in the flick are displayed in color photos across the top of the page: Rhonda Jo Petty (*Iron Horse* covergirl May 1985) wears a black leather corset as she stands in front of a Harley and stretches open her snatch with long-nailed fingers. Lucky Greenhog (February 1985) has big tits and a man's face buried in her crotch. Cindy "Tanktop" Smith (December 1984) has firm breasts and blue eyes that match her cut-off denim shorts. Sheri Hannigan (January 1985) wears more clothes than the rest put together. Candy Montana (January 1985) couldn't have been a covergirl—you can't get tits that big on one page. Elena Evans (May 1985) strikes a pose that makes her inviting from front and rear.

One of the still photographs from the video shows three of the topless lovelies gorging themselves on three upstanding dudes. The clip-out coupon guarantees that "this film contains scenes of explicit sexual activity between consenting adults." It offers a career opportunity to buyers of the video. Just circle the line that reads:

"I would like to appear in a Wylde Hoarse biker flick. Enclosed is my photo and telephone number."

The letters page of *Easyriders* magazine gives some insight into readers who make up the outlaw biker subculture:

In response to the letter titled 'Problems, Problems' in your Jan. 79 issue, the chicks who fuck, suck, and ride the way guys say they want chicks to fuck, suck and ride are not reading women's magazines. They read the same stuff men read.

If we all read women's rags, there wouldn't be a decent fuck among us. We'd all be too worried about messin' up our frizz-perms. To the chick who complained about all the tities—the more tits my ol' man sees, the better he knows he's got the best ones at home.—Balcony Babe, South Jersey, N.J.

Most Angels are heterosexuals, although they have been known to indulge in bumfucking and cocksucking. The most bizarre homosexual biker story told is not about the Angels, but the Lobos in Windsor, Ontario. Police wiretap the clubhouse in February 1976 and hear members talking over the telephone during a group bugger. The Satan's Angels in Vancouver, 16 years before they become Hell's Angels, kidnap a 20-year-old male hippie they call their butler and torture and bugger him silly all night.

Most Angels are family men and frown on kiddy diddling. Ronald (Big Cheese) Cheeseman, the 250-pound president of the Binghamton, New York, chapter and later the Mid-State chapter, has a 20-minute videotape in 1985 that shows him involved in sexual relations with a seven-year-old boy. A 10-year-old girl narrates: "You be sure to buy our tape, now."

A woman's main value for a Hell's Angel, aside from sexual gratification, is daily income—she must give all her money to her old man. Angels put their women to work in massage parlors, topless bars, cocktail lounges and strip clubs. Old ladies even set up men to be rolled—"Hey, hunk, let me suck your rod out back." Most jobs are covers for prostitution—the Angels' second most lucrative source of income after drugs. Old ladies are expected to bring home up to $250 a night. Some Angels have five or more old ladies. The luckier ones get to work for escort services, whose wealthy clients are often particular to thongs and whips.

A former prostitute for the Hell's Angels in Charlotte, North Carolina, describes how members suck in tighties to work for the club.

"Young girls just don't realize. They fall in love with these guys. They'll do anything to be around them. An older woman would have more sense. But a girl 13 to 15 hasn't been anywhere."

The Angels treat the girls well.

All the time they're setting you up. If you have something they
want—money, a piece of jewelry or your hind end—they'll find a
way to get it. These guys don't have any particular feeling for the
female, as long as she's making money.

The Angels pump girls with drugs when they put them to
work in massage parlors, strip clubs or on the street. Addiction helps bikers dominate them. Violence later replaces
drugs.

They tell the girl, after feeding her drugs, she can't have any
more. After a while the girl will slip out for more. They take the
girl and brutally hit her, really mess her up. Then they put her
back in the parlor. They lay her up for weeks until she heals. Then
she'll do anything they wish.

The Hell's Angels chapter founded in Stuttgart, West Germany, in 1981 takes over two saunas and controls 60 prostitutes. Old ladies who work as strippers and exotic dancers on
a circuit of hotels are couriers for information and drugs they
pass on to bikers who frequent the bars.

West German officials send 500 heavily-armed police into
a Hamburg bar on a Saturday in late August 1983 to arrest 24
Hell's Angels on charges of running a white slavery ring. Police seize weapons, drugs and cash in 80 houses and brothels.
More than 100 police in Zurich arrest nine Angels on the
following Thursday. The FBI arrests Andrea Roman Brown,
the 26-year-old president of the Hamburg chapter, in New
Hope, Minnesota, the same day and charges him with extortion and being a member of a criminal gang. The Angels allegedly run a prostitution ring that sells women to
Switzerland, the Netherlands and Austria; they are said to kidnap a prostitute and sell her for $5,500 to work in Switzer-
land; and they are said to control 60 prostitutes in Hamburg's
Reeperbahn red-light district.

An old lady also sells and carries drugs on the street for her
Angel to ensure he is never caught. She keeps his weapons in
her purse so he is clean when frisked, but ready for action if
trouble starts. Sandra Grieco, wife of James (Gorilla) Harwood, vice-president and security officer of the Troy, New
York, chapter until May 1985, carries a .22 Magnum revolver
in her purse. An old lady, because of fear, dependence on the

gang, or sheer viciousness, is as dedicated to the club as any male member and just as cold-hearted and deadly.

Old ladies are an important part of the Hell's Angels intelligence network. They work for telephone companies and in all levels of government offices where they can get blank birth certificates, drivers licences and other documents to help create fictitious identities and camouflage stolen goods. They get jobs in welfare bureaus, prisons and police departments, where they gather sensitive information for the club. They even fuck cops to compromise them or to gather intelligence.

The East Coast Hell's Angels make many of their old ladies dance and turn tricks in two topless bars in North and South Carolina—a club in Charlotte and one in Charleston. Both clubs are near military bases and the old ladies get all the weapons the club needs. The Cleveland chapter gets three light antitank weapon (LAW) rockets through old ladies in Charlotte. Most chapters get .45-calibre pistols and grenades through the two bars.

An old lady usually provides her Angel with a place to stay—a permanent address to which his welfare and unemployment checks are mailed. She also collects welfare, usually as a single mother, to supplement her unreported income as a stripper and prostitute. Many biker strippers use an alias and false identification when they sign up for a job. They cash their check at the hotel bar and move on to the next job and name. Tax officials never find them. Most Hell's Angels don't have jobs and can't launder drug and prostitution profits. They register vehicles, property, other assets and legal transactions in their old ladies' names to hide illegal gains. Angel women in Durham, Winston-Salem and Charlotte, North Carolina, are registered owners of up to 12 vehicles each in 1981. Patricia Jo Arnold, old lady of Terry Dale Hyatt, a Charleston, South Carolina, Angel, obtains permits for four pistols in 1979: a Colt .357 Magnum, a Colt 9mm, a .22-calibre and a Charter Arms Bulldog .38-calibre. A woman keeps her Angel's drug businesses going while he's in jail, delivers club messages and does his banking. Women drive the crash truck, or war wagon, on runs. Yet, they are not allowed to attend church or discuss business.

Love sometimes conquers lust and overrides business sense. The Hell's angels have their own marriage ceremony, performed by reverends of the Universal Life Church with an

Angels' bible—a Harley-Davidson motorcycle manual. One writes to the church headquarters in Modesto, California, to become ordained for free; $15 gets you a church charter. The Universal Life Church has ordained more than 15 million ministers. Many Hell's Angels are reverends, deacons and ministers who use the credentials to visit jailed club members. They also register motel rooms in the church name when booking in advance to prevent a sudden rash of no vacancy signs. It works at a Winchester, Virginia, motel they book in July 1981.

The Hell's Angels Manhattan clubhouse in New York City is legally registered as the Church of the Angels under a charter from the Universal Life Church. The chapter has stacks of church membership cards signed by reverends: Reverend Sandy Alexander, Reverend William Medeiros. Church property is tax exempt and revenue officials have a hell of a time fighting groups that don't qualify for religious property exemptions because the law doesn't define religion.

Reverend Edward (Deacon) Proudfoot wears a necklace of grizzly bear claws in the fall of 1983 to marry the infamous (Mouldy) Marvin Gilbert, 41, and young Jane Bickford in the name of the Hell's Angels. The ceremony, held at the Bass Lake campground near Fresno, California, where the Angels have partied since the early 60s, is complete with a three-tiered cake that Gilbert cuts with a large knife taken from another Angel's waistband. Gilbert has a note that reads "I will" pinned to his colors. His heavy gold ring, kept safe by 350-pound best man Albert Lee (Big Al) Perryman, is encrusted with the winged death's head in diamonds.

Marge Bickford comes from Las Vegas to witness the ceremony.

"I think he loves her. I wouldn't have her marry anyone else," she says of a man who beat a man to death with his fists. Mouldy Marvin and three other Angels rocket the club to international fame in September 1964 when they are charged with the alleged rape of two teenagers near Monterey. A frenzied press publishes lurid accounts of the girls' dates being pummeled by drooling, beer-guzzling, hairy Angels while club members take turns humping the recent virgins in the sand. There is little coverage when the charges are dropped for lack of evidence.

Few women get as far as Jane Bickford. During the long

evening of September 20, 1977, and painfully toward dawn, the Manhattan Hell's Angels torment 22-year-old Mary Ann Campbell on the roof of their tenement clubhouse at 77 East Third Street. The Angels want a gang bang and she won't put out. Vincent (Big Vinnie) Girolamo, the chapter's 31-year-old heavy, grabs her by the ankles, drags her screaming across the roof and holds her upside down over the edge of the six-story building. Angels on the street yell.

"Let her go. Let her go. I dare you."

Girolamo suffers a severe case of post-coital disinterest and drops his date. But the brute's gang banging days are running out. Girolamo visits Angels in California early in 1978. He argues with Michael (Irish) O'Farrell in the Oakland chapter clubhouse. The hulking Girolamo throws O'Farrell to the floor. Other Angels beat the New Yorker with baseball bats as he rolls their West Coast brother around. Girolamo takes his beating without complaint and returns to New York where he collapses. He dies of a ruptured spleen on the operating table. No animosity develops between the chapters over the death. Girolamo picks on a smaller man, has a friendly fight and dies. Them's the breaks.

The Hell's Angels harbor many men like Girolamo. They can't live without women, and don't want them to live. A woman is shot near the Hell's Angels clubhouse in Saint-Eustache, near Montreal in late March 1979—once in the head, once in the vagina.

Elizabeth Diane Gupton, a 20-year-old cock pumper in a Durham, North Carolina, massage parlor, is strangled on September 6, 1974, and buried in a shallow grave in Harnett County. Police indict her boyfriend—Durham Hell's Angel Charles Eugene (Tripp) Weddington, also known as James Earle Guthrie and Charles Eugene Trumbley—in the murder. He disappears with several witnesses in 1975.

Several Hell's Angels pick up a Charlotte hooker for kicks in January 1980. She refuses to have sex with them at the Wilkinson Art Studio, a massage parlor on Wilkinson Boulevard—the city's Miracle Mile. Angels Randall (Ronnie) Branch and Frank (Boots) Spell break her nose, leg, several ribs and teeth.

Clarence (Addie) Crouch has a hell of a reputation as a stud and woman beater among the Hell's Angels for his antics in Cleveland. The biker pimp at one time has 20 hookers in his

stable. Crouch has fathered about 13 children with various
women. He once bullwhips his naked black girlfriend and pins
a white girlfriend to the floor with a knife he plunges through
her foot.

The find'em, feel'em, fuck'em, forget'em attitude sometimes rubs off. Ian Everest, an 18-year-old asshole, drags a
14-year-old Girl Guide off a Winchester, England, street and
into the middle of a Hell's Angels party in a nearby dale in
mid-1972. He bangs her in front of cheering Angels.

Few women raped by Hell's Angels complain. In fact,
many women are raped so they don't testify against the club.
Angels go through a woman's purse and pockets while she is
being raped and note her address and telephone number, as
well as those of friends and relatives, and her place of employment. They call the next day to let her know they can
reach her anywhere.

Many old ladies would say Campbell is lucky to escape so
early, even if the decision isn't hers. When the fantasy fades,
when they have become addicted to the drugs the Angels
pump into them, when they have pumped too many cocks and
licked too many assholes in motel rooms as prostitutes, when
they have taken too many punches and kicks, few women
have the courage or desire to leave. They become slaves to
fear and their own inadequacies. Women are told their parents,
brothers, sisters or anyone else who matters will be killed if
they leave. They hang in until the Angels have no use for
them. Then they are murdered, sold or traded within the club
or to other gangs for motorcycle parts, drugs or to clear debts.
Some Angels even will their women to fellow members along
with their bikes, cars and weapons. The Hell's Angels, though
they abuse their women, are never hard up for good looking
pussy. They always find another hole to fill the gap.

5

THE ANGELS & THE MOB

ENIS Crnic, a security/intelligence officer with the Hell's Angels Cleveland chapter, raises the hood of John Delazappo's car in April 1977. Crnic executes a contract on the member of the city's Licavoli traditional organized crime family. He places the bomb near the firewall. BOOM. Murphy's Law. Crnic looks OK from the neck down. But even a hungry dog wouldn't eat what's left of his head. Cops change his name to No Face.

The Angels have a tense meeting. They're in deep shit. The James T. Licavoli mob now knows the Angels take contracts on them from a rival faction. The Angels send their president to bullshit the Italians and save their asses. The con: Crnic is not a member of the club when he plants the bomb. The Italians buy it. But they don't give the Angels contracts for two years. This leaves Kevin J. McTaggart, a mob associate who acts as liaison with the club, twiddling his thumbs.

The link between the Hell's Angels and traditional organized crime is, at best, tenuous. Mobsters are private men who appreciate a fine suit and a woman who can cook. They aren't into group sodomy or gang bangs on semen-encrusted mattresses. While the Angels flash their dicks to feed their macho image, the mobsters shelter their egos by keeping their dorks where they can't be compared.

But money forges strange alliances. The rough-edged Angels and slick traditional organized crime families across the continent reach an accommodation of convenience—like yin and yang: Angel muscle for mob money. The Angels break legs and kill for the mob in the early 1970s. The Angels strike a deal in areas where the mob runs strip joints, massage parlors, escort services and other fronts for cunt: they provide pussy, the mob keeps 40 to 50 percent of the take. They work out another agreement when the Angels' drug network gets sophisticated enough to compete with the mob's: no treading on toes. There are enough veins out there for everyone. The Angels, whose clandestine laboratories crank out prodigious amounts of methamphetamine daily, supply the drug to many mob families. The mob, in return, often provides the club with the chemicals needed to produce the drugs.

Muscle, pussy, drugs. Despite the mob's veneer of civilization, and the Angels' crust of scum, both criminal groups have a common denominator: a lust for money and power.

The Cleveland Angels, while on sabbatical from the mob's Licavoli faction, perform at least two contract murders for Daniel Patrick Greene, head of an Irish-dominated labor racketeering mob faction that fights with the Licavoli family. Cleveland becomes the bomb capital of Ohio from 1975 to 1977 as the Licavoli faction fights an all-out war with the faction led by Danny Greene and Jack Nardi for control of traditional organized crime activities in northeastern Ohio. The war begins when Greene and Nardi refuse to accept Licavoli, who takes over after boss John Scalish dies. Nardi, business agent with the teamsters, is blown up in his car on May 17, 1977, in the parking lot of the Teamsters Joint Council building in downtown Cleveland. The bomb is planted in the car next to his. Danny Greene is blown up as he gets into his car in the parking lot of the Brainerd Place Office Towers in the Cleveland suburb of Lyndhurst on October 6, 1977. The dent left in the parking lot by the bomb is still visible.

The Hell's Angels' dealings with unions flourish in the late 1970s when the president of an iron workers local gives four Angels letters of reference that say they have been workers in good standing for three years. He sends them to Pittsburgh, where the business agent of another local provides them with the answers to a test they have to write. He issues them journeymen ironworkers' cards and the Angels get high-paying jobs building a nuclear power plant—a favor for dirty work the club has done for the union.

Eight card-carrying Angels show up to support union members who picket a non-union job at the Geneva-on-the-Lake fairgrounds in Geneva, Ohio. The Angels stand near a gate and scream and holler at the non-union workers who try to prepare the site for a Johnny Cash concert. Union officials tell workers who complain to take their beefs to the Angels. The workers sign a union agreement within two hours.

The Hell's Angels have good days and bad days as hit men for the mob. The Licavoli mob hires the Cleveland Angels in September 1976 to kill an associate who has fallen out of grace with the family. They plant a bomb in his car and watch an unsuspecting neighbor—a victim of suburban trust—get blown up as he tries to move the car from the driveway.

The Cleveland Angels kill Joey Bonarrigo, another Licavoli associate, in 1978 after he delivers stolen liquor to the club, which fences hot items for the mob. Francis Curcio, a member of the Genovese traditional organized crime family in Bridgeport, Connecticut, uses Angel muscle to collect loan shark debts in 1981. Danny Bifield, president of the Bridgeport chapter, and "the most dangerous man in the State of Connecticut," shakes down debtors with the help of two other Angels.

A traditional organized crime family associate pays John (Pirate) Miller, a charter member of the Bridgeport chapter, to extort for the mob in the late 1970s and early 1980s. Miller plays the bad guy while a fellow Angel plays the good guy when they lean on debtors.

The Hell's Angels Manhattan chapter in New York City has strong ties with the Gambino traditional organized crime family in the 1970s and early 1980s. The Angels have a business arrangement with a New York club owned by the family. Sandy Alexander, former president of the chapter and head of the club's East Coast operations, deals with several Gambino associates. He also has close ties with Satan's Soldiers, an outlaw motorcycle gang that operates a legitimate business with the Gambino family on Staten Island.

Alexander consults with traditional organized crime families to ensure his club doesn't tread on mob turf with drug deals, thefts and other crimes.

Several Hell's Angels from the Manhattan chapter party in

an after-hours club frequented by mob figures in March 1979.
Angel Courtland (Chip) Candow gets into an argument with a
mob associate. The man pulls a gun and shoots Candow in the
hand. The Angels play it cool, but they are pissed off. Alexander calls a high ranking member of the Gambino family and
informs him the club has to do something.

"Do what you have to do," the mobster says. "There won't
be a problem with us."

The Angels stake out the mob associate's two pizza parlors
and figure out his routine. They sit in a car across the street
from one parlor for eight nights and wait for the right time to
send in an old lady who will leave behind a purse that contains
a bomb. A remote-control airplane guidance system is used to
trigger the C-4 plastic explosive. The pizza parlor is always
full of kids. The Angels don't want innocent victims. They
find the man's home in a quiet Queens neighborhood and plant
the bomb under the seat of his car. The man gets into the car
on May 9, 1979, and backs out of the garage. He remembers
something forgotten in the house and jumps out quickly to get
it. The Angels in a nearby car trigger the remote control bomb
as he hops out. The blast takes out the car's roof and floor as
well as part of the balcony above the garage. The mob associate escapes unharmed and moves away months later. He
hasn't been seen since. Two Hell's Angels prospects get their
patches 10 days later.

The Angels chapter in Troy, New York, deals drugs with an
associate of the Buffalino family. Fillmore (Crazy) Cross,
former president of the Hell's Angels San Jose chapter, has
ties with Angelo Marino, an operator of California Cheese.
Marino has links to traditional organized crime families of
Joseph Cerrito and James T. (The Weasel) Frattiano, former
boss of the San Francisco traditional organized crime family.

The Hell's Angels benefit most from their business dealings with traditional organized crime families. The Angels are
fearless goons when they first work for the mob. The mob
won't entrust them with tasks that require thought. The Angels
break legs, collect debts, torch buildings and kill. But the
more astute Angels observe how to run an efficient criminal
organization. They learn the value of graft and corruption, and
how to insulate themselves from prosecution by farming out
the dirty work.

Although the Hell's Angels aren't the only outlaw motorcycle gang to profit from associations with the mob, they are the best pupils. The Hell's Angels today are nearly equal to traditional organized crime in power and influence. The young generation of mafiosi laugh at the old men who speak solemnly of friendship and respect—men who will die rather than break the code of silence, the *omerta*. Today's mob punks don't want power bestowed—they take it. They snort, fuck and macho bullshit their time away. Fear and the lack of loyalty it engenders is the Hell's Angels major weakness; the mob has fallen prey to laziness and greed. Carelessness weakens the mob's once impregnable network.

A federal jury deals the US Mafia its most severe blow on Wednesday, November 19, 1986. It convicts eight mobsters—three family bosses—of being members of a commission that divides the country into territories, sanctions murder and keeps organized crime organized. The commission, which acts as the Mafia's board of directors, is formed by Salvatore (Lucky) Luciano in 1931 after he orders the execution of Salvatore Maranzano, the Mafia's *capo di tuti capi*—the boss of all the bosses. Lucky Luciano does away with the position and creates the commission to run the mob. Its existence is first proven in a court of law on November 19, 1986.

Seven of eight men are sentenced to 100 years in jail: Anthony (Fat Tony) Salerno, 75, boss of the Genovese crime family; Carmine (Junior) Persico, 53, boss of the Colombo crime family; Anthony (Tony Ducks) Corallo, 73, boss of the Lucchese crime family; Gennaro (Jerry Lang) Langella, 47, Colombo underboss; Salvatore (Tom Mix) Santoro, 72, Lucchese underboss; Christopher (Christy Tick) Furnari, 62, Lucchese counsellor; Ralph Scopo, 58, a Colombo soldier and former labor leader. Anthony (Bruno) Indelicato, 38, a Bonnano crime family soldier, is sentenced to 50 years only.

US Attorney Rudolph Guiliani sighs with lawmen across the country as the barrier against mob prosecutions crumbles.

"It can no longer be passed off as a prosecutor's theory. It's been proven beyond a reasonable doubt there is a Mafia. La Costa Nostra exists."

But it is no longer a bastion of honor. Santoro's reaction while he stands before US Federal Judge Richard Owen for his sentence illustrates the old mob style:

"Give me a hundred years and get it over with."

Gambino underboss Aniello Dellacroce bemoans the lack

of respect and balls among the new generation of mafiosi
when he chews out a young punk mobster in 1985. The punk
bypasses Dellacroce and takes a problem directly to the family
boss.

"I'm through with you," Dellacroce says. "You understand? I don't want to say hello to you."

The punk gets off easy.

"Twenty years ago, you would have found yourself in
some fucking hole someplace."

"You're right, Neil," the punk says.

> You know what I mean? [Dellacroce says]. But things change.
> Things change now because there's too much conflict. People do
> whatever they feel like. They don't train their people no more.
> There's no more—there's no more respect. If you can't be sin-
> cere, you can't be honest with your friends—then forget about it.
> You got nothing.

Fat Tony Salerno also suffers humiliation and frustration at
the hands of a new generation of mobsters who don't have the
guts and balls to stand up against almost maniacal outlaw
bikers.

"I don't know what to do," he complains to Tony (Duck)
Corallo. "I swear I don't."

The Hell's Angels' barbarism has it over the mob's put-on
civilization. *Respect* is the most common word in the Angel
vocabulary. It precludes friendship and makes the club less
vulnerable than the mob.

"I don't want to be your friend," William (Wild Bill) Medeiros, former security officer and charter member of the
Manhattan chapter, says. "Friends screw each other. In the
club, we weren't friends. We were brothers. If you respect me
and I respect you, we won't screw each other."

> We come from a basic concept of acquaintance. If we respect each
> other and I'm doing something you really don't like, we'll roll
> around in the mud. Then we've got it out of our system and forget
> about it. You citizens might say something and hold grudges for-
> ever and do things behind each other's backs.

The Hell's Angels' definition of respect coincides with
most people's understanding of fear. The definition of terror in

the 1960s is having your car horn get stuck while you tail a pack of Hell's Angels. The Angels have to let people know they're the toughest men around. They always provoke. An Angel walks into a bar and sits with the sweetie of a stud gone for a leak. What's a fucking guy to do when he returns? Play it cool. Put it on your Pay No Mind list. He'll appreciate the balls.

Angels, unlike the social butterfly greaseballs with gold chains matted to their jellied chest hair who now pass for mobsters, are truly men of respect.

6

THE POWER OF MONEY

Money is power. It buys policemen, judges.
            —Hell's Angels hit man James (Brett) Eaton.

I have been bought—Hell's Angels. #8.
—Juror's note to the judge in the Montreal murder trial of four
    Hell's Angels.

THE jury in the first-degree murder trial of four Hell's
Angels charged with killing five members of the club's
North chapter in Laval, Quebec, enters its 14th day of deliberation on Monday, December 1, 1986. Jurors tell Superior
Court Judge Jean-Guy Boilard twice during the weekend they
can't agree. They wrestle for days with the credibility of the
two main prosecution witnesses—former Hell's Angels with
less than spotless records. It looks like the trial will end in a
hung jury on Saturday, November 29. The foreman sends the
judge a note:
"After going over the evidence many times, we are unable
to achieve unanimity towards a final decision. What do we
do?"
The judge pleads with them to try again. They ask the
judge on Sunday to define premeditated murder and conspiracy.
The Sûreté du Québec, the provincial police force that

hounds the Hell's Angels, gets increasingly nervous as deliberations drag on. The trial is the result of a multi-million dollar investigation. Thirteen other Angels await trial on the same charges and warrants have been issued for another 10. The club has a licence to kill if these four Angels walk.

Police and justice officials have good reason to worry. They nearly blow the case with a cocky mistake less than one month before jurors are selected. The police, in the August issue of their glossy in-house magazine *Sûreté*, publish a less than flattering account of the evolution of outlaw motorcycle gangs in North America. The article says the lawless Hell's Angels control drug trafficking in Quebec and are involved in prostitution, extortion, bombings and intimidation. It also erroneously blames the Angels for 300 murders committed since their arrival in Quebec in 1977.

The Quebec Justice Department prints a six-page article on outlaw motorcycle gangs in its September issue of *Justice pour tous*, which sells on the newsstands for $1.50. It discusses 100 alleged killings by the Hell's Angels in the province, including the five deaths for which four Angels go to trial in September.

Although both magazines have a combined circulation of 49,000, the Montreal daily newspaper *La Presse* publishes a report of the *Sûreté* article for its 300,000 readers on August 25. The Angels' defence attorneys believe they have enough ammunition to have charges against their clients dismissed. Judge Boilard doesn't think so, but issues a publication ban effective until a verdict is reached and takes police and justice officials to task.

"The accused have established beyond any reasonable doubt that their right to presumption of innocence, a fair trial and an impartial tribunal were infringed upon by the actions of highly placed police officers and representatives of the Solicitor-General," Judge Boilard says. "This situation is inconceivable, deplorable and highly condemnable."

He charges seven senior government officials—including Jean-François Dionne, Quebec's chief Crown prosecutor, and Robert Therrien, the Sûreté's head of criminal investigations, both of whom he describes as "grossly inept"—with contempt of court. Other victims of the judge's wrath are André Dugas, the Sûreté's director of communications, Jean Latulippe, legal advisor for *Justice pour tous*, and Micheline Bouzigon, director of communications for the Justice Department. Judge Pierre Pinard, who hears the trial of Michel (Jinx) Genest, another Hell's Angel charged with the murder of North prospect Coco Roy, cites two more persons for contempt: Nicole Jobin, *Sûreté*'s editor, and Agathe Legare, editor of *Justice pour tous*.

Police fear another foul-up will cost them the trial. They even run security checks on the six men and six women picked as jurors to ensure everything runs smoothly. They find out, one day after 28-year-old journeyman carpenter Mario Hamel is sworn in on September 30, that he is convicted and fined $50 in 1983 for stealing gas by racing away from a service station after he fills his tank. The judge, prosecutor and defence lawyers see no reason to dismiss Hamel.

Judge Boilard unloads once more on the police in his address to the jury after a relatively smooth seven-week trial. He accuses the Sûreté of using "highly irregular" investigative techniques.

"I have no hesitation in saying that there is proof of incompetence. But there is no proof of dishonesty, although the line between the two is often very thin."

He is critical of how police handle two main witnesses— Hell's Angels who have rolled over. Curiously, police can't find their notes of the first interrogation of prospect Gerry (Le Chat) Coulombe to compare them with his official statement, which they forget to date. The judge upbraids them for a promise to withdraw murder charges against Gilles (Le Nez) Lachance in return for his testimony at a preliminary hearing.

"They should know that only the Crown has the right to make a decision to prosecute."

Police help Lachance find the .38-calibre police special revolver he buries in the woods near his Piedmont chalet in November 1985. Then they help him get a gun permit although he has a 1975 manslaughter conviction that prohibits him from carrying firearms. Judge Boilard cautions the jury in his summation against the testimony of such "unsavory characters."

The judge's comments about police and prosecution witnesses weigh heavy on the jurors on Sunday, November 30. Hamel lets them in on a dirty little secret late in the day: he has been paid to prevent them from reaching a verdict. The

next morning, December 1, he sends a note to Judge Boilard:
"I have been bought—Hell's Angels. #8."

Hamel refuses to enter the courtroom until reporters are excluded. The carpenter weeps as he tells the judge he accepted $25,000 to fix the verdict from a childhood friend who claims to represent the Hell's Angels. The four Angels on trial are "astonished and shocked" by the revelation, says their lawyer, Léo-René Maranda.

Corporal Yves Gravel tells Hamel's bail hearing on Wednesday, December 3, that the $25,000 is only a down payment—Hamel would get $100,000 if the four Angels are acquitted, $50,000 for a hung jury. The deal supposedly starts in October when Hamel allegedly buys hashish from Denis Larocque, a childhood friend with a criminal record for theft, being an accessory to a crime, and possession of stolen goods, an unregistered weapon, a prohibited weapon and break-in tools. He mentions he is a juror in the Angels' trial. The next time they meet, says Gravel, Larocque offers money from the Angels. Hamel discusses the offer with his common-law wife, parents, brothers and sisters. They tell him to refuse and to report the incident to Judge Boilard.

Larocque allegedly gives Hamel 25 $1,000 bills on November 7, 10 days before the jury is sequestered. Hamel hides $23,000 under the rug in his childhood bedroom in his parents' house, deposits $500 in the banks and keeps $1,500. Why does he take the money?

"It's simple," he tells Boilard. "I have three children and I earn $225 a week. He offered me $25,000 and me, I took it because I thought about my little ones."

Hamel tells fellow jurors of the bribe after his wife finds a $1,000 bill in the pocket of his pants hanging in the closet.

"I couldn't do anything but tell them. They were ready to flip out back there."

Hamel is later sentenced to one year in jail. Larocque is acquitted.

Judge Boilard ignores pleas from defence attorneys to declare a mistrial. The Canadian Criminal Code allows a trial to proceed with as few as 10 jurors. Boilard asks them in a soothing tone to ignore the bribe, praises them for their "intellectual honesty and intelligence," and ask that they continue deliberations. Maranda tosses his glasses onto the table and claims it is impossible for the jury to ignore the bribe.

"I just saw two jurors being physically supported by a guard in the corridor," he says and calls again for a mistrial.

The jurors are shaken up. But after 16 days of deliberations they acquit Robert (Ti-Maigre) Richard and convict Réjean (Zig-Zag) Lessard, Jacques (La Pelle) Pelletier and Luc (Sam) Michaud of first-degree murder in the shooting of five Angels at the Sherbrooke chapter clubhouse in Lennoxville on March 24, 1985.

"This is a triumph of justice over corruption," says Crown prosecutor René Domingue.

How often has corruption triumphed over justice? The Hell's Angels can't count the palms or dicks they've greased. Angels corrupt anyone who can make their life miserable or help business. They buy them wherever they run into them, usually while being arrested, in court or in jail. Police officers, who come into contact with the Angels more than other public officials, sell out most often.

A passerby finds the bodies of two Hell's Angels and a former club member in a flooded rock quarry near Andytown, Florida, on May 1, 1974. Their heads have been blown open by shotgun blasts. The two Angels from the Lowell, Massachusetts chapter—George F. (Whiskey George) Hartman, 28, and Edward Thomas (Riverboat) Riley, 34, both wanted for murder—were in Florida to ensure that former chapter member Albert (Oskie) Simmons removed his club tattoo. The Angels want the killers. Sandy Alexander, president of the New York City chapter, calls the police chief in a town near where the bodies are found and arranges special privileges for two Angels on a fact-finding mission.

One of those Angels is Clarence (Addie) Crouch, vice-president of the Cleveland chapter. He is one of 25 Angels attacked by the Breed at the Polish Women's Hall three years earlier in a fight that starts a war between the clubs. Crouch knows most of the Outlaws in Florida from his days as a Bandido and a Grim Reaper in the sunshine state. Many of the Outlaws are members of the Iron Crosses who party with Crouch in 1965 when he goes on runs to Daytona. The second Angel is Howie Weisbrod from the Manhattan chapter.

We were met at the plane by a couple of detectives, taken to the police station . . . and shown everything that they had on the case, shown all the autopsies, and we were guarded by policemen. We were shown files on all the outlaw motorcycle riders there. We read all their files and was [sic] given their addresses and things. Then they helped us lease a car and helped us in the investigation.

The two Angels in full colors, with police bodyguards, interview about 30 people—mostly Angel old ladies and drug dealers—in bars and stores for 10 days. Police are stationed around their motel so they can sleep peacefully in Outlaw territory. Plainclothes police surround the Angels during a sit-down in a restaurant with about 15 Outlaws. They get a police escort to the plane and report to Alexander in New York. The investigation leads to the biggest biker war in history. The police chief who aids it still helps the Angels.

A high ranking police officer in Cleveland feeds the club information about Outlaw troop movements when the war with that gang heats up in 1975. Police intelligence officers keep close tabs on bikers and know where most of them are at any given time. This source of information is so valuable to the Angels that they install a telephone in an upstairs closet exclusively for the police officer's calls. The phone is call forwarded to the chapter president's house when he goes home. The informant and a second police officer also tell the Angels about investigations, raids, search and arrest warrants, and when indictments are about to be handed down so they can lie low.

"There was one police officer," says Crouch, "the club furnished him with money to give a witness in a rape case. And he passed the money on."

Cleveland police officers set up break-ins since 1969 for an old childhood friend—Tommy, an Angel cat burglar with an affinity for diamonds and riding lawn mowers. Another Ohio police force turns over a small lakeside town to the Hell's Angels during their runs.

This police official let us have a free reign as far as beating up people [Crouch says]. We beat up a lot of people out there on the street, in the bars and everything else. They would just turn their backs and walk away. There was one incidence where there was a guy out there with a Hell's Angels—a phoney Hell's Angels patch—and they just stood by and watched us all go over and beat him up and take the patch away from him. . . . We could do anything, that included drugs, out in the open. . . . The town was ours.

We controlled the street. If people were racing up and down the street, we would kind of—we would stop them for this privilege of taking the town. They would let us have the town for stopping people.

During the two Racketeer-Influenced and Corrupt Organizations (RICO) statute trials in Oakland from 1979 to 1981, the Hell's Angels pay $100,000 for police reports on the club stamped "Confidential," "Secret," and "For official eyes only," and send copies to all chapters.

> These files were from California and they were prepared by some committee out there to investigate motorcycle gangs and it pertained to that RICO trial [says Crouch]. They had patches and pictures and things in it and it had all the information that they knew about these different clubs. . . . A lot of it was true and a lot of it was not. There were some parts in there that interested the club a lot, like parts pertaining to drug deals and things like that that members usually do outside, after church, after the meetings and all, they will go outside and arrange drug deals together on the sidewalk, where they will just whisper together, because they are afraid that the clubhouses are bugged by law enforcement or whatever. That statement right there kind of got everybody shook that they knew that one member was talking somewhere, because that was a true statement.

Hell's Angels in San Francisco County Jail across the bay use deputies to smuggle drugs to them in 1981. An Angel gives a deputy a telephone number to call. He receives drugs that he turns over to the Angel. The deputy is given a second number to call to confirm the Angel has received the drugs, and he is paid off.

A 36-year-old deputy with 14 years' experience is suspended in June 1981, three months after Hell's Angel Sergey (Sir Gay) Walton escapes from his seventh-floor cell and breaks out of the San Francisco County Jail. The former Oakland chapter president waits to be transferred to a federal prison to serve an eight-year sentence for possession of unregistered machine guns. Two keys are needed to get out of the cell, onto the roof and into the public area of the Hall of Justice. Someone has to turn off the door alarms before he walks through them.

Robert Banning, a member of the Hell's Angels in Bridgeport, Connecticut, says a guard at the Bridgeport Correctional

Facility also smuggles drugs for inmates. A police officer at the local jail removes cocaine from the pockets of two Hell's Angels before they are frisked in February 1985. He returns the drug after they are granted bail and drives them to the clubhouse where he and his partner often buy and use drugs with the Angels. The same police officer runs computer checks on guns and cars for the club.

James (Gorilla) Harwood, vice-president of the Troy, New York, chapter says a police officer named Pat tips him off when a grand jury hands down indictments for Hell's Angels so they can hide. He once brings the Angels a stolen motorcycle to have the vehicle identification number removed. Other police officers warn Harwood about police roadblocks and check licence plate numbers for the club. Hell's Angels from the Binghamton, New York, chapter wheel over to the Troy clubhouse to team up for a run on June 26, 1984. A uniformed police officer with the Troy Police Department shows up at Harwood's house in the early morning and tells him he will find out where the roadblocks are. He also says he'll try to help Gorilla with his recent arrest for destroying property. A sergeant with the same police force gives Harwood the police department's radio frequencies and a list of codes police use.

Sandy Alexander, at a July 4 party in the Manhattan clubhouse, points out the club's contact in the police department who checks out people for the Angels. The Charleston, South Carolina, chapter hosts a party on February 9, 1985, to celebrate its anniversary. Phillip Utley, visiting vice-president of the Durham, North Carolina, chapter boasts that the Charleston chapter will never get busted for its arsenal of weapons and drug stash because it has an in with local police.

The Hell's Angels are not the only outlaw motorcycle gang to sway police and prison officials. Speed, hash, grass and home brew are available in the section of the Toronto Don Jail where Outlaws president Robert (Pumpkin) Marsh is locked up with other gang members in 1985 and 1986. Marsh has ready access to the supervisor.

"The guards treated him like god," Outlaw Paul (Crazy) Paris says. "They were always talking to him, joking with him."

Judge James McGettrick of the Cuyahoga County Court of Common Pleas in Ohio gets pissed in a bar early in 1984. He dismisses a murder charge against a Cleveland Hell's Angel several months earlier. The Angel bombs a house he wrongly believes to be that of an Outlaw and kills three people. A ragged-looking agent with the Bureau of Alcohol, Tobacco and Firearms who works on the case sits with the drunken judge.

"Thanks for what you did for us on the Angels trial," he says without introducing himself.

"Yeah, I never got all the money I was supposed to get out of that," says the judge, who misses the sarcastic tone and mistakes the agent for an Angel associate.

The agent sets up a sting in April 1984. The FBI watches him pay the judge $5,000 in the video-equipped men's room of the bar. McGettrick is convicted of three counts of bribery on January 16, 1985, for fixing two murder cases against Hell's Angels. He is sentenced to four years in jail. He dies of a heart attack behind bars on July 17, 1986.

Judge McGettrick is not the only bencher in Ohio paid off by the Angels. A Cleveland Angel brags to Gorilla Harwood and an FBI informant outside the Jamaica Inn in Lumberton, South Carolina, on May 18, 1984, about McGettrick's bribe:

"How about that judge in Cleveland? They're saying we bribed a judge. Wait 'til they find out about the other two judges we bribed."

7

BORN TO BE MILD

THE Hell's Angels have an image problem. Since 1948, they've regaled with tales of gang-bang lust and chain-whipping terror the suburban deadbeat who fucks once a week and fantasizes about giving his wife a midnight snack that squirts. Newspapers, magazines and television tantalize the easy-chair conqueror with lurid details of a life he dares not lead, in a world he can't risk inhabiting. This domesticated mass of sexual repression drools over sordid tales of a sweet young thing losing count of beer-drenched hulks draining themselves into her, some twice. He knows that somewhere in the city, while he trudges off to work, a grease-encrusted horde of modern-day huns sleeps off a night of rape and carnage. He'd do it too, but for the wife, children, two-car garage, magazine subscriptions, Saturday night bowling and his job. Herb might want to hump his neighbor Fernanda from behind as she weeds the garden, but chances are he won't.

So the Hell's Angels bear the brunt of society's repressed sexuality. The Angels don't mind the responsibility while they try to impress the world in the 1950s and 1960s, but now that their billfolds are more likely to contain $1,000 bills than a token condom, they prefer to be seen as genteel rebels. The Hell's Angels, like the proverbial hooker, try to develop a heart of gold—and the sucker who goes with it.

The Hell's Angels, who define the fringe for several generations of dropouts, are trying desperately to change their image. Financial success fosters in the Angels a desire to be loved. They won't alter what they do, they just want people to see them differently. In fact, they don't want people to know what they do.

Sonny Barger, the respected president of the Oakland chapter, suggests at a high level officer's meeting in the late 1960s that the club clean up its image—literally. The Angels strip their colors of abusive patches, such as Nazi swastikas and wings earned for eating pussy in front of the boys.

The club undertakes massive publicity campaigns to purge its sordid reputation and lower its profile. It seeks the help of a public relations specialist. The colors—the grinning winged death's head—are no longer worn 24 hours a day, but hung in the closet beside three-piece suits and taken out for runs, parties, initiations, hits and the occasional jury intimidation. Motorcycles are relegated to weddings, funerals and runs. The Hell's Angels have exchanged their hogs for Cadillacs, Lincolns, Jaguars, Porsches and vans—a move not unwelcomed by the Harley-Davidson Motor Co. Inc. of Milwaukee. Although the company won't say so publicly, the Hell's Angels' affinity for their legendary 74 has at times been a public relations nightmare. How do you market the favored mode of transportation among rapists, drug dealers and hit men?

The Hell's Angels have done more than anyone to popularize the Harley-Davidson motorcycle and the company won't acknowledge their sordid reputation. Francis (Buzz) Buzzelli, spokesman for Harley-Davidson, comments on media stories about outlaw bikers and the Hell's Angels:

> That stereotype is not just. The Hell's Angel I talked to works in a body shop painting cars. I asked him about their reputation. He said that's why they licence their name. You can't put their name on a product without going through them. He said they go on runs and have a good time and don't want to be bothered. I wouldn't want these guys to get a bum rap. I'm concerned about our corporate image. We're trying to project a wholesome, all-American, clean-cut family image, not necessarily so hard core and rough. We're trying to round off the edges.

So are the Hell's Angels. They want to be notorious without seeming to be, and want to seem nice while being nasty. The Angels need a clean image to launder the big bucks they make illegally. Legitimate business will deal with illegal enterprise above board only when the appearance is right. No one wants a cop looking over his shoulder. The Hell's Angels go out of their way to appear like law-abiding citizens. The Manhattan chapter in New York City has a strict rule that when a car full of rival bikers or other enemies pulls up in front of the East Village clubhouse for a hit, you shoot everyone but the driver. He must be allowed to escape with the bodies so the Angels are not implicated in a shooting. The crime rate in neighborhoods with Hell's Angels clubhouses is nearly nil. The Angels don't shit in their own backyard and won't let anyone draw heat to their turf.

"They own the block and they take care of the kids," a police officer in Manhattan says. "Everyone is safe."

"You don't have to be worried if you live on this block," says Robert Mitchell. "You can come home at any hour of the morning."

"Better them than junkies," says Wanda Bianculli. "Crimes that would normally happen around here, like burglary and break-ins, don't happen."

"They're regular guys," says Ahmad El Tawil, who owns a deli on First Avenue. "I can tell them to go to hell and everything. They're the only people I give credit to in the neighborhood. I never have to ask them to pay their bills. . . . I'm not sure I would want to have to ask anyway."

Butch Garcia, a 29-year-old Hell's Angel, explains how the Manhattan chapter members get along with neighbors.

You show us respect, we show you respect. If you don't show the Angels respect, the Angels don't show you respect. And we're very good at disrespecting people.

The Angels have marked off parking space for a dozen motorcycles on East Third Street with orange cones. It is a show of respect not to take their parking spaces. And even though they try hard to keep the neighborhood clean of junkies and petty thieves, the Hell's Angels must suffer the humiliations of urban life. A men's shelter opens up nearby. The neighborhood, says Butch Garcia, has "gone to hell."

We live here with our families [Butch Garcia says]. We don't want those people here. But who can we complain to? We don't really think Mayor [Ed] Koch represents our interests. And I can't see us calling police and saying, "Hey, this is Butch from Hell's Angels. There is a homeless guy down here shitting outside our house. Can you do something about it?"

Gentrification is also taking its toll on the block, as apartment buildings are converted into cooperative apartments and the new neighbors sneak snapshots of the Angels on the street.

The Yuppies are giving this block a bad name [Butch Garcia says]. A realtor was down here the other day talking about how great it was to have Hell's Angels on the block. The realtors have started using us as a selling point. It's crazy.

Neighbors of the Manhattan chapter clubhouse at 77 East Third Street are shocked on June 1, 1987, when two Angels —Courtland (Chip) Candow, 42, and Edward Levie, 36—are charged with second-degree assault after a couple in a car are attacked with axe handles in front of the building. Ulisses and Janie Smith stop their car and honk the horn in front of a sign that reads "In Memoriam—Big Vinnie—When in Doubt, Knock 'em Out."

Four months after five Angels are gunned down in the Sherbrooke chapter clubhouse outside the rural college town of Lennoxville, Quebec, and only weeks after the bodies of six Angels and one old lady are pulled from the St. Lawrence Seaway, townspeople have few complaints about the club.

"They didn't disturb anyone," says Police Chief Richard Parenteau of nearby Rock Forest. "It wasn't like you see in the movies. They were clean here."

Neighbors of the Montreal chapter in Sorel, Quebec, hardly see the Angels.

Rosa Larivière, 78: "I'm not afraid, they've done nothing to me. We don't see them and they don't talk to us."

Rollande Vaillancourt, 71, lives in the house attached to the biker's clubhouse: "They're my friends. You see the lawn in front of their place? I pulled all the weeds out last week. In exchange, they put up some of their steel mesh on one of my windows—all for free."

Armande Bayeur, a widow who lives down the street: "Why are the police out to get those boys? All they do is make a bit of noise with their motorcycles. It's no worse than the noises motorists make with their cars. If they turn bad later, then there'll be plenty of time to go after them."

Solange Lavallée, storekeeper at the Miracle Mart Plaza: "They behave in town to avoid turning the citizens against them. People sometimes say they are safer here because the Hell's live in town."

Lucie Nadeau, jewelry store clerk: "We rarely see them and they're good clients."

Mario Peloquin, owner of Le Gateau des Anges bakery next to the Hell's Angels clubhouse and across the street from the parish church, has no beefs about his burly clients. "When they asked if I named my store after them, I said yes. The priest asked me the same question. I gave him the same answer."

Sorel Police Chief Jean Lalonde figures townspeople tolerate the Hell's Angels out of fear. Florian Ledoux, who runs a fruit stand next to the police station, refuses to talk about the bikers. "If someone has problems with the Hell's, it's up to him to do something about it." Ledoux is municipal councillor.

Most Angels appear straight around their homes. Members of the Quebec Symphony and the CEGEP de Sherbrooke community college are stunned to find out in the spring of 1985 that respected trumpeter Claude Berger is a member of the Sherbrooke chapter of the Hell's Angels.

The public perception of the Hell's Angels is summarized by a woman who complains after Sonny Barger and most of the Oakland chapter are arrested on drug charges in 1979:

"Why are they after Sonny? He's just a wild boy."

Angels around the world participate in charity drives to gain public and media support. They make sure they are seen contributing to the Statue of Liberty Fund. Photographs of hulking Angels, their Harleys ladden with stuffed animals, are featured yearly in newspaper reports of campaigns like Toys for Tots. Canadian Angels who donate to the Terry Fox Marathon of Hope fill the screen in a movie about the one-legged runner's attempted cross-country trek for cancer research. The Hell's Angels also donate blood. Why not, they draw enough of it.

Hell's Angels stop on freeways to help stranded motorists

or assist police officers make arrests. They even hand out courtesy cards in the 1960s after helping someone: "You Have Been Assisted by a Member of the Hell's Angels [chapter]." Angels come across as patriotic, right wing, sexist, anti-Communist and anti-black. In short, average Americans.

Magazine advertisements soliciting contributions to the Hell's Angels defence fund capitalize on patriotism and the Constitution. One ad in *Easyriders* magazine begins:

> HELLS ANGELS ARE AMERICANS. Show your support, wear a 'Hells Angels are Americans' T-shirt. In a joint effort, federal governmental agencies are calculatingly and systematically attempting to disband the Hell's Angels Motorcycle Club in America. These agencies have denied us due process; they have violated our rights guaranteed all Americans by the First Amendment of the Constitution, which includes freedom of religion, freedom of association and life style. If they can do it to us, they can do it to all Americans. Help us stop selective prosecution, and the systematic persecution of the Hell's Angels Motorcycle Club. Send us $10.00 or more donation to our Defence Fund and we will send you a T-shirt FREE! Send us $15.00 or more donation and we will send you a sweat shirt or thermal top FREE! We will send you FREE 'Keep America Free—Support Your Local Hell's [sic] Angels' Bumper Sticker with order of 2 shirts.

Fillmore (Crazy) Cross, president of the Hell's Angels San Jose chapter, undertakes one of the first major attempts to sanitize the club in 1974. Narcs finally clue in that the Angels are into heavy-duty drug deals in the early 1970s and turn on the heat. The Angels realize that many of their members are junkies whose first loyalty is to the needle. The club turfs out users and bans the needle.

"The guys couldn't function properly, couldn't be dependable members, didn't show up for meetings, forgot to pay dues," a concerned Cross tells the press. "You couldn't rely on them for nothin'. They weren't outlaws anymore; they were dope addicts."

The largest methamphetamine producers in the country rent three billboards that depict a syringe across a skull and crossbones warning: "No Hope with Dope." Reaction is instantaneous. The Angels have cleaned up their act. Their only interest really is motorcycles. Cross spreads his message on campus and on talk shows. His crusade is interrupted in 1975 by a jail sentence for possession of methamphetamine. The Hell's Angels are careful to point out in their brochures and speeches to students that they're against hard drugs; they consider marijuana, barbiturates and methamphetamines soft.

The 44-year-old Cross is added to the FBI's most-wanted list in August 1986, in connection with an attempt to extort $100,000 from a Santa Cruz, California, businessman who is beaten nearly to death on October 2, 1984, by two men allegedly hired by Cross. The six-foot, 175-pound weightlifter and martial arts specialist carries a handgun in an ankle holster. Contrary to the public image of the biker, his interests range from motorcycles to ancient Mexican artifacts, wines, expensive cars and rattlesnakes.

Perhaps the most enterprising public relations attempt by the Hell's Angels is the production of a feature length movie that portrays the club as a peace-loving family bound by love for the open road. Sandy Frazier Alexander, president of the Manhattan chapter in New York City and head of the club's East Coast faction, dreams up the idea for *Hell's Angels Forever* in 1972. He co-produces and acts in the movie, which premiers in San Antonio, Texas, in 1983.

"It's the first Hell's Angels movie that isn't a Hollywood script," says Sonny Barger, Oakland chapter president. "It's the first time we get to show our side of it."

For those who like to goo-gaw over stars, the 90-minute Dolby stereo movie also features country singers Willie Nelson and Johnny (*Take This Job And Shove It*) Paycheck, rhythm and blues singer Bo Diddley and quintessential San Francisco acid rocker, Jerry Garcia of the Grateful Dead. The same camera that shows Angels as they frolic with their offspring also eavesdrops on a conversation during which one Angel recalls beating a man unconscious with a hammer. The celluloid apologia culminates with the US Department of Justice dropping its racketeering case against the Oakland chapter in 1981 after a jury acquits the Angels for a second time on the charges. The message: if they can't nail us, we ain't doing it. Those with long memories will recall that all the feds got on Al Capone was tax evasion.

The Angel flick gets its New York premier on October 3, 1983. More than 100 polished Angel choppers line the street and celebrities arrive in horse-drawn carriages. Don Imus, a celebrated New York radio personality renowned for his off-color routines on air, MCs the event on the curb. Crowds cheer stars like Bo Didley, Carole King and Johnny Paycheck. The party continues at Studio 54, which the Angels have rented for the evening.

The Hell's Angels also use the courts in attempts to sanitize their image. Forty-five Angels file a $3-million damage suit against police in Alameda and Solano counties, Oakland, Sacramento, San Jose and Vallejo, as well as the California Highway Patrol and the state Department of Corrections on January 17, 1979. The suit alleges that these agencies have engaged in a "persistent, pervasive, deliberated pattern . . . and plan" of harassment and intimidation since the fall of 1977 to destroy Angels' rights of free speech, assembly, due process of law and freedom from unreasonable search and seizures. Why? As a means "of forcing individuals to renounce membership in the club or their association with such club members in an effort to destroy" the Hell's Angels.

The Hell's Angels Montreal Inc. sue the *Hamilton Spectator* for libel when the southern Ontario newspaper publishes a story about Noël Mailloux two years after he murders Cindy Lee Thompson and four-year-old Stewart Hawley through a haze of paranoia and coke.

"The plaintiff states and the fact is, that Noël Mailloux was not a member of the Hell's Angels at the time of the publication of the article, nor at any time thereafter. By reason of the foregoing, the plaintiff has suffered serious injury to its character, credit and reputation."

Angels from across the country stage a $15-a-head fundraiser at New York's Limelight disco in November 1985 to help defray about $1 million in legal bills for more than 100 Hell's Angels and associates the FBI's Operation Roughrider nabs on drug and weapons charges on May 2 that year. Rocker Joan Jett, who weeps and threatens to stop the show when someone throws a hot dog at her during a concert at Toronto's Exhibition Stadium in August 1982, performs at the party. Old standby Willie Nelson donates an item for the celebrity auction. Butch Garcia, president of the New York City chapter, bemoans the club's poor image outside the disco.

"We're not racketeers, we're not Al Capone, we're not

Marlon Brando. We're human beings. . . . The media has sensationalized our image."

The Olympic torch relay in 1984 is one charity event that garners the Hell's Angels loads of publicity. Its tortured denouement also exposes a tender spot in one Angel's heart. A heavily tattooed George (Gus) Christie, president of the Hell's Angels Ventura, California, chapter, collects $3,000 from biker friends to run one kilometer in the 15,000-kilometer cross-country Olympic torch relay. Christie runs his kilometer in Point Mugu, cheered on by Hell's Angels, Crucifiers and Heathens. He asks that the money be given to the Special Olympics, an international charity that sponsors events for the mentally retarded. More specifically, he wants the money to go on to the Special Olympics program in Pottstown, Pennsylvania.

Christie first hears of Pottstown when its Special Olympics committee writes him after learning he is interested in retarded people.

"May God bless you for your willingness to help others," writes the committee's Joan Carlson.

"You've got a friend in Pennsylvania," writes Rosemary Haflin, who has a retarded son.

Christie calls Pottstown from the pay phone inside the Angels' Ventura clubhouse, the red steel door of which sports a sign that reads: "No Bozos. No Wimps." Pottstown still hasn't received the money in early 1985. Christie takes his complaint to Kennedy heiress Eunice Shriver, chairman of Special Olympics Inc. She finds out that the money is split between the state Special Olympics committees in California and Pennsylvania. Nothing for Pottstown.

Christie passes the hat around again in March 1985, and has blue-and-white windbreakers with the Pottstown Special Olympics logo made up for the kids.

"It meant so much that this rough, tough Hell's Angel was soft enough to care about some mentally retarded kids," says Haflin.

Christie reveals why his heart has a soft spot:

I once saw a documentary on television showing mentally retarded people competing in sports and I was overwhelmed. I felt that retarded children is an area that people don't want to deal with. It's like the Hell's Angels. They know we're there, they don't understand and they don't want to deal with us.

Christie is arrested in a Ventura motel parking lot on Thursday, September 25, 1986, and charged with attempting to arrange the murder of a federal prisoner in Arizona. He allegedly gives a man $500 and the ownership receipt to a car to arrange the killing.

Most people are suckers for stars. The Hell's Angels and the stars themselves are no exception. The courts are lenient with celebrities and the public accepts their flaws as necessary artistic idiosyncracies. The Hell's Angels have a genuine interest in partying with stars, many of whom are big drug consumers. The Angels also understand that cavorting with North America's only royalty and society's court jesters helps legitimize the grinning skull on their backs. Hollywood's wackos bring out the best and the worst in the Hell's Angels.

James (Gorilla) Harwood tenses as he watches a crouched figure pounce from car to car to sneak up on the Hell's Angels Troy, New York, clubhouse. Harwood pulls guard duty this night and faces an enemy bold enough to tackle the club alone. Before he can squeeze off a shot, Harwood recognizes the enemy as a friend re-enacting a scene from his hit movie, *Animal House*. John Belushi, who dies in a Hollywood bungalow at age 33 on March 5, 1982, of a drug overdose administered by Toronto groupie Cathy Smith, is just goofing around on his way to visit Harwood.

Belushi is one of the many stars attracted over the years to the death's breath mystique of the Hell's Angels. He is also one of the most embarrassing. John (Pirate) Miller finds the rotund, drug-addicted comedian whining for methamphetamine outside the clubhouse. The Angels let him into their drug supply to shut him up.

The Hell's Angels aren't without a sense of humor and count many comedians among their hangers on. Dan Ackroyd, Belushi's bosom buddy, is a friend of the Angels' New York City chapter. Ackroyd, the world's most famous Ghostbuster, owns a trendy Toronto restaurant bar called Crooks after co-owner and former policeman Richard Kruk. Two orange-yellow Illinois licence plates with the letters BDR

528 hang over the bar. The plates are taken from the backup Bluesmobile in the Blues Brothers movie starring Belushi and Ackroyd. The star car has the licence plate BDR 529. The letters BDR stand for Black Diamond Riders—the legendary Toronto outlaw motorcycle gang led by the even more legendary Johnny Sombrero, known to his mother as Henry Paul Barnes.

Humor is a fine line between life and death among Angels. Normal people shrug off a lapse in taste. The teller of a bad joke risks having his asshole torn out through his ears in the company of Angels. Robin Williams can't nanoo nanoo his way out of a joke that offends Sandy Alexander in the late 1970s. Pirate Miller and sergeant-at-arms Vincent (Big Vinnie) Girolamo visit the set of "Saturday Night Live" on a day Williams hosts the show. They pull a knife on him in a backstage elevator and threaten to make sliced pork of Mork's dork if he doesn't apologize on national television. Williams is a saner man that he lets on. He complies after he changes his wet pants.

A New York City radio mega-star has a run-in with the Hell's Angels in the mid-1970s. The radio personality runs into a group of Angels on the NBC set of "Goodnight America," which profiles the gang. Alcohol and pills loosen his mind and tongue.

"You guys don't look so tough," he boasts.

An NBC security guard saves his ass. The radio personality realizes while he sweats in a locked room that he must apologize or die. The Angels don't want to talk to him. A telephone caller warns he'll get stiffed. Mr. Cool's throat tightens and his sphincter loosens. He apologizes several times during his morning radio show. Big Vinnie Girolamo walks into the studio and nods OK through the window.

"I'm so afraid of them I'll contribute to their defence fund if they ask me to," he says.

Charles Alfred (Chuck) Zito, former member of the Manhattan chapter and founder and president of the Hell's Angels Nomad chapter in New York, owns Charlie's Angels Security. He hires his musclemen gym friends to wear Charlie's Angels T-shirts to keep the crowd under control at the New York premier of *Hell's Angels Forever*. The one-time runner-up in

the New York State Golden Gloves tournament works as a
bodyguard for several stars, including Liza Minnelli. The pro
boxer gets along well with Judy Garland's daughter and invites her to the clubhouse at 77 East Third Street to freak out
the boys. She arrives in a chauffeur-driven limo.

Zito is also bodyguard for Sylvester Stallone while the Italian Stallion cuts his first two Rocky movies. Zito teaches
Stallone how to box and wears around his neck a boxing-glove
charm the star gives him. Zito also spars with his friend
Mickey Rourke, for whom he provides limousine service.
Rourke says the men are still good friends despite Zito's conviction on drug charges and suggests the entrepreneur is being
hounded by police because he is a Hell's Angel. Rourke,
decked out in his finest biker leathers, poses for photographers
with Hell's Angels in front of the Georges V Hotel in Paris in
April 1987 while on tour promoting his controversial movie
Angel Heart. Zito joins celebrities Walter Cronkite, Glenda
Jackson, Cicely Tyson, Christopher Walken and the cast of
"Saturday Night Live" at Radio City Music Hall on April 4,
1985, for the opening night of Liberace's 17-day engagement.

Hell's Angels protect the precious fingers of Norman
Wexler, writer of the screenplays for *Saturday Night Fever*
and *Serpico*. Why Wexler needs protection is a mystery. He
has been arrested for biting a stewardess and threatening Richard Nixon. Writer Geoffrey Hunter sues Wexler for $4.5 mil-
lion at the end of 1985 for sicking an Angel on him. Hunter's
jaw is broken and he suffers a concussion.

The Angels meet many of their celebrity friends while they
work as movie stunt men. Sandy Alexander, besides being a
pro boxer and trapeze artist, is an accredited, card-carrying
stunt man and actor. Alexander monopolizes the first 10 minutes of a film that Rourke gets him a part in as a bad guy who
gets blown up in a boat.

Angels are paid in cash and pussy when they work as
heavies for stars. Some become friends, such as country
singers Johnny Paycheck and Willie Nelson. Angels get
choice seats at Nelson concerts. The Oakland Hell's Angels,
before they fall out with the Rolling Stones, run the concessions at their concerts, providing cuties to sell T-shirts and
paraphernalia.

Mick Jagger has come closer to death than any other star

because of his association with the Hell's Angels. The Altamont killing is bad for business. It gives the Angels bad publicity and severs their relationship with the hippies—their best
customers. Clarence (Addie) Crouch, a founder and former
vice-president of the Hell's Angels Cleveland chapter, describes the club's feelings for Jagger.

The club felt that the band did not stand behind them, they had
hired them to do security for them.... They felt that this rock
band should have stayed behind them and said that they had hired
them for security around the bandstand, or whatever, but they did
not. They just left.

And it has always been a thorn in the side of Oakland and a lot
of the chapters and a lot of the clubs. So, there has always been
more or less of an open contract, an open contract on this band,
and this person. And there have been two attempts that I know of
that failed.... They will [kill him] someday.

It is Mick Jagger of the Rolling Stones. It is from the Altamont
thing. I was in this town where this chapter is in New York, in the
city, and this had been discussed many times about killing him,
killing the band for that. And people want to do it to get in the
good graces of California.

Whoever does it, it is quite a trophy for them or whatever.
There is a lot of hate there, too, to the extent that no Hell's Angel
will listen to Mick Jagger music.

One attempt was made where they sent a member with a [.22-
calibre] gun and a silencer to a [New York City] hotel, and he
stalked that hotel for a long time, but they did not show up. Then
the next attempt was a few years later, somewhere around 1979,
when they were in New York City for a concert. They had some
place near water, and I was told that they took—they were ex-
plaining to me how they did it, they had swam over and checked
the place out. It was some house near water or something, and
they were going to put a bomb up underneath it. And they were
going to blow up the whole band and everybody at the party.

And they were crossing [Long Island Sound], and they had a
pontoon boat, a little rubber raft thing with plastic explosives in it,
and they lost it in the water [one of the hitmen drops the plastic
explosives overboard]. That is how it had come up, because they
had gotten in trouble with some intelligence officers in Cleveland
and all because they had lost some—they had lost a big amount of
plastics for TCB. It was a large amount of plastics. And they had
described to me how much trouble they had gone to to set this all
up and everything, but they had failed. But they swore they would
still do it, they would get him sooner or later.

Barger's reaction in 1983:

I personally don't like the guy, but that don't mean I want to kill him. Let's just say that there are seven chapters in England and he comes over here enough that if there was a contract out on him, he wouldn't be singing anymore.

The Hell's Angels only like stars that like Angels. They plant a bomb under the van of country singer David Allen Coe while he plays in New Jersey because he parties with Outlaws. Coe places a desperate phone call to Sandy Alexander when he returns to his Florida home on Big Pine Key. Coe cries like a baby as he explains to Alexander he is just an entertainer, not a biker. The hard humping, shit kicking former death-row convict has a rider in his contract that guarantees no biker is turned away from his shows. He arrives with an entourage of Outlaws at radio station CFGM's Summer Picnic at Molson's Park in Barrie, Ontario, on August 11, 1985. The Outlaws flex muscles and tattoos for local police photographers and make everyone backstage nervous with their brawn. Organizers fear the brutes will eat all the performers' steaks if they put them on the barbeque too early.

How successful has the Hell's Angels' attempt to sanitize the club's image been? Cleveland Angel Matt Zanoskar complains in June 1986 that things have gotten so bad the club has trouble finding priests to bury its dead.

PART

II

8

THE BIG FOUR: MOTORCYCLES, MURDER & MAYHEM EN MASSE

CHARLES Darwin would recognize in outlaw motorcycle gangs his missing link. Sigmund Freud would marvel at the id unleashed. Karl Marx would see capitalism run wild. The evolution of the 1,000 or so outlaw motorcycle gangs in the US and Canada recapitulates these men's contributions to knowledge. Gangs go through a metamorphosis that starts with budding assholes and ends with a shitpile of money. Not all gangs have reached the same stage of growth. Some bikers still get their jollies slapping out gray hairs who get in their way and gang banging on Saturday night. Others have a bit more class—they just steal the old fart's heart drug and wolf it down for a cheap high.

The Hell's Angels are boss. They're the toughest, meanest, wealthiest and most sophisticated outlaw motorcycle gang in the world. But try as they may, they don't have the monopoly they want. Three other motorcycle gangs compete with the Angels for drug trafficking territory: the Outlaws, the Pagans and the Bandidos. All are based in the US. Only the Pagans don't have international chapters.

The Big Four outlaw motorcycle gangs claim to be the one percent of motorcyclists who won't conform to society's laws and morals. They are guided by their own code of terror. They strive to maintain their reputation as outlaws by instilling in people a fear they interpret as respect. The gangs keep members in line and eliminate the opposition with squads of killers: the Hell's Angels' Filthy Few, the Outlaws' SS, the Pagans' Black T-shirt squad, and the Bandidos' Nomad chapter.

Most motorcycle gangs are nothing more than groups of gonad-driven greaseballs on wheels. The Big Four hide behind the illusion. They are in reality highly organized criminals who use violence, intimidation, extortion, fear and corruption to gain territory and wealth. They invest their illegal profits in legitimate businesses rather than squander the money. All four gangs boast self-made millionaires whose ambition, shrewdness and business savvy rate with those of the continent's top corporate executives. They have one talent most executives don't: a killer instinct kept finely honed by political infighting that leaves more than figurative knife wounds in the back.

The Big Four are paramilitary operations fueled by greed and run on fear. Members are armed with the latest in military technology, including blast simulators for the cruise missile. They are protected by the best lawyers. The most successful live in the poshest houses in the best neighborhoods and pamper themselves with cars, yachts and planes. The day of the biker with nothing but the colors on his back and the engine in his crotch is gone for the Big Four. These outlaw motorcycle gangs are a new breed of organized crime: lean, hungry and deadly. They're grabbing what they thought they'd never have. And they want more.

Traditional organized crime looks tame next to bikers, who are learning to beat the mob at its own game. There are 24 traditional organized crime families in the US with about 2,500 made members. The migration to Florida has left about 200 mob members in Canada, mostly in Toronto and Montreal. The Big Four have about 3,500 color-wearing members, each with 10 associates.

The Big Four earn most of their money making and selling drugs. They control 75 percent of the North American methamphetamine market. Prostitution, extortion, theft, arson, robbery, bombings and contract murders are among the crimes that bring in millions more. Bikers commit many of the crimes on their own while protected by the club.

The bikers who make up the Big Four are not young punks.

More than half are older than 35 and their leaders are pushing 50. Ralph Hubert (Sonny) Barger Jr., the most respected Angel and the world's best-known outlaw biker—a near cult figure—is 49. Paul (Ooch) Ferry, the Pagan's national president, is 48. Donald Eugene Chambers and Ronald Jerome Hodge of the Bandidos, and Henry Joseph (Taco) Bowman and Stairway Harry Henderson of the Outlaws, are no longer young men.

Many Big Four bikers are experienced criminals who accumulate an impressive amount of frequent-flyer points as they criss-cross the world on business. They are more comfortable in suits than colors and prefer Cadillacs or Jaguars to arm-wrenching choppers. They are careerists—neo-Yuppies hungry for the trappings of power.

Two of the Big Four motorcycle gangs are locked in a death battle since 1974. The Hell's Angels and Outlaws kill each other's members at every opportunity. They also assimilate smaller clubs to expand their territory and bolster their strength. Gangs that resist takeovers don't last long; their drug supplies dry up or they are killed.

Law enforcement agencies are unable to control outlaw motorcycle gangs. Only warfare and infighting limits their drug and prostitution enterprises. The police had better get their act together. Representatives of the Big Four gangs met twice in 1986—once on the West Coast, once in the Chicago area—to discuss ways to improve relations between the clubs and tone down the violence that hinders their profitability. The Hell's Angels and the Pagans have also had a sitdown in York, Pennsylvania.

Similar meetings were held in 1936 when the young generation of business-oriented mafiosi wanted the mustache Petes to restrain their kneecapping and headsplitting. Cooperation has proven to be financially healthy for the mob. The bikers are catching on and already imitate traditional organized crime's low-key approach to doing business. They will become unstoppable if they ever stop fighting each other.

9

THE PAGANS: DO UNTO OTHERS & SPLIT

*And in the end there was Surtyr. He had defeated Zeus,
Apollo, Thor, and Ocles. In all their savagery, they
could not match Surtyr's vengeance. He called his followers Pagans. So it was written in the blood of the
defeated Gods that Surtyr's followers would rule the
earth, and make citizens tremble at the mention of their
name.*

*I left the Pagans because I had had enough. I had been
shot three times, stabbed twice, and poisoned once. I
served time in prison and nearly destroyed myself with
the constant use of drugs. I joined motorcycle gangs to
raise hell, ride bikes, and enjoy the camaraderie of a
brotherhood. Instead, I ended up leading a life of crime
and greed.*
—A Pagan who cherishes anonymity.

JOHN Vernon (Satan) Marron becomes Pagans president
shortly after the club absorbs his gang—the Sons of Satan
—in the early 1970s. The drug-abusing Marron eliminates all
threats, real or perceived, with death. Ralph (Lucifer) Yanotta

130

has enough of Marron's paranoid rule in 1973 and wants out of the club to join the Outlaws.

It's one thing to terrorize citizens, he feels, but law-despising bikers shouldn't live under a rule of fear. The club is supposed to be a brotherhood. But when one brother falls out of favor, Pagans weld him inside an oil drum, plug it with bullets and dump it into a bay. Pagan Dale Mason demonstrates the same disregard for brotherhood a decade later when he executes Pagan William (Yukie) Tomlinson and his wife Toni in a Cumberland County, New Jersey, gravel pit. They are the only witnesses in an assault charge Tomlinson files against Mason.

Yanotta isn't wimping out. He foresees the continuing infighting and just wants to get down to business dealing drugs, weapons and violence. Marron sees it differently: a quitter is an enemy. Satan puts $1,000 on Lucifer's head during a run. Yanotta is taken to a quarry in Bucks County, Pennsylvania, the next day and injected with sulfuric acid from a car battery, stabbed 37 times and shot in the head. Like a festering impetigo sore, he lives.

Lucifer Yanotta recovers in Florida where he joins the Outlaws Motorcycle Club. Marron sends two Pagan hit men after him. They return in boxes. Lucifer Yanotta participates in a cold-blooded execution in another rockpit the following year—1974—that triggers a war between the Outlaws and the Hell's Angels. Yanotta has nothing against violence; he just feels uneasy around unbalanced people like Marron.

The Pagans rank among the fiercest outlaw bikers in the US, with about 900 members in 44 chapters between New York and Florida. They are the only gang without international chapters, although they have ties to gangs in Canada. Most chapters are in New Jersey, Pennsylvania, Delaware and Maryland, where Lou Dolkin starts the club in Prince George's County in 1959. Threat of death for fuck-ups makes the Pagans a well-disciplined network of drug and weapons dealers, thieves and killers.

The Pagans learn in the mid-1970s that their shield of violence can also be their Achille's heel. The club is based between Baltimore and Washington, DC, from 1959 to 1975. The Pagans get involved in a territorial dispute with the Confederate Angels in Richmond, Virginia, when the Hell's Angels start courting the southern gang. The Pagans tolerate local biker gangs on their turf, but don't want competition from national clubs. They send a hit team to Richmond to waste one biker and wound several others.

Police pressure forces the Pagans to move their home base to Marcus Hook, in Delaware County, Pennsylvania. They choose the small port town for good reason. It is near the state lines of Delaware and New Jersey. Delaware County has a fragmented police network, with 42 different departments. The Pagans outmanoeuvre the police and kidnap, rape and fight. They also go to war against the Warlocks. Police have 15 unsolved murders on their hands within one year. The bodies of six women are found in rivers and swampy areas in 1975, the year the Pagans come to town. The public outcry causes police forces to band together and drive the gang out. The Pagans settle in Suffolk County, New York.

The Pagans are more nomadic than other clubs. Chapters, like a skip tracer's nightmare, have been known to move overnight. The club also doesn't have a geographically fixed mother chapter like the Hell's Angels in Oakland, the Outlaws in Detroit and the Bandidos in Corpus Christi. Pagan operations are guided by a mother club made up of 13 to 20 former chapter presidents. They wear a black number 13 on the back of their colors to indicate their special status. The mother club alternates meetings between Suffolk and Nassau counties in Long Island, New York. Members meet at each other's homes or elsewhere, rather than at clubhouses. The Pagan president and vice-president are figureheads who don't really run the club, although the president sets the price of drugs the gang sells. As a show of class, the Pagans give their president, Paul (Ooch) Ferry, the same salary paid the President of the United States—about $200,000 a year. Promotion within the club comes quick to members who bring in money through drug trafficking or prostitution, who own businesses that front for the club, who operate labs or control chemists, or who can corrupt police, politicians and judges. Pagans who do this best may get to wear the number 13 under the club colors: a horned Fire God who brandishes a sword of fire and sits cross-legged on an arch of flames.

Pagans, like other outlaw bikers, go to great lengths to prove their loyalty to the club's colors. Michael (White Bear)

Grayson, Pagan leader in Pilot Mountain, North Carolina, is a carpenter and auto body repairman who reads J.R.R. Tolkien and Hermann Hesse. The number eight ranking Pagan in the mother club hierarchy in 1981 drinks two bottles of Jack Daniels to kill the pain when he has the Pagan colors tattooed on his back.

The Pagan mother club sets national policy and directs all club business. It gives advice and guidance to chapters, rules on accepting new chapters, and disciplines with violence. The mother club operates like La Cosa Nostra's national commission: each member is responsible for the chapters in an area. Mother club members reap a handsome percentage of profits from the criminal operations of each chapter.

Edward Jackson—a pseudonym for a Pagan who, during his six years with the club, holds the positions of mother club member, Pagan national vice-president, sergeant-at-arms (who is responsible for members inside the club) and Pagan enforcer (who takes care of business outside the club)—explains the club's workings:

> Mother club members run the Pagan operations. Each mother club member establishes his independent moneymaking activities. Chapters are controlled by the mother club. A mother club member must know everything that is happening within his chapters. I had chapter presidents report to me; however, I also planted spies within the chapters to insure I knew everything that was happening.

"As a mother club member, I was responsible for generating income for myself and my chapters," says Jackson, who attended college on a sports scholarship and played tight end for four years on the varsity football team. "I would devise and oversee schemes and operations which would bring in money. The chapters under my control would carry out any criminal activity to make money."

> I have orchestrated Pagan-related criminal activities such as prostitution, extortion, drug trafficking, gun trafficking, counterfeiting and auto theft. Money generated by these operations went to me and my chapters. With the exception of narcotics operations, money generated was applied to the Pagan treasury and bail fund. Money in the treasury was used for legal fees, the president's salary, parties, the support of clubhouses and Pagan women and

various investments. The club supported the families of those
members who were sent to prison—as long as they were in good
standing with the club.

There is a standing rule that you have to do anything a member
tells you. If you say no, the member will do it, then he has the
right to kill you.

In 1973, the mother club had a Pagan chapter in Bucks
County, Pennsylvania, rob a Pennsylvania bank. The chapter received one-third of the stolen money and the mother club received
two-thirds of the take. In recognition of this, the mother club had
special patches made for the members who did the bank job. The
patches resembled small money pouches with dollar signs.

Pagans were continuously used and paid by landlords or credi-
tors to collect overdue rents or debts. Pagans were used in this
capacity because we could easily intimidate people.

I remember distinctly in Long Island there was a bar that
hadn't paid up the money that they owed. I called, made a call,
told the members that somebody's old lady had been assaulted.
They went down and wrecked the bar. Of course, the payment was
made the very next day because you can't afford to have your
establishment wrecked every day.

Prostitution was an extremely profitable operation. Many of
the Pagan girlfriends or female associates generated money for the
club and me by selling themselves. In or around 1974, as a mother
club member, I had Pagan women get jobs in massage parlors in
Alexandria and Arlington, Virginia. At first, the women obtained
the jobs through their own initiative. However, it became so profitable that I worked out deals with the owners of the parlors to
supply the women and also provide protection by having Pagan
members serve as bouncers. While I was managing this prostitution operation, I also distributed drugs throughout Virginia and
Maryland. It was, to say the least, a very successful moneymaking
operation.

Many of the women the Pagans put to work as prostitutes
are runaways. The bikers gang rape them—they call it training—and sometimes photograph them for blackmail. Some
girls are abused then let go; some stay with the club; others are
never found. Edward Jackson's three houses, two cars and
three motorcycles are registered in the names of Pagan women
while he is with the club. Registering property in someone
else's name is one of many ways outlaw bikers keep prying
eyes out of their affairs. Jackson explains why bikers use
nicknames and often don't know each other's real names.

We do a job together. I don't know your real name. The only people that know the real names are the president and the treasury, for bail purposes. We do something together. They can put a polygraph on me, I still don't know your name. . . . They could ask me your real name . . . and I wouldn't know it.

Codes are another protection against snoopers. The most important of these is TCB.

Any criminal activity that goes on has to be told to the chapter president, in turn to the mother club member [Jackson says]. I established a policy where because of the fear of the conspiracy charge, people would come and say I am going to take care of such and such. I would say wait a minute, go do what you have to do, just tell me you took care of business. That is where TCB, or taking care of business, came from.

While I served as a Pagan enforcer, I formed a black T-shirt gang—13 members that any time there was a problem, anywhere in the country, we got in two vans and we went and took care of it. Reprisal from a Pagan consists usually of a .38-calibre double automatic Colt, two shots in the back of the head, stomping on him just like a fish wrapped up in newspaper. That is the telltale signs of a Pagan hit.

The Pagans, like the other Big Four motorcycle gangs, maintain a security and intelligence operation that includes a spy network of women who work in courthouses, motor vehicle administrations and police departments.

The women in the courthouse apprised us in advance of such things as wiretaps, search warrants, arrest warrants, and raids [Jackson says]. The women at the motor vehicle administration provided us with blank licenses for phony identification purposes. In fact, Gus, Ike [both New York City mobsters] and I assembled a package of false I.D.s and sold them for $200 apiece. The package included blank driver's licenses, which were provided by our women, blank social security cards, and blank draft cards.

The intelligence network is effective. Pagans track down a federally protected witness relocated to Fairmont, West Virginia, from California and leave him for dead after beating him.

Fear and corruption are the Pagans' greatest weapons

against prosecution. Some parole officers, out of fear, will not return to jail Pagans arrested while on probation. And some Pagans, curiously, receive minimum fines and jail sentences.

A member of the Warlocks motorcycle gang shoots and kills a Pagan in Marcus Hook, Pennsylvania, in November 1975. Pagan Glenn Turner shows up with a .45-calibre handgun, which is either stolen or has been used in another crime, as police arrest the Warlock. Constable Donald Lewis replaces it with a .38-calibre gun to protect Turner. Lewis also buys cars and receives favors from Turner's father, who owns an automobile parts store, junkyard and towing business.

Glenn Turner pulls another .38-calibre revolver in the early hours of March 24, 1982, and shoots New Jersey State Trooper John Jacobs in the face when the cop stops Turner's 1980 Cadillac in Gloucester Township for speeding. The burned Cadillac is found within an hour. Turner, who lives in Marcus Hook, is caught five days later. He posts $150,000 cash bail and $25,000 for pending weapons charges after spending several weeks in jail. He forfeits the money, fails to appear for a court hearing and isn't caught until December 1982.

The Pagans ensure that jailed members don't roll over and testify against the club. Many lawyers assigned to arrested Pagans are club members. The lawyer's presence during questioning by police leaves a Pagan little chance to strike a deal. Such is the trust among brother bikers.

The Pagans constitution reflects not only the club's stated purpose of motorcycling, but also reveals its propensity for violence and its affinity for drugs. The following is a complete version of the club's rules:

PAGAN'S M.C. CONSTITUTION

Club Organization

The Pagan motorcycle club is run by the Mother Club. The Mother Club has last and final say so on all club matters. Any violation of the constitution will be dealt with by the Mother Club.

Chapter Organization

Six (6) members needed to start a chapter. Four (4) officers, no new chapter may be started without approval of the Mother Club.

Many original Hell's Angels were aviators who named the club after planes they flew during World War II. This B-17 bomber was photographed during a refueling stop in north Africa.

Sonny Barger (center with striped shirt) and his Oakland chapter.

(Above) Big Vinnie
Girolamo of the
Manhattan chapter in
New York City:
"When in Doubt,
Knock 'em Out."

(Right) Edward Levie
of the Manhattan
chapter on the cover
of a 1985 brochure for
the Hell's Angels Legal
Defense Fund.

A biker's colors are his most sacred possession.   (POLICE PHOTOS)
(Top Left) Howie Weisbrod from the Manhattan chapter on a run
in Canada.

The Angels have skinned non-members caught wearing club tattoos. (POLICE PHOTOS)

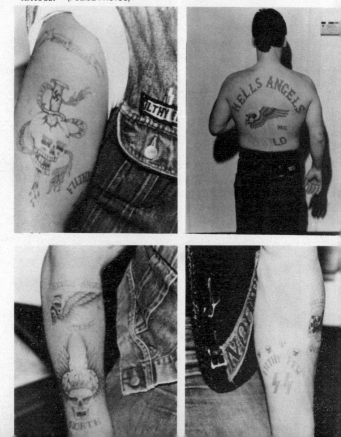

Anything can be found or done in a clubhouse. Gerry (Le Chat) Coulombe's authentic Nazi flag adorns the walls of the Missiles clubhouse in Chicoutimi in the late 1970s. Angel clubhouses, such as that of the Montreal chapter in Sorel, are equipped with video cameras and motion sensors that are monitored 24 hours a day.
(POLICE PHOTOS)

Daniel Matthieu, (left) a prospect with the Hell's Angels Montreal chapter, was killed September 1984 when a car driven by a priest rushing to see the Pope on his tour of Canada ran a stop sign and crashed into a cavalcade of Angels. Walter Stadnick, seen before (below left) and after the accident, was severely burned and lost several fingers. (POLICE PHOTOS)

WANTED BY FBI
NORMAN EDWARD RISINGER

FBI No. 196 922 D

ALIASES: J. E. Owings, James E. Owings, James Edward Owings, Norman Edward Reisinger, Norman Edward
Risinger, N. E. Risinger, Norman Risinger, Norman Edward Patrick Risinger, "Spider"

19 L 1 U tat. T U T U T U T T

NCIC: 1901TTAATT16SRAA04AA

M 1 U >4   A A T T R K U 3

Photographs taken 1977

Norman E. Risinger

DESCRIPTION
AGE: 38, born March 17, 1942, Port Arthur, Texas
HEIGHT: 6'
WEIGHT: 160 to 180 pounds
BUILD: medium
HAIR: balding - graying brown
OCCUPATION: mechanic
EYES: brown/hazel
COMPLEXION: light
RACE: white
NATIONALITY: American
SCARS AND MARKS: scar between eyebrows, scar on stomach and back,
left ear pierced, tattoos; devil with words "Born to Raise Hell" on left
forearm; skull with crossed pistons and words "Outlaws Forever" and
"CHICAGO" on left upper arm, and others
REMARKS: wears mustache and beard; reportedly a member of the Outlaw
Motorcycle Gang

CRIMINAL RECORD
Risinger has been convicted of theft, aggravated assault, and aggravated
battery.

CAUTION
RISINGER IS BEING SOUGHT AS THE ALLEGED GUNMAN IN THE EXE-
CUTION-STYLE, SHOTGUN MURDERS OF THREE RIVAL MOTORCYCLE GANG
MEMBERS, WHOSE BODIES, WEIGHTED WITH CONCRETE BLOCKS, WERE
LATER FOUND FLOATING IN A ROCK PIT. CONSIDER RISINGER ARMED
AND DANGEROUS.

Federal warrant was issued on August 20, 1978, at Ft. Lauderdale, Florida, charging Risinger with unlawful interstate flight to avoid prosecution for the crime of murder (Title 18,
U. S. Code, Section 1073).

YOU HAVE INFORMATION CONCERNING THIS PERSON, PLEASE CONTACT YOUR LOCAL FBI OFFICE.
TELEPHONE NUMBERS AND ADDRESSES OF ALL FBI OFFICES LISTED ON BACK.

Identification Order 4855
June 25, 1980

William H. Webster
Director
Federal Bureau of Investigation
Washington, D. C. 20535

Most Angel deaths are not accidents. Outlaw Norman (Spider)
Riesinger blew the brains out of three Angels with a 12-gauge
shotgun in a southern Florida rockpit in April 1974. Hundreds of
bikers from both clubs have died in the ensuing war.

The fiercest Hell's Angels in the world, the redoubted North chapter in Laval, Quebec.

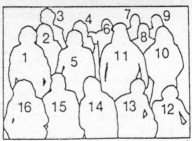

1. Jean-Marc Nadeau 2. Jean-Yves (Boule) Tremblay 3. Gilles (Le Nez) Lachance 4. Réjean (Zig-Zag) Lessard 5. Michel (Willie) Mayrand 6. Jean-Pièrre (Matt le Crosseur) Mathieu 7. Michel (Jinx) Genest 8. Marcel Simard 9. Guy-Louis (Chop) Adam 10. Jean-Guy (Brutus) Geoffrion 11. Robert (Ti-Maigre) Richard 12. Régis (Lucky) Asselin 13. Yves (Apache) Trudeau 14. Laurent (L'Anglais) Viau 15. Yvon (Le Père, Gorille) Bilodeau 16. Luc (Sam) Michaud

TOO WILD TO LIVE: Among the North chapter Angels slated for death by Montreal chapter president Réjean (Zig-Zag) Lessard (1) were North president Laurent (L'Anglais) Viau (2), Guy-Louis (Chop) Adam (3) and Michel (Willie) Mayrand (4).

(POLICE PHOTO)   (POLICE PHOTO) (POLICE PHOTO)

Police pull the rotting bodies of slaughtered North chapter Angels from the St. Lawrence Seaway in June 1985. Note the trademarks of Hell's Angels handiwork: chains, cement blocks and sleeping bags. (POLICE PHOTOS)

The slaughter of Angels by Angels has caused many members to turn against the club. Yves (Apache) Trudeau (above left), Gerry (Le Chat) Coulombe (above) and Gilles (Le Nez) Lachance (left), of the doomed North chapter, all testified against the club to save their lives.

ON THE ROAD AGAIN: The Hell's Angels are inveterate travelers who rack up more frequent-flyer points than most businessmen. Michel (Jinx) Genest (left), a North chapter member whose life was spared, was shot at by Outlaws at a bus depot in Wawa, Ontario.

Yvon (Le Père or Gorille) Bilodeau (right), the oldest Angel in Quebec and another North member allowed to live, visits New York City so frequently the Manhattan chapter lets him wear their patch.

(POLICE PHOTOS)

Funerals are major social events for outlaw bikers. Here, members of the Outlaws Motorcycle Club, at war with the Hell's Angels, gather in Florida from across North America to bury a club member. Outlaws security officers photograph all onlookers while police photograph them.

This patch commemorates a brotherhood pact the Outlaws signed with the Satan's Choice in Canada in the mid-1970s to ensure each club harbored the other's fugitives. The Outlaws spread their tentacles north and took over four of 12 Choice chapters in the spring of 1977. The Hell's Angels followed.

(PHOTOS BY BROWARD COUNTY SHERIFF'S DEPARTMENT)

The Outlaws have their own
funeral traditions. (Above) The
pallbearer on the left is Peter
(Greased Lightning) Rogers, the
man responsible for triggering the
war between the Outlaws and the
Hell's Angels.
Only an Outlaw throws dirt on an
Outlaw (right). Club members take
turns shovelling dirt into the grave.
Former club president Stairway
Harry Henderson stands on the left.
Current president Henry (Taco)
Bowman stands on the right.
(Below) Mourning Outlaws fire a
last salute to a fallen brother.

(PHOTOS BY BROWARD COUNTY SHERIFF'S
DEPARTMENT)

Women are attracted to outlaw bikers for many reasons. Most are young, good looking and willing. And they're just as deadly.

A HAPPY THREESOME: Big Jim Nolan, president of the tough South Florida chapter of the Outlaws until jailed in the mid-1980s, frolics with friends.

Women are nothing but property to bikers and they're proud to advertise it. Christine Deese, 18, (below right) was nailed to a tree in Florida by her boyfriend—Norman (Spider) Riesinger—for failing to turn a $10 trick. She says the man never showed up.

President

Runs chapter under the direction of the Mother Club. Keeps chapter organized, makes sure chapter business is carried out and inspects all bikes before runs and makes President meetings.

Sergeant At Arms

Makes sure Presidents orders are carried out.

Vice President

Takes over all Presidents duties when the President is not there.

Secretary Treasurer

In charge of minutes of meetings and treasury. No members may change chapters without the Mother Club members permission in his area. All present chapter debts are paid and is approved by the president of the new chapter he wishes to change to. If a member has a snival, he must use chain of command, in other words, (1) His Chapter President, (2) Mother Club member in area, (3) President of Club.

Meetings

1. Chapters must have one organized meeting per week.
2. Chapters meetings are attended by members only.
3. Members must be of sound mind (straight) when attending meetings.
4. If a Mother Club member attends a meeting and a member is fouled-up, he will be fined by the Mother Club member.
5. Miss three (3) meetings in a row, and your out of the club.
6. Members must attend meeting to leave club and turn in his colors and everything that has the name "PAGANS" on it. (T-Shirts, Wrist Bands, Mugs, Etc.)
7. If a member is thrown out of the club or quits without attending meeting, he loses his colors, motorcycle, and anything that says "Pagans" on it, and probably an ass kicking.
8. When a member is travelling, he must attend meeting of the area he is travelling in.
9. If a vote is taken at a meeting and member is not there, his vote is void.
10. Members must have colors with him when attending meeting.

Bikes

1. All members must have a Harley Davidson 750–1200CC.
2. If a member is not of sound mind or fouled-up to ride his

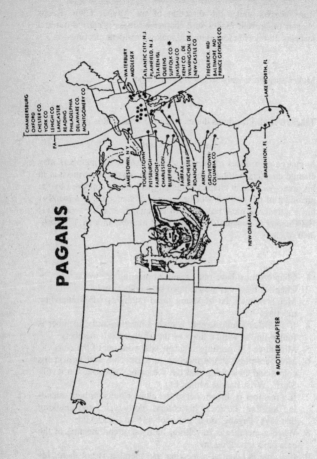

PAGANS

CHAMBERSBURG
OXFORD
CHESTER CO.
YORK CO.
LEHIGH CO.
LANCASTER
READING
PHILADELPHIA
DELAWARE CO.
MONTGOMERY CO.

PA.

WATERBURY
MIDDLESEX
ATLANTIC CITY, N.J.
PLAINFIELD, N.J.
STATEN ISL.
QUEENS
SUFFOLK CO.
NASSAU CO.
KENT CO. DE
WILMINGTON DE /
NEW CASTLE CO.
FREDERICK, MD.
BALTIMORE, MD.
PRINCE GEORGES CO.

LAKE WORTH, FL

JAMESTOWN, N.Y.
YOUNGSTOWN
PITTSBURGH
FAIRMONT
CHARLESTON
BLUEFIELD
FAIRFAX
WINCHESTER
ROANOKE
AIKEN
GROVETOWN/
COLUMBIA CO.

BRADENTON, FL

NEW ORLEANS, LA.

★ MOTHER CHAPTER

motorcycle in the opinion of another member, his riding privilege may be pulled by said member until he has his head together.

3. All bikes must be on the road April 30th, or otherwise directed by the Mother Club.
4. All members must have a motorcycle license.

Mandatories

Two (2) mandatories, July 4th, and Labor Day. Mother Club may call additional mandatories if need be.

Funerals

1. If a member dies in a chapter, it is mandatory for all members in his chapter to attend funeral.
2. Chapter is in charge of taking care of all funeral arrangements, parties, police, procession, etc.

Parties

Pagan parties are Pagan parties only. Each chapter must throw (1) party or run per year.

Respect

1. Respect is to be shown to all Mother Club members, officer members, members personal property, Bike, Old Lady, House, Job, etc. In other words, if it's not yours, "Don't Mess With It."
2. No fighting among each other is allowed, any punches to be thrown will be done by the Sgt. Arms or a Mother Club Member.
3. No stealing from members.
4. Respect your Colors.

Colors

1. President gets colors from Mother Club member in area when new member is voted in.
2. When a member leaves club, the president of his chapter turns over his colors to the Mother Club member in his area.
3. Respect your Colors, don't let anyone take them from you except the president of your chapter or a Mother Club member.
4. No colors are worn in a cage, except during funerals and loading or unloading a bike from a truck.

5. Nothing will be worn on the back of your jacket except your colors, Diamond, 13 patch.
6. No Hippie shit on the front.
7. Colors are to be put on cut off denim jackets only.
8. The only member who may keep his colors if he leaves the club is a Mother Club Member.

Old Ladies

1. Members are responsible for their old ladies.
2. Members may have more than one (1) Old Lady.
3. Members may not discuss club business with their Old Lady.
4. No Old Ladies allowed at meetings.
5. No property patch is worn on an old lady. So if you see a chick you better ask before you leap.

Prospects

1. Prospect must be at least 18 years old.
2. Prospect must be sponsored by one member who has known him at least one year.
3. Sponsor is responsible for prospect.
4. Prospect must have motorcycle.
5. Prospect must ride his bike to meeting at time of being voted into club.
6. Prospect can not do any drugs.
7. Prospects can not carry weapons at meetings and Pagan functions, unless otherwise directed by his President.
8. No stealing from Prospects.
9. Prospects must attend all meetings and club functions.
10. Prospects must do anything another member tells him to do, that a member has done or would be willing to do himself.
11. Prospects must be voted in by all members of the chapter and Three (3) Mother Club Members.
12. Prospects must pay for his colors before receiving them.
13. Prospects period is determined by Mother Club Member.
14. Pagan's M.C. is a motorcycle Club and a non-profit organization.

The Pagans' propensity for violence and their proximity to mob turf earns the club the best connections to traditional organized crime among the Big Four outlaw motorcycle gangs. Pagans act as drug couriers, enforcers, bodyguards and hit men for the mob, mostly in Pennsylvania and New Jersey, and associate with the Genovese and Gambino families in

New York. Pagans kill members who jeopardize business with too much talk. This strict code of discipline is not unlike the Mafia's code of *omerta*, or silence. The similarity in business practices eases the way for Pagans into the family fold.

Two Pagans have blood links to the mob: Anthony (Rocco) LaRocca Jr. is nephew of John LaRocca, head of La Cosa Nostra family in southwestern Pennsylvania; Joey (Sir Lancelot) Anastasia is nephew of Albert Anastasia, founder of Murder Inc.

Cooperation between the groups starts slowly, with Pagans being given menial tasks. Two prospects are asked to prove they are worthy of becoming Pagans by clubbing a trade unionist with baseball bats when he fails to vote the way the mob wants him to. Pagans and mobsters gradually cooperate in extortions, counterfeiting, car thefts and drug trafficking.

Allan Morrow, the Prince of Porn, hires eight Philadelphia Pagans in 1976 to muscle out the competition in Scranton. The bikers pump carbon monoxide into the building then charge in with attack trained dogs. The owner of the Paxton Plaza Building in Harrisburg, Pennsylvania, plans to defraud an insurance company and hires four Pagans to bomb the building on October 6, 1978. Six of 10 dynamite bombs explode to cause extensive damage.

A common interest in methamphetamine production and trafficking strengthens the Pagan link with traditional organized crime. Ronald Raiton, of Dresher, Pennsylvania, is one of the biggest East Coast suppliers from 1977 to 1981 of the chemicals needed to make methamphetamine. He supplies P2P to Ronald Kownacki, a New Jersey businessman aligned with the Pagans, and to Ignazio Raymond Anthony (Long John) Martorano, a member of the Bruno organized crime family. Chemists who work in houses, apartments and trailers in public campgrounds turn the P2P into methamphetamine.

Kownacki is the Pagans' major methamphetamine supplier. He sells the drug to a southern New Jersey Pagan called Buckets, who distributes it to Pagan mother club members in New Jersey, Delaware and Philadelphia. Kownacki pays the Pagan president $500 a week for protection and buys a bar for gang members to hang out in.

Kownacki's business runs something like this: he pays Rai-

ton $4,500 for one gallon of P2P and forks over an additional
$10,000 to the Bruno crime family for every gallon; he then
sells each pound of methamphetamine to Buckets for $9,000;
Buckets dilutes each pound 50 percent and sells each new
pound for $10,000 to mother club members. They further di-
lute it and sell it to other Pagans for $900 an ounce. (The
Pagans learn how to manufacture methamphetamine from P2P
when Kownacki is jailed in 1981.)

Outlaw bikers are opportunists. A few Pagans realize in the
early 1980s that the club can outmuscle Philadelphia's strife-
torn Bruno crime family. (Hunchback) Harry Riccobene, a
caporegime, or lieutenant, has broken away from the family.
Riccobene runs drug, gambling and loansharking networks.
He is the Pagans' main mob contact and uses the bikers as
enforcers and drug runners. (He even uses two members of the
Pagans' Black T-Shirt hit squad as bodyguards at a 1982
trial.) The 70-year-old, four-foot-ten mobster is embroiled in a
power struggle with Nicodemo Domenic Scarfo that weakens
the family. Scarfo becomes the third boss of the Philadelphia
Bruno family in two years after a remote-control bomb kills
Philip Charles (Chickenman) Testa as he walks into his house
on March 15, 1981. Scarfo wants Riccobene's action.

Factions led by (Hunchback) Harry Riccobene and Long
John Martorano vie for power within the Bruno organized
crime family and weaken the organization through warfare.
Martorano controls drugs; Riccobene makes his money
through gambling, loansharking and extortion. Riccobene
aligns himself with the Pagans to develop his own drug network. Martorano woos the Pagans because he knows they are
stronger and he doesn't want competition or war. The Pagans
are divided on who to side with.

"The Pagans are much larger than organized crime," Pagan
Edward Jackson says. "They are in the ruthless aspect of organized crime between the twenties and thirties. In other
words, organized crime figures are wearing suits now. The
Pagans are out in the street doing the dirty work."

There is little honor among eastern seaboard hoods and
much tension between the Pagans and the mob. Two Bruno
associates and hit men Peter Rinaldi and Victor DeLuca take

$80,000 in Pagan gold from Kownacki in December 1980. They claim the gold is back payment for protection money the club owes the family. Kownacki asks the Pagan president for help. Pagans James DeGregorio and Eddie Condon try to abduct Rinaldi, DeLuca and Hunchback Harry Riccobene at gunpoint in a downtown Philadelphia parking lot in February 1981. DeLuca bolts while being shoved into the back seat of a car. DeGregorio shoots him in the shoulder. Riccobene fades into the crowd.

Riccobene, DeLuca and Joseph Pedulla later meet DeGregorio and fellow Pagan Glenn Turner at Pedulla's house to discuss returning the gold. Turner knows Riccobene from three years spent together in jail. It is at this meeting that the Pagans and Riccobene talk about joint drug ventures.

Relations between the two groups sour again in April 1982, when DeLuca, Pedulla and Long John Martorano demand that all methamphetamine traffickers, including the Pagans, pay the Bruno family 20 percent of their profits for the privilege of dealing in the Philadelphia area. Martorano has a near stranglehold on the importation of P2P, the precursor to methamphetamine, in 1982 and controls mob production and pricing of the drug. His influence extends into Canada, where he is involved with members of Paul Volpe's Toronto crime family.

DeGregorio, Kenneth DeRosa, a former Bruno chemist, and Charles (McNut) McKnight meet soon after with Long John Martorano, Joseph Ciangalini and Salvatore (Sonny) Merlino at Cous' Little Italy Restaurant, formerly the Piccolo 500 Restaurant, in south Philadelphia. About 30 Pagans race their Harleys around the restaurant as a show of force. The mob and Pagans discuss contract murders the bikers can carry out for the family. The Pagans are also exempted from paying the 20 percent tribute to the mob and both groups agree to respect each other's boundaries.

"We will just stay out of each other's way," the acting boss of the Bruno family says.

The concessions anger 42-year-old family underboss Sonny Merlino, who storms out of the restaurant. John (Egyptian) Kachbalian's motorcycle is parked near Merlino's car. He asks Kachbalian to move it. The Pagan is too slow. Merlino pushes the bike with his car and injures the biker. Pagan retribution is swift. They shoot at Merlino's mother's house. The car of

Anthony Ricciardi, one of Merlino's associates, is fire-bombed. Shots are fired through the front door window of Salvator Testa's house. The mob pays $5,000 for injuries to the Pagan and motorcycle run over by Merlino.

Several Pagans meet with Bruno family members at the Oregon Diner later in April 1982 to smooth over differences. The mobsters include Long John Martorano, George Martorano, Nick Virgilio, Phil Leonetti, Larry Merlino and Frank Verdino. Harry Riccobene, Victor DeLuca and Joseph Pedulla are also there.

The April 1982 meetings that cement ties between the mob and the Pagans reflect the power of brains over brawn. The agreement ends two tense years for Philadelphia's strife-torn mob. The Pagans are more powerful than the mob during the meeting at the Oregon Diner. They can overthrow the mob in Philadelphia, but fail to do so because they aren't united. The deal with the mob, however, helps consolidate the Pagan hold on the methamphetamine market.

The Pagans make and distribute most of the methamphet-amine and PCP in the northeastern US—about $15 million a year. They intimidate competing dealers to corner the market. They have their own chemists and laboratories, which supply dealers in Connecticut, New York, New Jersey, Pennsylvania, Virginia, Maryland and Ohio. They also deal in cocaine, mar-ijuana and killerweed—parsley sprinkled with PCP. The Pagans are unsophisticated and lack business ethics, even though they are highly organized. The greedy Pagans, unlike the Hell's Angels, don't care about the quality of the metham-phetamine they sell. The mother club controls distribution and everyone else down the line wants part of the action. The drug is cut every time it moves from one level to the next. It's a rip-off by the time it hits the street.

The Pagan drug network is extensive and intricate.

I had one person that I took, dressed him up in a three-piece suit, I put him on an airplane [Jackson says]. He stopped with PCP and traded PCP even up for speed from a club called the Para-Dice Riders from [Toronto] Canada. He would stop in Pittsburgh. The next stop would be Stairway Harry, who is a national president for the Outlaws. He would stop and see the Buzzards in Wisconsin. In

Flint, Michigan, the Flying Wheels. The El Foresteros in Iowa.
Then to the West Coast, see the Coffin Cheaters, Satan Slaves,
come back around the bottom of the country through Arizona,
Texas, with the Bandidos, who were our brother club. End up with
the Outlaws down in Florida, and then stop back in Virginia and
the mother club would have a stash of drugs and $25,000 in cash.
That went on once a week. He would start out with just killerweed. He would deal even up for speed, have different speed and
killerweed, get hallucinogenic from the West Coast, downers from
Texas and Arizona.

William Terrance (Lance) Costello, a former Marine reser-
vist and machinist who joins the Pagans in 1970 to drink beer
and fight, learns quickly that bikers are unforgiving businessmen.

Dealing drugs in the Pagan organization is quite different from the
activities of an individual dope dealer on the street [Costello says].
The very nature and structure of the Pagan organization breeds an
element of fear among its members which characterize Pagan drug
dealing and other illegal activities. When you deal drugs for the
Pagans, you know without any question that, should you perform
less than expected, the people above you would cut you off from
drugs or kill you.

Many members launder their drug and prostitution money
through legitimate businesses, such as motorcycle repair
shops, which they also use to fence stolen parts. The club
owns a trucking company in the northeastern US. Pagans con-
sistently obtain sophisticated weapons, which they use or sell
to radical groups and other motorcycle gangs. They have automatic weapons, plastic explosives, dynamite, hand grenades
and blast simulators for the cruise missile that they distribute
through the club network.

It's surprising their network works—Pagans are stoned
more often than not.

During meetings it would almost come to a contest [Pagan Edward
Jackson says]. In fact, one mother club meeting where I was at,
we actually chose up teams and we put so many lines of speed
down, so many tuinals, so much coke, and we just did three
tuinals, two on speed, two of killerweed; it became a contest.

Everybody used drugs all the time. During the six years I was

a Pagan, I was fearless, ruthless, and always under the influence
of narcotics. My personality drastically changed because of my
narcotics habits. On a given day I would awake, take speed to
wake up, do cocaine, take some downers, and smoke killerweed.
It's not difficult to have Pagan members carry out illegal and often
ruthless acts because they are generally extremely high from some
sort of drug use. In fact, most Pagan members simply follow in-
structions from mother club members and chapter presidents. They
really have no concept of the overall operations.

But even the drugged-up Pagans have standards. They
measure a man's impairedness by his ability to handle his
motorcycle.

It was my understanding as sergeant-at-arms and Pagan enforcer
inside the club that if you could start your motorcycle and ride it,
then you could ride it. . . . During funerals, when there was more
than one chapter, the national sergeant-at-arms would carry a bat
with him and would ride up alongside of the pack and anybody
who wasn't riding properly would get swatted in the back. That is
why we always had trucks following the pack. They would pick
up the people that were discarded to the side of the road.

Lance Costello considers himself a victim of Pagan overin-
dulgence:

I feel I have lost some of my intelligence. I have lost my memory.
During the times I was using these drugs, my thoughts weren't
coherent. A friend of mine was stabbed—one of the members—
and if I could have loaded my gun at that time, I would have killed
the person. But I couldn't get the bullets into my gun because I
was so messed up. . . . When I worked in the liquor store for Mark
Fox [Pagan national treasurer], I could add up about 15 different
items in my head without using a cash register. I am lucky to do
two or three now without some paper.

Costello let his prodigious drug profits slip away as easily
as his thoughts.

I bought a van. I always spent it on parties. A day wouldn't go by
that I spent less than $200 a day. Most of the people in my chapter
were idiots. They had been using drugs much longer than I had.
Most of them came from a disadvantaged background, where it
wouldn't be as true in some of the other chapters. But providing

these people with drugs, they owed me, when I left, large amounts of money. And I, for a long time, supported them.

At one time I rented a house for about $400—five bedroom house where I had four or five of them living with me because, even though I would give them drugs, they still couldn't support themselves. They would sell the drugs, they would spend the money, they would party on the drugs. Some people after a period of time aren't capable of looking after themselves.

10

THE BANDIDOS: SOUTHERN FRIED PUSSY

We are the people our parents warned us about.
—Club motto.

DONALD Eugene Chambers sits in his Houston living room in March 1966 mulling over plans to form an outlaw motorcycle club to control drug trafficking and prostitution in Texas. The three major North American gangs have impressive names: Hell's Angels, Outlaws, Pagans. What do you call a band of Texas desperadoes?

The television's cathode flicker illuminates the recesses of Chambers' brain. The Frito Bandido tears across the screen raising hell to sell chips, nachos and other mutilated potato forms. A bunch of outlaws falls victim to mass marketing. Chambers calls his gang the Bandidos. He even adopts the fat, machete-and-pistol-wielding cartoon cowboy as the club's colors. In keeping with the racist bent of the other Big Four gangs, the Bandidos constitution states provokingly: No fat Mexicans.

Chambers has a sense of humor, but he is not a funny man. The Bandidos president and two club members force two men who rip off the gang during a drug deal near El Paso to dig their own graves in 1973. They shoot them and set the corpses on fire.

The Bandidos, also called the Bandido Nation, are the fastest growing outlaw motorcycle gang in the US. The club has about 30 chapters and 500 members. It even has an Australian chapter, acquired with much bloodletting. The club is concentrated in Texas and extends into Louisiana, Mississippi, Arkansas, New Mexico, Colorado, South Dakota and Washington State. The Bandidos are run by a mother chapter made up of a president, four regional vice-presidents and regional and local chapter officers. The current president, Ronald Jerome Hodge, of Rapid City, South Dakota, sets club goals and policies and has final authority. Bandido chapters don't have clubhouses. Members meet at their homes, which often are as fortified as the clubhouses of other clubs, with spotlights and guard dogs to protect the perimeters.

The Bandidos file articles of incorporation with the secretary of state for Texas in February 1978, to establish the club as a non-profit motorcycling organization. They let the incorporation lapse when they realize it can be used against them in prosecutions under the Racketeer-Influenced and Corrupt Organizations (RICO) statute to prove that crimes are committed by the club as a whole and not individual members.

Bandido Michael Smith files a $22-million lawsuit against the US Government in September 1985, in which he claims he is being persecuted because of his membership in the club. Smith, of Mobile, Alabama, files the suit in New Orleans after being released from prison. He claims he is the victim of a widespread conspiracy by federal authorities against political and social organizations.

The Bandidos, like other outlaw motorcyclists, are routinely stopped by police, as they are more likely than not to be committing an offence. Gang members carry miniature tape recorders and bait police officers in attempts to get compromising statements that can be used as a defence during trial.

A Nomad chapter takes care of Bandido security, counterintelligence and internal discipline. The chapter is made up of charter members who have been with the club for more than five years. Hodge wears a Nomad rocker on his colors. This elite group does not live in one area, although many of its members gravitate to Lubbock, Texas. The chapter compiles files on police forces and outlaw motorcycle gangs they con-

sider enemies. Corruption is an integral part of security for
any organized criminal enterprise. A deputy sheriff presigns
and certifies blank birth certificates for the Bandidos in Little
Rock, Arkansas. They are used to hide fugitives and commit
frauds.

The Bandidos kill if they can't corrupt. A van stolen near a
Bandidos' hangout in Austin, Texas, cuts off US Attorney Jim
Kerr as he rolls out of his drive in November 1978. Seventeen
.30-calibre machine-gun slugs plug his car. He is slightly
wounded. Texas Judge John Wood isn't so lucky. Maximum
John shows little mercy for Bandidos who appear in his court.
He is shot with a rifle as he gets into his car on May 29, 1979,
shortly before he is to hear another Bandidos' trial.

The Bandidos are involved in drug trafficking, prostitution,
arson, contract murder, fencing, extortion, stealing and running weapons, as well as welfare and bank fraud. A 50-year-
old Bandido owns 15 to 20 small businesses worth $12 million
in 1981. The bikers make most of their money manufacturing
and selling methamphetamine. Two Bandidos die when their
twin engine Cessna crashes in Tucumcari, New Mexico, in
1979. Three weapons and cocaine are found in the fuselage.
Club members and associates who are pilots smuggle drugs
and guns across the border and state lines. Bandidos in Albuquerque have 140 pounds of dynamite stashed away in 1979.
Bandidos break into homes and stores to steal guns. They also
get machine guns, submachine guns and C-4 plastic explosives through military contacts.

The Bandidos' alliance with the Outlaws, which begins
with Hodge's visit to Florida in 1978, expands their drug network. The Outlaws provide the Bandidos with cocaine they
get from Colombian and Cuban suppliers. Both clubs socialize
in Bandidos-controlled towns and they own a nightclub together in Oklahoma City. The clubs consider themselves sister
organizations and wear each other's tattoos. This sisterhood
causes some tension in July 1983, when the Satan's Angels in
British Columbia, which the Bandidos in Washington State
supply with cocaine and methamphetamine, bury their colors
and become Hell's Angels. The Outlaws frown on anyone
associating with their mortal enemies. And Angels sell drugs
made in Angel laboratories.

The Bandidos, like most good old boys, like their wheels.
They are first-rate motorcycle and car thieves. It is only when

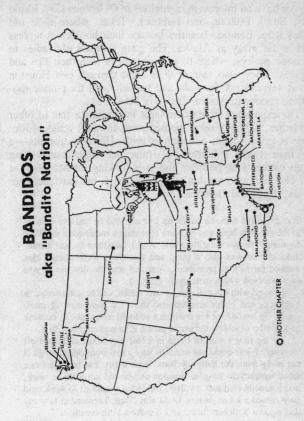

BANDIDOS
aka "Bandito Nation"

they discover the joy of selling sex that peddling pussy replaces auto parts as their number two pastime. The Bandidos own or have an interest in nightclubs in Oklahoma City, Rapid City, South Dakota, and Lubbock, Texas, where their old ladies strip. Bandido beauties bounce their boobies in topless bars as far away as Alaska. The gang supplies old ladies to massage parlors, where they soothe dicks with their lips and vaginas. They also market their meat through two Houston escort services. A Bandido and his wife sell their nude modelling agency in Austin, Texas, in May 1981.

The experience of Barbara Opie is not unlike that of other old ladies, although biker women come from all walks of life. Opie is given up for adoption at birth. Her grandparents—a psychiatrist and a housewife—raise her. Opie starts using drugs on her 11th birthday and goes looking for her father at 12. The man who wouldn't see her through life introduces her to sex, drugs and violence.

The day I met him, he pulled up in a car, and he had five women in the car with him, and he wasn't wearing a motorcycle jacket or anything. He was wearing a suit. And I found out he was a Bandido and he was also a pimp and that these were women that worked for him as prostitutes. And that was the first time I was ever involved with a motorcycle gang.

I stayed with my real dad for two weeks, and he got arrested in Lubbock, and I was arrested also there for possession of marijuana. He handed me his marijuana and told me to take it, because he knew he would be thrown in prison if he was caught with it.

By the time I was 16 I was in a half-way house and it wasn't working. I just could not seem to stay away from doing drugs. I ran away from the half-way house with a guy that belonged to a small motorcycle gang in Houston and he did not want to work, and I remembered that my dad's old ladies would go to work, and they earned a lot of money. I told him "Well, I remember how my dad made a birth certificate, so I'll make a birth certificate."

You just take white paper ink, and you blot out all the dates and you run it through a copying machine a couple of times, so it comes out looking blank and you type in what you want, and then you run it through a couple more times so it looks original. And, so, I made me a birth certificate, because I was only 16 and I went and started working as a stripper in Houston, and I made a whole lot of money, and that satisfied my husband.

My first old man I turned tricks for, but it was not anything like—I did not go stay in a hotel and you know—I had specific

sugar daddies that just really liked me and I liked them and I
would sleep with them for money. But after I became his old lady,
I never tricked. He would not allow me to turn tricks.

The marriage breaks up and Opie becomes involved with
the Bandidos when she seeks their protection against an ex-
convict who tears up her apartment in search of his girlfriend.
She meets Chilite the Fox. "He was the kind of guy that parents don't ever want their daughters to meet."

He was really good looking and he wore all kinds of diamonds and
he drove a big car and he was a Bandido, and he just sort of—I
was swept off my feet by him. . . . And at that point, I became
probably addicted to drugs. I had always messed around with
drugs and I always used—especially LSD frequently—but I became addicted to a drug called THC [tetrahydrocanabinol].

Belts or colors identify women as Bandido property.

I had a property belt, and then when I was Chilite's old lady, there
was another old lady there that was his wife, and she had the
property colors. When she ran away from him and left, she left,
ran off and left with a sugar daddy, I inherited the property colors.
It signifies that you're the property—instead of a second old lady
or something—you are property of that specific Bandido and the
other Bandidos cannot misuse you sexually or physically.

Some bikers have as many as five [old ladies] and then there
are some that restrict themselves to just one. So many guys are
different. There are a lot of them that just do not get serious and
they will keep a lot of them to keep a lot of money coming in.
Then there are some that will get kind of serious and just have
one. Because obviously, if you are really serious about each other
or you really like each other, another woman just does not fit in
well. But if it is just a guy who just does not really care about the
girls, he will usually have more than one.

[Chilite the Fox] held me in sort of a fear type pattern. He was
OK. He could do all the drugs he wanted to and he was fine until
he started drinking. And when he would start drinking he would
just go completely crazy. And when we were at work, the girls,
and we saw that [Chilite] had come into the club, if he started
drinking, we would become terrified, because he would just commit terrible acts of violence when he was drinking.

[Chilite] threw an ashtray at me one time from across the
room. I was so loaded I couldn't even move, I was just sitting
there. And he threw an ashtray at me because I wasn't up making

sure that the other guys had plenty of stuff to drink, and he broke
my front tooth. This is the kind of guy he was. He was all right at
first, and then we kind of got into a trap and we became held there
by fear.

The bond lasts until Chilite the Fox is jailed for violent
rapes. She takes up with and marries Jim Opie, president of
the Bandidos Shreveport, Louisiana, chapter and operator of a
topless bar in Corpus Christi.

When Chilite went to jail, Jim came to town and he told me that I
would go with him. He would call me his old lady and I could work
in El Paso and nobody would bother me, and so I said all
right. I was in that type of lifestyle because I wanted to be. I was
never forced into anything. And I had options. I really did. I
always had a good option and a secure option background that I
could fall back on. He did not force me to go with him. I wanted
to go.
    When I was a nude dancer for my first old man in Houston, I
had to make $150 every night. When I became Jim's old lady and
I was not a nude dancer and I was not prostituting, the amount fell
to $50 a night as a topless dancer. Every bit of money that I ever
earned went directly to my old man. Almost all the women,
though, regardless of whether they were biker old ladies or not,
they gave all their money to some man.

Says Jim Opie: "Everybody that graces the door of a topless club can almost bet he is putting dollars in some biker's
pocket."
Barbara and Jim undergo religious conversion in May 1978
during an evangelical revival meeting in Shreveport, where
they are now active members of the Broadmoor Assembly of
God. Faith gives her a new outlook on the biker lifestyle.

I feel that our society has basically degenerated so far, that there
are so many things that threaten the American home, that threaten
the American family, and Bandido motorcycle gangs, or Pagan
motorcycle gangs, or Outlaws, or Hell's Angels are only part of
the things that threaten our society.
    I feel that teenagers, when they're lonely and they're lost and
they're looking for someone to care for them, they will accept it
from whatever point of view it comes in. All these big boom
growths of these satanic churches and the Jim Jones thing, the
Bandido motorcycle gangs, the other motorcycle gangs, there are

kids out there and they are lonely and they are hurting and they are turning toward something that will give them security.

And they will turn toward motorcycle gangs for security; they see those guys as being really strong, as being able to protect them, and they will turn toward—especially a female, because they see it as a different type of lifestyle and an exciting type of lifestyle and they do not realize at all what they are getting involved in, until they become so involved with drugs that they don't care.

Another former Bandido old lady warns that the only thrill a girl gets is her first ride with the biker. Everything after that is a white-slave-market nightmare.

"A biker will take the girl to a club meeting where she will be sexually abused by each club member."

The punishment for refusal to participate in club wife swaps?

I was bound with tape around my wrists, elbows, knees and ankles, and then my wrists and ankles were bound for five days. Each day I was beaten when my husband woke up. I was kicked until my entire body was swollen.

The Bandidos export violence, besides selling drugs and pussy, much to the dismay of Australian police. Tony Spencer, who uses the alias Snodgrass, and Anthony Sciberras, both members of the Commancheros in Sydney, visit the US in the summer of 1983 under pretext of arranging the export of motorcycle parts to Australia. They visit the Bandidos chapter in Albuquerque, New Mexico, and decide they want to form a chapter of the gang in Sydney.

They return to Sydney, inform their Commancheros mother club of their intentions, and recruit. The 18-year-old club splits after months of arguments. The Commancheros retain their identity. Defectors to the Bandidos must burn their Commanchero colors. The Bandidos colors can't have Sydney on the bottom rocker.

Friction builds when both clubs run into each other at their favorite watering holes. Members of both clubs who live near each other fight—verbally at first, then with fists. Jock Ross, president and founding member of the Commancheros meets with Bandidos president Tony Spencer in mid-July 1984. They formally declare war and agree, in true British colonial spirit, that members' homes and places of employment will not be attacked.

Three Commancheros are severely beaten in a Bandido hotel on August 9. The hotel is empty of Bandidos when 10 Commancheros show up the next day. Shots are fired near the Bandidos' clubhouse at Balmain, a Sydney suburb, later that night. The Commancheros shoot up the clubhouse two nights later. The tit-for-tat battle continues the following week when the Bandidos shoot up the Commancheros' clubhouse. Both clubs buy guns, walkie talkies and baseball bats. Two Commancheros discharge a shotgun into the rear of a car driven by two Bandidos on August 20. The gentleman's war gets nasty on August 26. Members of both clubs have a gunfight near their homes. The scene is set for a rumble and what better place for a biker fight than a flea-market swap meet for motorcycle parts sponsored by the British Motor Cycling Club.

About 1,000 people fill the parking lot of the Viking Hotel in Milperra, a southwestern suburb of Sydney, on Sunday afternoon, September 2—Father's Day in Australia. The Commancheros arrive on motorcycles and in three vehicles at about 1:30. In true down-under style, they remove rifles and shotguns from saddlepacks and scabbards and load them. Some bikers pull out baseball bats—one branded Tennessee Thumper—knives, machetes, wrenches, chains and screwdrivers. They circle the parking lot and look for Bandidos. They tell the hotel owner there won't be any trouble if the rival gang doesn't show. Sixteen Bandidos motorcycles and a war wagon pull into the lot and the shooting begins at 1:50 p.m.

Seven people are shot dead and 21 are injured within minutes. Four Commancheros and two Bandidos die. Leanne Walters, a 14-year-old who rides with another gang, is shot in the face. Both gangs retreat to their war wagons and keep their guns sighted on the parking lot. It takes an unarmed detective 50 minutes to convince them to allow paramedics to treat the wounded. The fight continues in hospital corridors, to the horror of doctors and nurses. Police try to arrange a truce between the clubs, but can't find the leaders.

This kind of bloodletting makes the Outlaws proud to be the Bandidos' sister club.

II

THE OUTLAWS: TRAVELS WITH CHARLIE

God forgives, Outlaws don't.

—Club motto.

If you see my cunt, make her write me a letter or break her arm.

—Charlotte Outlaw Mike 1%er writes to another Outlaw from prison on June 3, 1979.

CHRISTINE Deese is a tall, shapely redhead on whose nose the West Palm Beach sun has drawn out a loose cluster of freckles that mock her attempts to appear older than her 18 years. She's a dumb broad, but knows enough to stay alive. So she doesn't complain when Norman (Spider) Riesinger, a 25-year-old member of the Outlaws Motorcycle Club, smashes a beer bottle over her head and nails her to a tree.

Spider has every right under outlaw biker code to beat his old lady in November 1967. He sends Christine to turn a trick for $10 and she comes back empty handed. When an Outlaw tells his old lady to put out, she puts out: for whoever and however.

Spider Riesinger is an impulsive, cruel man, as he demonstrates seven years later when he blows the heads off three

157

Hell's Angels in a murder that leads to the ongoing war between the two clubs. Four other Outlaws help Spider crucify Christine to a tree with spikes hammered through her palms. She doesn't scream, she doesn't fight.

"They said they would bash my face in with a hammer if I did."

The appeased bikers pull out the spikes after 15 minutes. They take Christine to hospital when the wounds infect. A sick hooker can't bring in the bucks. The Outlaws, as they become more involved in prostitution, forbid their "cunts" from visiting doctors or health clinics where their poor condition would be noticed.

"They try not to beat them around the face so they won't look abused," says a 33-year-old former old lady who helps runaways from the club. "But one girl came to me with cigarette burns all over her breasts and her butt. They'd done this to her while she was messed up on drugs, just to see if she'd flinch."

William Heidtman, sheriff of Palm Beach County, is dumbfounded by the control Outlaws have over women. "These females seem to blindly follow any direction from the men. She [Christine Deese] apparently just stood there when they told her to and they just nailed her hands to a tree."

The Outlaws Motorcycle Club, also called the American Outlaw Association, is the Big Four outlaw motorcycle gang most prone to prostitute its women. White slavery is the club's greatest source of income after drugs. The Outlaws' quest for profits pits the club against the Hell's Angels in a guerrilla war that has seen scores of bikers killed since the early 1970s.

The Outlaws revere twat power, but hate women. They degrade and abuse them at every opportunity.

"Goddam, bitch, I'm about to piss in my pants," an Outlaw screams at his old lady in a Charlotte, North Carolina, cemetery during the February 1981 funeral of Outlaw Tommy Stroud.

The old lady unzips his pants and holds his dick while he pees.

"We all did that," says a former old lady. "It was the neat thing to do."

Outlaw Robert (Fingers) Winecoff lays a Buck knife across the left pinky of a woman who visits the Lexington, North Carolina, clubhouse in 1975. He hits the knife with a hammer and cuts the finger off. The woman refuses to lay charges.

A 16-year-old girlfriend of Garnet (Mother) McEwen, president of the St.-Catharines chapter, dies in a fire in a Fort Lauderdale massage parlor where she works while on holidays.

A former old lady describes what happens to a woman hitchhiker the Outlaws pick up on I-85 near Charlotte.

> After everyone in the van took a turn with her, they named her T.C. for Training Cunt and put her to work for the gang. They took her back to Louisville and put her in a house. She was making $1,000 a week.

Training cunts or train chicks are kept humping.

"They'd go 100 guys a night (at club parties)," the old lady says.

The Iron Crosses motorcycle gang in West Palm Beach

becomes the first Outlaws chapter in Florida in September 1967. The gang hangs out in Hollywood and gains notoriety on December 5, 1965, when they follow a farm labor worker, who accidentally cuts them off on the Florida turnpike, to his cabin in a Pompano labor camp and blow away his wife with a shotgun.

John Davis founds the Outlaws in Chicago, Illinois, in 1959. The club has about 34 chapters in the US and Canada with about 900 members. The club also has chapters in Australia. The Outlaws divide their US territory into four regions, with the westernmost chapter in Oklahoma City, the headquarters for the south region. Atlanta is the headquarters for the southeastern region, Chicago for the central region, and Detroit the northern region. The Outlaws are well organized, disciplined, and have a military-like chain of command where chapter presidents answer to a regional president, who reports to the mother club. Like the Hell's Angels, Outlaw chapters have elected officers, including a president, vice-president, enforcer, treasurer and road captain.

Chicago gives up its claim as Outlaws powerbase in the summer of 1984 after 25 glorious years, when Harold Cecil (Stairway Harry from Gary) Henderson loses the club's national presidency to Henry Joseph (Taco) Bowman of Detroit. Taco is former northern regional president of the Outlaws and former president of the Detroit chapter. He often wears a floor-length black cape adorned with a swastika.

The club rallies under an emblem—the Outlaw colors—affectionately known as Charlie: a white skull with crossed pistons on a black background—a modern Jolly Roger with due deference to technology. The skull has beady red eyes, which are supposed to look out for trouble behind the wearer's back. The pistons are outlined in red. Charlie is borrowed from the back of Marlon Brando's black leather jacket in *The Wild One*. The emblem is briefly visible in a fight scene as Brando falls backwards. The club has added its name to the emblem. The word Outlaws appears in a semi-circle above the insignia on the upper rocker. The chapter name, usually a city, state, or in the case of Canada, country, appears on the bottom rocker. The initials *MC*, for motorcycle club, denote status depending on where they are placed on the colors. The letters *MC* under the crossed pistons indicate a regular member. A chapter president wears the initials above Charlie. A chapter enforcer wears them below the bottom rocker.

No outlaw motorcycle gang allows women to wear colors. The Outlaws let their women wear a leather vest with the words "Property of Outlaws," a literal meaning of their status. One old lady is kidnapped and tortured by members of the Outlaws for being irreverent enough to wear the club colors on the seat of her jeans. Her abusers include William Elbert (Gatemouth) Edson, a member of the club's elite SS hit squad who participates in the murder of three Hell's Angels in 1974 that starts a war between the two clubs.

The Outlaw constitution says that a member who throws his patch on the ground during a dispute is automatically ejected from the gang forever. The constitution doesn't mention that this entails a severe beating, even death. The constitutions of all Big Four outlaw motorcycle gangs contain a similar restriction: all members must be white.

Although they swear to live on the fringe of society, the Outlaws abide by a creed that ensures they never have to face that society alone:

> A 1%er is the one (1%) of a hundred of us who have given up on society. And the politicians' One Way Law. This is why we look repulsive. We are saying we don't want to be like you or look like you.
>
> So stay out of our face.
>
> Look at your brother standing next to you and ask yourself if you would give him half of what you have in your pocket. Or half of what you have to eat. If a citizen hits your Brother, will you be on him without asking why? There is no why. Your Brother isn't always right but he is always your Brother! It's one in all and all in one. If you don't think this way then walk away. Because you are a citizen and don't belong with us.
>
> We are Outlaws and members will follow the Outlaws' way or get out. All members are your Brothers and your family. You will not steal your Brother's possessions, money, woman, class or his humor. If you do this your Brother will do you.
> O.F.F.O. (Outlaws Forever Forever Outlaws)

While Outlaw chapters operate independently, regional and national officers control drug trafficking, relations with other motorcycle gangs and the distribution of the club's profits. The Outlaws are involved in extortion, contract murder, motor vehicle theft, gun and explosives running, armed robbery, rape and mail fraud besides drug trafficking and prostitution. The Outlaws are one of the most violent criminal groups operating today. They kill 80 people in Florida alone from 1974 to 1984. They murder 15 people in North Carolina from 1979 to 1984. It will never be known how many people they've killed.

Outlaw members must sell drugs and own at least one handgun. Members must work in pairs to prevent fuckups and to avoid situations where the club can lose face—a lone biker is a tempting target for punks trying to impress each other. The Outlaws can't bear losing any battle, on the street or in court. Like other outlaw motorcycle gangs, they spare no money or effort to intimidate witnesses or tamper with juries to stay out of jail.

Drug trafficking is the Outlaws' main source of income. "Canadian Blue" diazepam (known to housewives as Valium) manufactured in clandestine Ontario laboratories and smuggled across the border, usually to Chicago, is one of the mainstays of their drug operation. It is distributed from Chicago to different chapters. Some pay cash for the drugs, others trade weapons, women or methamphetamines. The Florida chapters buy the club's cocaine from Colombian and Cuban suppliers. The Outlaws also manufacture and distribute cocaine and methamphetamine in the Fort Lauderdale area. They own property in south Florida where smugglers dock and unload their boats.

The Milwaukee chapter, called the "wrecking crew" because of its violent tendencies, controls the methamphetamine market in Wisconsin. The Outlaws also control methamphetamine laboratories in Georgia and, along with other outlaw motorcycle gangs, plan to supply the US eastern seaboard and midwest with marijuana from Hawaii.

Money and drugs have become so important to the Outlaws that Toronto Outlaw Murray (Moose or Hulk) McConnell chews out fellow member Maurice Couling, who buys a chopper with part of $15,000 he defrauds from an insurance company on a false claim that his motorcycle has been stolen.

"He was calling me stupid and an idiot. [He said] I could have invested the cash in coke and tripled my money."

Pussy is the Outlaws' vice of preference after drugs. If it weren't for hookers, the world's oldest profession would be masturbation. The Outlaws try their damndest to put one-armed lovers out of business. Most women in the Outlaw entourage are between 16 and 20 years old. Most are rebellious teenagers or runaways lured with easy sex, drugs, a community of strong men and freedom from responsibility.

The Outlaws take prostitution seriously. An old lady is a biker's exclusive girlfriend. The fact she pumps 10 cocks a night doesn't mean she's unfaithful; it shows she loves her man enough to bring home hundreds of dollars a week. To ensure their young women are properly groomed for the task, the Outlaws send their protegees to finishing schools called "lockups." They are, in intent, if not form, the Vassars and Radcliffes of the outlaw motorcycle world. A woman first learns that she or her family will be beaten or killed if she runs away. Then she works as a prostitute for weeks, sometimes months, to learn the finer points of satisfying men. After a woman is properly broken in, the Outlaws get her a job in a topless bar, a massage parlor, or on the street, where other old ladies keep an eye on her. Because an old lady is an Outlaw's property, she has to give him all the money she earns, sometimes more than $1,000 a week. When she is worn out at 22, if she complains too much, if she can't meet her quota, if she becomes a security risk, she is killed. She is lucky if her old man sells her for quick cash or motorcycle parts.

Somewhere, in some small town, there's always another sweet young thing itching for action and a one-way ticket to easy street.

But not all horny women want to be hookers. And not all hookers want to be Outlaw old ladies. William (Gatemouth) Edson, an Outlaw hit man on the run, makes $3,000 a week when he puts his two old ladies to work in massage parlors while he hides in Chicago.

"Sixty percent of the women with the gangs are there out of fear," Edson says. "If they aren't dragged off a street corner, then it's a girl who has been told if she leaves her boyfriend he'll kill her parents."

Such is the case of Betty Darlene Callahan who peddles pussy in her home town of Asheville, North Carolina, to tame a taste for heroin. Her boyfriend, Tommy Forrester, doesn't mind her line of work. He's busy dealing drugs, like "Canadian Blue," that he buys from Allan Ray (Red) Hattaway, who also lends him money. The 31-year-old Hattaway runs drugs and collects debts for the Outlaws. He is also a club hit man.

A $20,000 diamond and gold Outlaw ring attests to his disregard for human life. He dumps the bodies in wood chippers.

Callahan slips out of her room at the Town Motel to pick up a post-coital snack at the restaurant next door on Saturday evening, December 12, 1981. Hitman Hattaway and drug runner Gary Miller stop her at gunpoint in the hallway when she returns. Forrester, it seems, owes the hit man $1,500. The gunmen strip search the couple. Forrester gets roughed up. Miller tells a cop who knocks at the door that all is fine. Hattaway announces that Callahan will have to accompany the killer north to work off the debt. Betty Darlene Callahan, 25, becomes a white slave destined for the Chicago market by being in the wrong place at the wrong time. But first, Hattaway has to take care of business.

Forrester and Callahan are forced into a van at 10 p.m. and driven to the Starlite Drive-in where they are tied together and transfered to Miller's Chrysler Cordoba. Hattaway drives into Tennessee and back into northern North Carolina. He stops at Paul Wilson Bare's rural junkyard near Laurel Springs at 2 a.m. Sunday to pick up strips of cloth to gag and blindfold the prisoners. The car stops on a dirt road after another five miles. Hattaway and Bare take Forrester for a walk. Miller tells Callahan that her boyfriend's chances of dying are 50–50. He gives her a choice: stay with him and "if he lives, you live, but if he dies, you die." The alternative is going with Hattaway to Chicago to work as a prostitute for the Outlaws. Callahan nods yes. Miller, for whom killing is a business decision, molests her.

Hattaway and Bare take Forrester for a 10-minute walk at the end of which they cut off his left ear and shove him into the 250-foot-deep shaft of the Ore Knob Mine, abandoned since the Civil War.

Hattaway and Miller prime themselves with cocaine and Canadian Blue Valium and drive all day Sunday to Chicago. Miller gets horny and fucks Callahan in the back seat. They arrive in Chicago at 9 p.m. Hattaway tells Callahan she will either work for him or he'll sell her to Thomas (Westside Tommy) Stimac, a member of the national ruling board of the Outlaws and former president of the Chicago chapter. Miller warns Callahan at Sullivan's Motel:

"It goes without saying you don't leave this room."

Hattaway adds: "If you do leave, it doesn't matter where

you go, we will find you. We got people all over the United States. If you do get away, and the police hide you out, we'll kill your mother and we'll kill your sister."

Marty (Scarface) Curran, a walking powderkeg armed with a .357 Magnum, shows up at the motel on Monday, December 14. Hattaway orders Callahan to give his brother Outlaw a blowjob.

They move to the Chalet Motel in Lyons on Tuesday where Westside Tommy Stimac inspects a naked Callahan. The next night, she's Stimac's property. He asks her what kind of sex acts she's willing to engage in on the way to the LaGrange Motel. Callahan spends the night screwing Robert George (Snoopy) Burroughs, the 35-year-old president of the Montreal chapter, overseer of the Outlaws' Canadian operations, fugitive in his own country and main US supplier of Canadian Blue. He keeps a .22 Magnum revolver in his boot. Burroughs teaches Callahan how to fight with a knife since she will work as a prostitute for the club.

Callahan is taken to Westside Tommy Stimac's house in Hinsdale, Illinois, on Thursday where she meets his girlfriend, Toni Summers. The Iowa girl works as a prostitute at the Club Algiers in Lyons. She shows Callahan around the house and points out her 31-year-old boyfriend's office, which she is forbidden to enter. Paperwork in the office details how to take over existing prostitution businesses in the Chicago area. Snoopy Burroughs, the Canadian, instructs Stimac in one printed note to "check out the connections" of a "fashion show":

1) Who are these jerks—what connection
2) No heavy backing—Let's take over
3) Send cunt for job interview to find out pay + other details + find out where people put on their shows—maybe they go out of business or we give better cunts at better rate
4) Maybe use cunts for new escort service also
5) Maybe use at Private Party Stages, etc., with couple whores thrown in to fuck + suck for $
   . . .
7) Check with Larry the Printer others to see if we are stepping on toes
8) Least we will get to meet more cunts even the ugly ones (Pussy is Pussy)

OUTLAWS

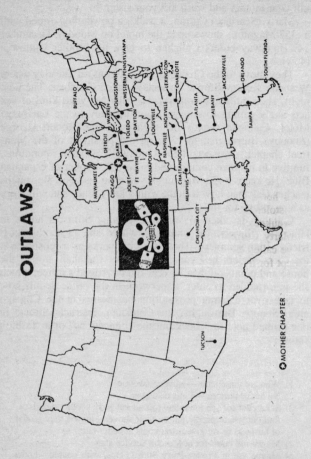

BUFFALO
WARREN
YOUNGSTOWN
WESTERN PENNSYLVANIA
TOLEDO
DAYTON
LOUISVILLE
LEXINGTON
KNOXVILLE
CHARLOTTE
DETROIT
GARY
JOLIET
FT. WAYNE
INDIANAPOLIS
NASHVILLE
CHATTANOOGA
ATLANTA
ALBANY
JACKSONVILLE
ORLANDO
SOUTH FLORIDA
TAMPA
MILWAUKEE
CHICAGO
MEMPHIS
OKLAHOMA CITY
TUCSON

⊕ MOTHER CHAPTER

Marty Curran orders Callahan to a bedroom where she has to suck off Stimac after Summers leaves for work. He gives her cocaine in return. Stimac, Curran and Burroughs then discuss with Callahan how she will prostitute for them. Westside Tommy Stimac will get her on the mob-controlled circuit of topless bars and whorehouses through his connections. The mob gets 40 to 50 percent of the girl's money. The bikers get the rest. The Outlaws deal with traditional organized crime families in Chicago since 1975 when they form an alliance that allows the bikers to supply women for night clubs and bars. Outlaws work as enforcers and hit men for the mob. Members of the Youngstown, Ohio, chapter supply guns and explosives to the mob in Pittsburgh. They also supply women for mob bars in Florida.

Callahan can't work until they get her false identification. Her new name, they tell her, is Julianne Alvarado. Curran gives her a Wisconsin driver's licence and a social security card stolen from the real Julie Alvarado one year earlier at a Milwaukee club where Outlaws hang out.

Marty Curran then drives Callahan to an Outlaw probate house called the Flats near Michigan City, Indiana, where she is kept for five days.

While I was there, the guys, they had those guns that looked like AR-15s, automatic-type weapons. They went out and target practiced on some silos. . . . The men were inside one night and there were some rats, some field mice running around, and they got out the gun and target practiced inside the house, shooting at these rats.

At the Flats I also met a guy by the name of—what I knew him by was Fabe. I later learned his name was Fabian. He told me that he was going to law school to be a lawyer, which I later found out he was, but while he was—while I was there, in my presence, I saw him do cocaine. I saw him with his colors on, by that I mean the jacket that said: Chicago Outlaws. He seemed to me to be like the lawyer to the whole bunch. He advised them on numerous things. When they had a little problem, he would tell them what was best to do.

Hitman Hattaway goes south, while Callahan is at the Flats, to take care of a pusher called Lonnie Gamboa, whom he claims owes the club money. He drives once again to Paul Bare's junkyard with Gamboa in the trunk of a black Monte

Carlo and a machine gun on the back seat. "Gamboa went in a lot easier than the guy that went two weeks before. We had to fight him," Hattaway comments to friends later in the evening.

Callahan is taken to Westside Tommy Stimac's mother's house for Christmas dinner.

> They all had their guns with them and their colors on that night [Callahan recalls]. She showed us Christmas cards that her son had sent that had an insignia of the Outlaws on the front of the Christmas card, and had a saying inside, I do not really recall. It was some kind of vulgar statement.

Stimac takes Summers and Callahan to the Sybaris-Inn Motel later in the evening where Callahan is ordered to perform various sex acts on the couple. The evening is recorded with photographs, a penchant of Stimac who has drawers full of color Polaroid pictures of women licking, sucking and fucking him. He sells them for pocket money.

Asheville police charge Miller the pusher on Monday, January 4, with kidnapping Callahan and her boyfriend. Stimac tells Marty Curran to take Callahan to a phone booth to call the Asheville police and tell them she has not been kidnapped. The bodies of Gamboa and Forrester are pulled from the Ore Knob Mine on Monday, January 25, and Curran makes a big mistake. He takes Callahan to the Brookfield Motel, gives her $15 to eat, and leaves her alone for the night. She calls her mother, then the Federal Bureau of Investigation.

Miller tells Clifford Haller, a fellow inmate at the federal Metropolitan Correctional Center in August 1982 he needs a hit man to kill Callahan, who is now a federally protected witness about to testify against the Outlaws. Haller contacts the Bureau of Alcohol, Tobacco and Firearms. They set up a fake hit man with an undercover telephone number that Haller gives Miller. But the drug dealer is no fool. Before he calls the number, Miller checks it out through a sister-in-law who works with Southern Bell Telephone Company of North Carolina and finds out it is a government number. These street smarts allow Miller to make $971,400 in six months dealing marijuana. His trafficking in cocaine, methamphetamines and Canadian Blues was more lucrative.

* * *

Betty Darlene Callahan is no longer an Outlaw sex slave, but she is a prisoner of fear. The Outlaws can't afford to let her live. A rat who gets away encourages others to tell tales. Kimberly Kalas brags once more to a woman in a nightclub on July 27, 1982, that she will testify against the Outlaws when the Callahan case gets to court. The 17-year-old stripper has been dancing at the Club Algiers for two weeks to raise money to get a friend out of jail. Kalas tells the woman at 3:30 a.m. she's made arrangements to meet Westside Tommy Stimac, who will take her home. She is slowly strangled to death at 5 a.m. by someone who draws a knife lightly over her body, enough to cut, but not to kill. It is torture to make her talk. Kalas' body is found in Black Partridge Forest Preserve five miles southwest of Stimac's Hinsdale house. There's no sign of a struggle. She hasn't been raped. She knows her killer.

Kalas is the second person in 10 months to die after making an appointment to meet Westside Tommy Stimac. John (Burrito) Klimes, a 32-year-old Outlaw officer, wants out of the club. Stimac beats him severely at the Chicago clubhouse. Members are upset at his success providing strippers for mob-run Chicago nightclubs. He also gets the club in hot water while on guard duty at the clubhouse on Roosevelt Road on May 30. He shoots three black men that night, killing one. The Outlaws don't like fuck ups.

Burrito Klimes tells two non-biker friends in late September 1981 they shouldn't be seen with him because he's having trouble with the club. Westside Tommy Stimac calls Burrito Klimes at 10:30 p.m. on October 8, to find out when he'll leave home to meet him at the Showcase Lounge at First Avenue and Ogden in Lyons. A bomb under the seat of Klimes' Blazer van explodes at 10:50 as he approaches the Santa Fe Railroad tracks on First Avenue. An Outlaw demolition expert called Arab allegedly makes the bomb in Florida. A former Chicago Outlaw called Vulture allegedly transports it to the windy city.

The Outlaws' success with illegal enterprises prompts them to diversify into legitimate businesses. They own pornographic bookstores, massage parlors, boat shops and storage yards, and have connections with the Basic Bible Church. The Outlaws cross paths with traditional organized crime families as their power and income grow. One of the first deals be-

tween the two groups is struck at a North Chicago pizzeria in
1975. Pete (Greased Lightning) Rogers (alias Courtney), national enforcer for the Outlaws and head of their infamous SS
Death Squad, meets with John Lee (John L.) Ash, a Tennessee
racketeer, and representatives of Tony (Big Tuna) Accordo,
who starts as Al Capone's chauffeur and becomes one of the
windy city's top crime bosses. The odds of leaving the meeting dead are so great that Greased Lightning is flanked by
Outlaws hit men Willy (Gatemouth) Edson, armed with two
.45-calibre automatics, and Crazy Joe Spaziano. The artillery
isn't needed. Both sides agree to cooperate.

Other Outlaw chapters also get involved with traditional
organized crime families. Clarence Michael Smith, of the
Outlaws' Tampa chapter, is convicted of the murder in New
Orleans of Robert Collins, who testified against the nephew of
the city's La Cosa Nostra boss, Carlos Marcello. A member of
a traditional organized crime family in Palm Beach hires Detroit Outlaws to collect an illegal debt in 1979.

Prosperity makes the Outlaws as fanatic about security as
the Hell's Angels, although they aren't as sophisticated as the
Angels. The Outlaws don't screen membership candidates as
stringently as do the Hell's Angels and end up with more
losers and cavemen on the club roster. Even so, they still
know how to take care of business.

Their clubhouses are heavily fortified with brick, steel
walls and windows and heavy doors. Most of their clubhouses
are in poorer working-class neighborhoods where police can't
set up surveillance units without arousing suspicion. The poor
are also less likely to complain about goings on at the clubhouse. The Outlaws' buildings, like Angel clubhouses, are
equipped with floodlights, closed-circuit television monitors,
trip alarms, radio frequency scanners, telephone tracking
equipment and whatever else they can get their hands on. The
Toronto clubhouse is laced with chicken wire to deflect grenades, surrounded with sandbags to stop bullets, has shuttered
and barred windows, watchdogs, an eight-foot wire fence and
video monitors.

The Outlaws demand that probationary members and
women provide the club with names, addresses and full physical descriptions of family members and relatives, as well as
the vehicles they own. The information intimidates members
and associates from leaving the club. It becomes part of the hit

list when someone rats. The Outlaws keep similar intelligence files on police investigators and lawyers. The crafty Georgia Outlaws watch the parking lot at the Bureau of Alcohol, Tobacco and Firearms to identify agents and their cars. A close female associate of the club is found working in the intelligence division of a major Georgia police department. The Toronto Outlaws pay an Ontario Government employee to run computer checks on driver and vehicle licences of probationary members in 1984 and 1985 to make sure they aren't undercover cops. He also deletes traffic violations from their records.

The Outlaws seek alliances with other gangs to thwart attacks by the Hell's Angels. They have forged, since 1980, links with the smallest of the Big Four—the Bandidos. Gang members sometimes tattoo themselves with each other's colors or identify themselves as sister organizations. Six Outlaws from Oklahoma City are arrested with four Bandidos at the house of Bandido Gary Fogle in Fort Smith, Arkansas, in October 1982. The Outlaws visit Bandidos in Corpus Christi, Texas, and Lafayette, Indiana. Outlaws look up Ronald Jerome Hodge, national president of the Bandidos, at his Rapid City bar, The Dallas West Forty, when they attend the Sturgis Classic Motorcycle Races held each August in South Dakota. The Outlaws also own a topless bar with the Bandidos in Oklahoma City.

Outlaws have three goals: money, power and territory. Their push into Canada months ahead of the Hell's Angels in the spring of 1977 is the result of heavy politicking and partying that culminates with the Outlaws absorbing four Satan's Choice chapters in Ontario and Quebec. The Satan's Choice are the most powerful gang in Canada. The US-based Outlaws become an international gang overnight when they absorb four Choice chapters and gain access to some of the best chemical drug laboratories in the world, expand their market and inflate their membership with some of the toughest and conscienceless bikers on the continent.

The groundwork for the takeover is laid in June 1975, when the Choice and the Outlaws agree to recognize each other's members as equals. The bikers have a special brotherhood patch made that incorporates a piston from Charlie and a star to symbolize the US, and a trident, flame and red maple leaf to symbolize the Choice. The agreement gives bikers on both sides of the border a place to stay while on the road or on the run. The pact also gives the Choice an outlet for their PCP and methamphetamine.

Canadian police arrest US Outlaws less than a year after the agreement to shelter each other's fugitives is signed. James (Blue) Starrett, a 30-year-old Outlaw who escapes from a Florida jail in 1974, is caught on July 22, 1976, in St. Catharines where he has a house painting business called Charlie Brown Painting Contractors. Starrett is wanted in the killing of a Fort Lauderdale woman with a shotgun in 1970 when she refuses to be gang banged.

William (Gatemouth) Edson, wanted in the murder of three Hell's Angels, for torturing a Bandido female associate, and for burning a Fort Lauderdale go-go dancer with cigarettes and heated spoons for wearing Outlaw colors to a party, is caught walking into a liquor store in Kitchener on August 27, 1976. Edson is smuggled into Canada across the Detroit River by boat in a scheme arranged by Lenny Braund, Outlaw president in Detroit, and Stephen Dow, president of the Windsor chapter of the Choice. Joseph (Sonny) Lacombe and Dr. John Arksey from Montreal provide Edson with false identification that transforms him into Dennis Lupo. He monitors police frequencies with a radio scanner while in Kitchener and never strays far from his sawed-off M-1 carbine.

Choice bikers also take advantage of the pact. Howard (Pigpen) Barry, the foulest biker in the gang, is stopped in Fort Lauderdale in 1975 with a driver's licence that identifies him as Tim Jones. He also sports Outlaw colors. He escapes, but is caught in North Carolina with the president of the Lexington chapter of the Outlaws. Barry is wanted for the attempted murder of a Peterborough woman.

The quick takeover by the Outlaws of four of the Satan's Choice 12 Canadian chapters can be attributed to a police raid on August 6, 1975, of a clandestine PCP laboratory on a remote island on Oba Lake, 150 miles north of Sault Ste. Marie in northern Ontario. Police pose as sports fishermen to raid the lab in small boats. They seize nine pounds of PCP, or angel dust, and 236 pounds of chemical stew one step from completion, worth $60,000,000 (Cdn.). Two Choice members are sent to jail: Alain Templain, owner of a $60,000 lodge and a seaplane, and Bernie Guindon, founder and national president of the Satan's Choice. Guindon entrusts the club's presidency to Garnet (Mother) McEwen, of the St. Catharines chapter, while he serves a 17-year sentence. McEwen convinces Windsor chapter president William (King) O'Reilly and Sonny Lacombe and Doctor John Arksey from the Montreal chapter, as well as the Ottawa chapter to join the Outlaws.

The transition is rough. Many Satan's Choice members don't want to bury their colors and traditions. Outlaws from both sides of the border throw a party to celebrate the club's international status at Crystal Beach, Ontario, in July 1977. The Satan's Choice chapters who don't want to become Outlaws are excluded, although many other bike gangs are invited. Some dissenters are forced to leave Ontario and Quebec while tempers cool. The Choice have now re-established themselves in Ontario, with 45 members in Toronto, Kitchener, Peterborough, Thunder Bay and Hamilton.

The price for selling the club's colors is a $10,000 contract Guindon puts on McEwen's head from his jail cell. It still hasn't been carried out. McEwen flees when the Outlaws accuse him of skimming $30,000 from the club's treasury. He gets a job at a Calgary hotel after he convinces the Chosen Few he isn't establishing a bridgehead for the Outlaws. McEwen returns to Ontario in 1980 after a biker beats him severely with his own wooden leg.

The Outlaws' attempts to get a good grip on the Toronto market are frustrated for eight years. Several gangs ally to prevent the Outlaws' small chapter from expanding and to keep the Hell's Angels out of Canada's largest city. The gangs know that the warfare that comes with the two clubs will draw too much police attention and ruin the lucrative businesses they have carved out. The barrier crumbles in September 1984, when Toronto's 35 Iron Hawgs—one of the city's largest, although not smartest, gangs—don Charlie and form the biggest Outlaws chapter in North America.

Robert (Pumpkin) Marsh is elected Iron Hawgs president in March 1984, after he argues that members should sell more drugs and join the Outlaws. His opponent wants the club to return to its old ways, riding hard on weekends. Marsh convinces the club to join the Outlaws because he fears the Hell's Angels are about to invade Toronto. He wants to plug into the Outlaws' drug network to strengthen the club's war fund for guns and grenades. Stan (Beamer) McConnery, former national president of the Outlaws and member of the St. Cathar-

ines chapter once headed by Mother McEwen, warns the
Hawgs' drug supply will dry up like that of the Para-Dice
Riders if they don't take sides in the war with the Angels. The
Para-Dice Riders, who embark on a one-month, cross-country
run in the summer of 1986 to celebrate their 25th anniversary,
are a powerful, but low-profile outlaw motorcycle gang with a
strong foothold in Toronto's working class east end.

The Iron Hawgs appreciate the chance to add muscle to the
gang. They'd like to avoid embarrassments like that suffered
at the hands of the Para-Dice Riders six years earlier. Rider
members walk into a Danforth Avenue bar on Friday, June 22,
1979, and beat a group of Hawgs. The Hawgs split, but return
with reinforcements for a second fight. Three Riders armed
with a sawed-off shotgun, a rifle and a pistol walk into the
Hawgs' Dufferin Avenue clubhouse at 2:30 a.m. Saturday and
order everyone to kneel. One Hawg refuses and is kicked and
punched until he falls. The Riders order the Hawgs to hand
over their colors. President Murray McConnell refuses. The
Rider with the shotgun bashes him on the head with the butt.
It discharges a load of buckshot into 29-year-old Karen Po-
well's ass. The Riders beat a hasty retreat.

The Outlaws expand quickly in Ontario. They force the
Queensmen in London to re-organize in 1982 and become the
Holocaust—an Outlaws prospect club. They become a full-
fledged Outlaw chapter one year later. The Ontario Outlaws
have chapters in Windsor, London, St. Catharines, Hamilton,
Toronto, Ottawa, Sault Ste. Marie and Kingston by 1986.
They make up the club's northern district. Many of the cities
are border points. There are nine penitentiaries within 20
miles of Kingston and much money to be made controlling the
drugs that go into them.

A new alliance is forged in Toronto. The Outlaws, Vagabonds, Para-Dice Riders and Satan's Choice agree to co-exist
and share the wealth by sticking to their territory. They don't
want the Angels in the city, although individual gang members
party with Angel politicians who drop in. The Angels court
the Henchmen in Kitchener, the Wild Ones in Hamilton until
they fold, and the Coffin Wheelers in Sudbury.

Ontario bike gangs have every right to worry about an in-
vasion by the Hell's Angels. They watch with trepidation as
the Outlaws move into Canada in 1977. Their worst fears are

realized on December 5 that year: the Popeyes in Montreal bury their colors and don the red and white winged death's head of the Hell's Angels. The first shots are fired two months later to begin the bloodiest biker war in North America. Montreal, which produces the best hold-up men on the continent, is also a breeding ground for its most ruthless killers. In a confrontation of hit men, guts, luck and artillery determine the outcome.

12

HARVEST OF TERROR

THE war between the Hell's Angels and the Outlaws begins in the United States, but causes more blood to be shed in Canada. The province of Quebec, a historic battleground where the French and English settle their differences with weapons and words over the centuries, may have seen more biker murders in the last two decades than all of the United States. Bikers are responsible for more than 300 killings in Quebec in the last 10 years. There seems to exist in the Quebec gene pool a psychopathic bent that gives rise to a disproportionate number of cold-blooded killers. Hit men for the Italian traditional organized crime families, the French-Canadian Dubois gang and the Irish-dominated West End Gang are feared across the continent. Even its legendary Vandoos—the 22nd Regiment—returns from Europe after World War II with a sordid reputation for merciless fighting.

Quebec has been home to outlaw motorcycle gangs for more than 40 years. Most gangs stake out their turf in the hundreds of small, insular Catholic parishes that make up the province. The larger gangs move into the cities, such as Montreal, only to find that they are safer from prosecution in towns and villages where police forces are small and easily intimidated.

There are few successful attempts to curb gang violence

and crime in Quebec. An organized crime commission publicly pats itself on the back in 1979 for weakening outlaw motorcycle gangs with a series of public hearings. The Hell's Angels grant their second charter in the province that year to the fearsome North chapter. The Sûreté du Québec fruitlessly spends millions of dollars investigating the Hell's Angels from 1983 to 1985. They successfully prosecute club members in 1986 and 1987 only because the Hell's Angels fight among themselves and rat on each other.

The Hell's Angels' North chapter in suburban Laval continues the tradition of mindless, gratuitous violence practiced by outlaw motorcycle gangs in rural Quebec. This lust for drugs and death eventually forces the other Hell's Angels in the province to close down the chapter and slaughter five members they feel are too wild for the club's good. The Hell's Angels, as they become businessmen, try desperately to shed the caveman image that outlaw motorcycle gangs thrive on.

The Quebec countryside is a pastiche of motorcycle gangs at various stages of development: from insecure, long-haired Neanderthals who continually try to reaffirm their masculinity, to Corvette cowboys who ride their Harleys to the bank on sunny days to deposit the previous night's drug profits. A walk along the streets of many rural Quebec towns is a step through a time warp. These gangs imitate the Hell's Angels of the 1940s, 1950s, and 1960s. They all want to be the most feared motherfuckers in the parish. The dream comes true for the most enterprising and violent among them. Hell's Angels head hunters are always on the lookout for talent to recruit. The club is a way of life that offers little chance of retirement. It needs a steady infusion of dispensable muscle and aggression. The boonies are full of suckers whose idea of retirement doesn't extend past who they're going to lie down with tonight.

The seeds that blossom into the wild North chapter are sown across the countryside like wild oats. These are some of the outlaw motorcycle gangs out of which the Hell's Angels in Quebec have grown. Only their colors distinguish them. They are all mindless brutes.

THE PACIFIC REBELS AND CITOYENS DE LA TERRE:

Bored 18-year-old greaseballs smothered by the burgeoning flower generation of the 1960s tear around the historic and picturesque Ile d'Orléans, 20 miles from Quebec City. They call themselves the Pacific Rebels. They rumble, steal and drink. The throb of their motorcycle pistons wets the crotches of quite a few 13- and 14-year-old girls. To ride and bang is fun as long as that's all there is in life. But there comes a time when a man has to work. Selling drugs is the easiest way out of a regular job for a biker. The aging Pacific Rebels move into the underworld of drug trafficking. They're also into armed robbery, theft and rape by the time they're 30. They add murder to the list in 1973.

A handful of Marxist influenced dirtbags form Les Citoyens de la Terre on the Ile d'Orléans in 1973. The gangs clash immediately. Raymond (Che Raymond) Cardinal, the 28-year-old leader of the Citoyens, gets shoved around by several Rebels in the downtown square. Gang members take pot shots at each other on the street. Cardinal leads nine Citoyens on a raid of the Rebels' clubhouse shortly before midnight on July 26, 1973. Michèle Blouin, the 20-year-old girlfriend of Rebels president Serge (Gallo) Beaulieu, watches television in an upstairs room lit by a red light. Two cars and a motorcycle stop in the street. The Citoyens get out with guns and clubs and shoot at the clubhouse. Blouin fires back. The lady can shoot. She juggles a 12-gauge shotgun and a .22-calibre rifle. A .22 bullet plugs Yvan (Stuntman) Lapointe in the head. He falls dead beside his .22-calibre rifle bought earlier in the day. The Citoyens retreat.

Michèle Blouin lies at the trial to beat a murder rap and insists she used the 12-gauge shotgun only. One of the Rebels must have used the rifle. The Citoyens vow revenge as they walk out of court.

The hostilities start again when 24-year-old Rebel Ghislain Fiset is found dead in a snowbank near the Orsainville penitentiary on New Year's morning, 1974. He has a .22-calibre bullet hole in the leg. His head is hacked open with a hatchet. Former Rebel Jacques Barrette is shot in the stomach as he gets out of his car in a downtown parking lot on January 22.

Michel Lapointe, who resembles Rebel Jean-Claude Talbot, is shot in front of a downtown shopping center the next night.

Two Sherbrooke men mistaken for bikers are attacked on January 29. Mario Bruneau and Mario Demers, both 18, wait for a friend in a parked car on a downtown street when a car pulls up and three hooded men get out and open up with a shotgun and submachine gun. Bruneau dies.

Four Rebels walk out of the Quebec City courthouse on February 4 and get into their car parked in front of the historic Hotel Frontenac on one of the city's main squares. Driver Serge Létourneau dies immediately when a bomb under the seat explodes. The three others are injured. Police arrest four Rebels, including Beaulieu. They stop a car later that night and find a .410-gauge shotgun, a sawed-off 12-gauge shotgun, and two .303-calibre rifles, one of which is sawed off. Blouin commits suicide in her suburban apartment the next night with a .22-calibre bullet in the right temple. She confesses in a note left on the kitchen sink that she killed Lapointe the night of the Citoyens raid on the Rebels clubhouse. The Pacific Rebels spread their violence to the countryside as police pressure drives individual members out of Quebec City.

THE BLACK SPIDERS—SAINT-MICHEL DE BELLECHASE:

The six-year reign of rape and terror by the Black Spiders in the farming community of Saint-Michel de Bellechase from 1972 to 1978 is a sad tale of opportunistic crud, gutless men and spineless politicians. The insular village of 1,500 people 18 miles south of Quebec City lives off the land, tourists and cottagers. Village teenagers don't have much to do except hang around. Jean-Marie (Tony) Leclerc and Guy Bernier form the Black Spiders motorcycle club in a rented clubhouse early in 1972. They hold a few open houses to acquaint villagers with the club. Some complain about the noisy motorcycles. Leclerc and Bernier are immune to criticism. They're former members of the Pacific Rebels in Quebec City.

Local boys go wild after their first taste of outlaw life. Gang bangs are the main club activity for two years. The Black Spiders introduce marijuana and hash to Saint-Michel in

1974. Drugs are sold among gang members at first. They turn on and supply local teenagers. They deal with another motorcycle gang, also called the Black Spiders, in nearby Montmagny.

The Black Spiders terrorize the countryside by 1976. They roar into bars and throw their weight around. Yvan Denault, leader of the Montmagny gang, lays one heavy too many in 1976 and the owner of the Trois-Chemins inn blows him away. Leclerc takes over the gang and introduces the community to real terror. Leclerc rips off gang members by exacting dues to pay the mortgage, taxes, electricity and telephone bills of a gang-owned clubhouse in Saint-Michel. He's already bought and paid for the house and pockets the mortgage money.

Leclerc establishes a gang hierarchy based on length of membership, age and number of criminal acts committed. Gang members have specific responsibilities: Serge (Baloune) Leclerc and Jacques (Coco) Rocheleau obtain drugs; André (Curé) Brochu recruits jail bait for orgies; Yves (Bébé) Laverdière is the club extortionist; Simon (Scott) Cadrin is vice-president, treasurer and administrator. The Black Spiders beat people in the streets and rape women at random. No one complains. They continue. They abduct and gang bang most of the teenage girls in the village over two years. Fathers and mothers are too scared to complain. They lock the doors. No one ventures into the streets after dark. Rumors circulate about the rapes. Some girls refuse to leave the house. Some leave the village.

Drug trafficking increases. Gang members supply local teenagers, who are assigned districts. The gang lucks into an importer who brings in shipments from Mexico and Colombia through Boston and Miami. They sell to Quebec City pushers. Leclerc keeps his profits in a bank account he opens in his 16-year-old girlfriend's name.

Villagers put up with the abusers because they are local boys. They can't tell family friends their son screwed their daughter. They also fear the gang will beat them if they talk. The girls put up with the rapes for fear the bikers will reveal they've bought drugs from them. They are also ashamed to reveal they've had cocks inside cunt, ass and mouth simultaneously. The Black Spiders sell drugs and extort money from 12 and 13 year olds at the local community center by 1978.

"Go get some money from your mother's purse or I'll kill your little brother," one biker tells a 12-year-old girl.

The local police cover their asses. They say they can't do anything unless someone complains. The villagers are too scared to talk for fear police won't protect them. And the chickenshit backwater city council passes a motion that requires written complaints before they call for police action. Even the courts won't convict the Black Spiders when an outsider complains about being shot at in the Saint-Laurent de Saint-Michel campground. The judge rules that the outsider "blundered" by following the bikers too closely with his car.

Only Paul Vézina in Montmagny is man enough to take on the Black Spiders in 1978. They kill him. The gutless villagers finally form a mob and 100 people armed with clubs and farm tools ransack the Black Spiders clubhouse.

THE FLAMBEURS—MONT-JOLI:

The public history of outlaw motorcycle gangs starts with their rampage through Hollister, California, during the weekend of July 4, 1947. There are many tales of gangs taking over towns, frightening people for a few hours, even a few days. The Flambeurs in Mont-Joli make these exploits seem petty. They control their town for six years—from 1972 to 1978. Even the local police are too scared to take them on.

The Flambeurs form in the late 1960s in the exhaust of two dying gangs: the Dragueurs and the Jokers. They let the town of 6,700 know in 1970 they won't tolerate interference in gang activities. They explode a bomb near the house of alderman Charles Gagnon, who bad mouths the Flambeurs at city council meetings. The gang takes over the downtown business section, where stoned bikers sell drugs and piss on the street. The Flambeurs hold motorcycle drag races day and night. They throw empty beer bottles at passing cars. No one stops to complain to a pack of 20 bikers. They smash store windows and overturn displays. They gouge and kick parked cars. They frighten tourists. They give drugs and alcohol to children. They take their violence indoors at times: a customer who enjoys a prostitute at a hotel is robbed of $280 by two Flambeurs who crash into the room. They even collect a $2 toll from motorists on rue de la Gare. Cars that don't pay must turn back or get smashed. Drivers pay to keep the peace.

No one complains. They just avoid the downtown. Stores go bankrupt. The Flambeurs, like outlaw motorcycle gangs across the province, carry on because local police are scared. The mayor explains the apathy:

> You know, you mustn't blame the people who, here and else-where, are terrorized by groups, real organized gangs, who make a show of their numbers and their strength and set up as lords and masters in lots of places and really make the people believe that they are better off suffering in silence than calling in the forces of law and order to establish the peace.

Crap.

THE MISSILES—SAINT-GÉDÉON:

The Missiles are the most dangerous and violent motorcycle gang in the Saguenay-Lac-Saint-Jean area in the 1960s and 1970s. Most of the bikers sell drugs and pussy to supplement their welfare checks. Their favorite pastimes include drug trafficking, extortion, blackmail and target practice on down-town streets. Some of the scuzbags are destined for greater things: Luc Michaud, whose nickname at the time is Bardot; Jean-Yves Tremblay, then called Bébé; and Gerry (Le Chat) Coulombe are all future Hell's Angels. Coulombe has the flair of an interior decorator. He tacks an authentic Nazi flag on the wall of the Missiles clubhouse. A police officer steals it during a 1979 raid and he still asks around for it.

The Missiles fight three other area gangs in the 1970s for drug trafficking territory—streets and bars. The Lacmas, Hondix and El Conquatcheros are punks, but not real outlaw material. A Missile slices up two Lacmas in a bar fight in 1978. The same Missile walks away with Lacma Gilles Gag-non's finger after another fight. Gagnon isn't very lucky. Sev-eral Missiles beat him with baseball bats several months later. The Missiles are hard on their own members. They threaten Herman Bélanger with blackmail for breaking a club rule by not leaving his motorcycle, or its worth in cash, behind when he quits.

The Missiles and Lacmas rumble several times early in 1979. The Missiles decide to finish the gang off. They plant a bomb outside the Lacmas clubhouse on April 21. It knocks down a wall and several people. The Lacmas, Hondix and El Conquatcheros hold an emergency meeting. They decide to burn down the Missiles clubhouse with Molotov cocktails. They drive up in their van. Shots come from all directions as the first biker steps out. The Missiles are prepared. The police arrive to prevent a massacre.

The Missiles party with the Popeyes and continue the relationship when this gang becomes the Hell's Angels in 1977. Luc Michaud and Jean-Yves Tremblay run the Sunshine agency for dancers in Montreal one year later with two Angels: Laurent Viau and Charles Harvey. Each of the eight girls on staff turns over $30 weekly to Michaud. It's a poor return, but he eventually learns to milk them for more.

THE GITANS AND THE ATOMES—SHERBROOKE:

The bloodiest biker battles outside Montreal take place between the Gitans and the Atomes in Sherbrooke, 90 miles east of Montreal. The Gitans, called the Dirty Reich before 1970, cultivate ugliness and stench. The gang is led by Georges (Bo-Boy) Beaulieu, and includes Charles (Cash) Filteau, Yvan (Bagosse) Tanguay, Guy (Junior) Auclair and Robert (Couleuvre) Tremblay—who later become Hell's Angels. They take over a Rock Forest bar between 1976 and 1979 where the bikers sell their drugs. They threaten to kill the owner, employees and even their children if they complain. Gitan bouncers screen clients and turf out possible rats and darkies. A Gitan is available at the bar 24 hours a day to supply high school pushers. The club is wealthy enough to loan a local merchant $10,000. The Gitans also run a ring of teenage thieves who steal welfare checks from mail boxes. Young girls cash them at the bank. The Gitans have blank birth certificates, driver's permits and credit cards they sell for $25 to $100 apiece. Three Gitans are expert safe crackers, with more than 30 safes to their credit. Two others like to lure faggots into laneways and beat them. The Atomes also sell drugs. They specialize in spreading venereal disease to jail bait through gang bangs.

The Gitans are the Popeyes' favorite gang. Yves (Le Boss) Buteau and Yvon (Gorille) Bilodeau supply them with drugs.

The relationship continues when the Popeyes become the Hell's Angels. Buteau encourages his farm team to take on the Atomes in 1973–74. It starts when one biker trashes another's motorcycle. Both clubs like to rip the colors off rivals' backs. The killing starts on Friday, March 15, 1974. Atome Robert Provencher, 20, and Gitan Jacques (Boubou) Filteau, 25, scrap in a Sherbrooke parking lot. Provencher is shot in the back. Filteau is knifed in the stomach. Members of both gangs show up at the hospital. They rumble in the hallways and another biker is stabbed. Five Gitans armed with two baseball bats and three guns chase a car full of Atomes and stop them on a main street half an hour later. They shoot Marc Distefano, 20, in the face and Michel Lamoureux, 19, in the chest with a .303-calibre rifle. Both Atomes die. Philip Demers is shot in the knee. Claude (Burger) Berger, 24, a trumpet player, is one of the four Gitans charged with murder and attempted murder.

Six bikers die during the 12-month war, shot with rifles, revolvers and submachine guns supplied to both sides by Popeyes Marcel (Le Grec) Auger and Michel Roy. The clubs call a truce in 1974. It lasts, with the occasional fight, until the expansionist Hell's Angels tell the Gitans in 1984 they can become an Angel chapter if they wipe out the Atomes. Atome Michel (Ballon) Fortier hustles since 1974 to make Sherbrooke the drug distribution center of Quebec. The Angels don't like competition. The Gitans quickly kill Jean-Noel Roy, Réjean Gilbert and Ronald (Big) Sigouin. The Atomes bury their colors. The Gitans become the Sherbrooke chapter of the Hell's Angels on December 5, 1984, and set up their clubhouse in nearby Lennoxville.

THE MARAUDEURS—ASBESTOS:

The Maraudeurs wreak havoc in Asbestos from 1974 to 1979, when several members—Michel (Willie) Mayrand and Réjean (Zig-Zag) Lessard, among others—quit to join the Hell's Angels. The gang deals drugs in large enough quantities to require submachine guns for protection. Members hang out in a municipal park and induce 10-year-old children to get stoned and drunk. Threats keep the police at bay. One police officer is told to back off or the club will fuck his wife raw. The police chief claims he doesn't know the bikers are a problem. The Maraudeurs party with the Popeyes. One night, in 1976, nine of them gang rape a 19-year-old girl who doesn't complain for three months out of fear. Some gang members show signs of intelligence. One biker sells a truck without telling the buyer he hasn't paid off the loan he bought it with. The new owner gets stuck with the bill. The same biker sells a Camaro for $6,500. The new owner has to pay an additional $5,500 to the finance company.

THE POPEYES—ALL OVER THE MAP:

The Popeyes are the most powerful gang of fuckups in Quebec in the 1960s and 1970s. Most of the stringy greaseballs are candidates for deviants anonymous—the kind of scuz who would rape their mothers then boast they've had better.

Fifty Popeyes converge on the Hôtel des Pins in Saint-Andre-Avellin near Papineauville, 70 miles west of Montreal, on Saturday, August 14, 1976. They come from Laval, Montreal, Trois-Rivières, Sorel and Repentigny. They drink beer all afternoon and harass clients. The owner's wife and her daughter are too scared to tell them to cool it or call police. Many merchants fear the gang since they've adopted their community as a hangout. Business drops off when biker violence drives away clients and tourists.

Ten members of a local parachute club drop by the bar at 10 p.m. The owner's daughter suggests her regular clients go drink elsewhere. Five leave. The bikers smash bottles and glasses on the floor and against the walls. One biker walks up to a parachutist at the bar and asks him to cut a deck of cards. The Canadian Armed Forces instructor refuses. Another Popeye climbs on the pool table, rips the light from the ceiling and smashes it against the wall. The fight is on. The bikers splinter tables and chairs with crowbars and axes. They throw bottles across the room. Someone starts shooting. They attack the instructor. He slips into the basement, out a window and crawls to safety a mile away on his hands and knees.

Owner Vital Myre comes home from his second job and calls police from a neighbor's house. The bikers beat an employee from whom they steal $300 before police arrive. They hit the cash register for $500. They smash and set fire to cars in the parking lot. More than half escape arrest. Most of those arrested bear the tattoo FTW: Fuck The World.

The Popeyes become Canada's first Hell's Angels chapter one year later. Some of those arrested for trashing the hotel become prominent Angels: Louis (Ti-Oui) Lapièrre, 22; Jean-Pièrre (Matt le Crosseur) Mathieu, 26; Denis (Le Curé) Kennedy, 24; Robert (l'Italien) Bonomo, 29; Yves (Le Boss) Buteau, 25.

The Montreal chapter recruits gangs from around the province shortly after it is formed on December 5, 1977. They work out business deals with affiliate gangs. Some gangs are so promising they become prospects—one step from winning the Hell's Angels colors and becoming official chapters. Other gangs disappear as the Angels absorb their best members. The Montreal chapter is so large that it splits on September 14, 1979, and the North chapter is formed. Michel (Willie) Mayrand and Guy-Louis (Chop) Adam join the Angels that year. The North chapter, although formed after Montreal, has most of the club's original members.

Laurent (L'Anglais) Viau, Jean-Pierre (Matt le Crosseur) Mathieu and Jean-Guy (Brutus) Geoffrion are founding members of the Hell's Angels in 1977. All are Popeyes then, as is Gilles (Le Nez) Lachance. But he doesn't become an Angel until he gets out of jail in 1981 after he serves six years of a manslaughter sentence he starts in March 1975.

Lachance, then 26, and 19-year-old Popeye Normand (Dog) Labelle cruise Laval streets for trouble on September 14, 1974. Brian Levitt, 18, and his 31-year-old brother Gary are in town from Sainte-Marthe-sur-le-Lac to spend an evening at la Chaufferie disco.

We were driving when another car pulled up right beside us [the younger Levitt says]. Someone threw something into our car and hit me on the head. We stopped our car. They stopped. There were two of them. We had a few words and just as things were about to get violent, they left. We continued to the discotheque. My brother and I sat down at the bar and ordered a beer. A little later, Gary got up and went to the can. I was sitting alone with my beer when two guys walked up—the same guys who were in the car. They had long hair. They shoved me. One held me and the other hit me. I broke away and tore my shirt. I ran to the washroom to warn my brother.

I started to tell him what happened but the bathroom door opened. I saw one of them (Lachance) in the doorway. I think he was holding it open. The other guy in the car was behind him. He had a revolver in his hands. It was the same guys who tried to beat me up at the bar. Shots were fired. I was hit in the left hand and a bullet grazed my face. Gary fell to the floor, bleeding and starting crying for help.

Gary Levitt is shot in the lung. He dies at l'hôpital Sacré-Coeur in Cartierville one week later.

Lachance learns to craft leather while in jail and dreams the time away. He joins his former Popeye friends in the Hell's Angels when he gets out and talks about making a bundle selling drugs and sailing away on his boat. He denies he plans to renovate his boat to smuggle cocaine from South America.

Lachance sells mescaline in bars to stay alive: he keeps $100 for every 25 grams he sells. The rest goes to L'Anglais Viau, president of the Hell's Angels North chapter. Viau pays off Montreal's West End Gang and snorts the profits. Unlike other Hell's Angels chapters, North doesn't tone down its drug use as its drug business expands. The richer the chapter gets, the more drugs the members consume. The habit kills them in the end.

PART

III

13

TAKING CARE OF BUSINESS

The Hell's Angels are not involved in anything but motorcycling.
—Ralph Hubert (Sonny) Barger Jr., guiding light, elder statesman, frequent spokesman and most respected member of the Hell's Angels Motorcycle Club, in April 1986.

For us, the era of greaseballs who go around terrorizing people is over. Our company's goal is to make profits.
—A Quebec Hell's Angel in August 1985.

Montreal, Canada
This letter is to inform you that the North Chapter has been closed down. This was a joint decision taken by Montreal, Sherbrooke and Halifax charters. Four of the members (Jinx, Dick, Gorille and Mike) has [sic] been absorbed by Montreal along with three of the Prospects. The rest are out dishonourably. Ted from NYC has been up since and has been made aware of all the circumstances. The charters on the US West Coast can see a member from British Columbia the next time they are in California. There will be someone from Sherbrooke in Paris on the 18th April for the overseas brothers who want more informatins [sic]. Of course anyone is welcome to Montreal if they want first-hand information.

The Montreal chapter of the Hell's Angels sends its mandatory monthly letter in late March 1985 to the club's East Coast regional office—the Hell's Angels Manhattan chapter clubhouse at 77 East Third Street in New York City. The regional secretary compiles all letters and sends copies to chapters around the world to keep members abreast of what brothers are doing. The Montreal chapter's letter ends months of speculation by Angels around the world about serious problems among Quebec Angels.

Réjean (Zig-Zag) Lessard, president of the Montreal chapter, complains to his superior in the US early in 1985 about the North chapter's heavy use of cocaine and booze, as well as its unruly behavior. Sandy Frazier Alexander, president of the Manhattan chapter as well as the club's East Coast faction, hears him out. He tells Lessard to deal with the problem locally. Alexander expects some violence, but not a slaughter.

Hell's Angels chapters across the US query Manhattan about rumors of heavy tension among Quebec chapters during the month before the Montreal, Sherbrooke and Halifax chapters take care of business. The question comes up every Thursday at church. No one has a satisfactory answer. The weekly Wednesday night telephone call among chapters on March 27 puzzles and frightens the Angels. Another US chapter tells Manhattan that North is out. Sandy Alexander decides at church the next night to send vice-president Ted DeMello to Montreal. Important club business is not handled over the telephone.

DeMello is a former member of the San Jose chapter who fills in as Manhattan president a few months later when Alexander is arrested in May 1985. DeMello sits in on a few chapter meetings in Quebec. He's cautious enough not to ask questions about touchy matters, but makes it known he's there to help. Angel chapters operate independently. They deal with problems internally and don't advertise them to the club. DeMello backs off when he realizes what has happened. He returns to New York and reports he doesn't know the details, but it looks like Angels are dead and North no longer exists.

The entire club is stunned. East Coast officers can't believe it. Angels liquidate members, but never an entire chapter. The outlaw fratricide confirms fears among Hell's Angels around the world: Quebec Angels are bloodthirsty maniacs. Even re-

doubted Cleveland and Manhattan Angels find convenient excuses to avoid Montreal parties. Quebec Angels relish taking
the extra step beyond the threshold of civilization.

Several incidents over half a decade contribute to the
slaughter of the North chapter. The shooting death of Quebec's most sensible and far-sighted Hell's Angel is key among
these. Yves (Le Boss) Buteau drags the Quebec Hell's Angels
out of the Neanderthal mire in which most of the province's
bikers wallow and teaches them to take care of business. He
also underlines the value of subtlety and tolerance—a lesson
quickly forgotten after he is buried. His killer, now a member
of the rival Outlaws Motorcycle Club in Montreal, can claim
to have set in motion the incidents which have taken the Hell's
Angels in Quebec to the brink of destruction.

Gino Goudreau ekes out a nervous living selling drugs in
neighborhood parks around Sorel, Quebec, during the summer
of 1983. He's a small time pusher, too lazy to work, not ambitious enough to tackle more profitable crimes. Given a
choice, he'd rather fuck his girlfriend and ride his motorcycle.

The omnipresent Hell's Angels run into Goudreau several
times during the summer. Their message is clear: "Get your
fucking ass and your fucking drugs out of our territory." Goudreau's laziness fogs his sense of survival. He's also cocky
because his brother is an Outlaw in Montreal. The 22-year-old
pusher and his girlfriend Sylvie Therien park their motorcycle
by Le Petit Bourg bar, a Hell's Angels hangout on rue Elizabeth, shortly after 1 a.m. on Thursday, September 8. Three
men stand outside the door: Yves (Le Boss) Buteau, the 32-
year-old president of the Hell's Angels in Canada, René Lamoureux, a 36-year-old Angel who is the club's main link
with US Angels, and Guy (Frenchy) Gilbert, a 34-year-old
Satan's Choice from Kitchener, Ontario. Gilbert is in Sorel to
discuss his chapter's desire to become Angels. He and other
Choice resist the Outlaws takeover of three Satan's Choice
chapters in Ontario and one in Quebec in 1977.

Goudreau pulls a .38-calibre revolver and shoots Buteau
twice in the chest, Gilbert once in the stomach, and Lamoureux once in the stomach and across the scalp. The stripper
inside the bar hops off stage and hides. Patrons turn over
chairs and tables as they rush for the washrooms. Goudreau
hops on his bike and roars away with his girlfriend. The shots
are fired so quickly that Buteau doesn't have time to pull a

gun from his belt. He dies face down near the gutter. Gilbert clutches his bleeding stomach, stumbles into the bar and falls dead on his back. Lamoureux lives. Goudreau gets his Outlaws patch after a court rules the killings are an act of self defence.

Buteau is Canada's most powerful and clever Angel and the architect of the club's intricate drug trafficking network before his death. Sonny Barger and his lieutenants in Oakland respect the man who controls the most murderous Angels in the world. Buteau is the only Canadian member allowed to use the title: Hell's Angels International. He helps convert the Popeyes into Angels in 1977 and fuels the bloody war between the Gitans and the Atomes in Sherbrooke. The Gitans become the Hell's Angels Sherbrooke chapter one year after Buteau's death, as do the 13th Tribe in Halifax. The Satan's Angels in British Columbia form three Hell's Angels chapters two months before Buteau's death. Three months after the funeral, the fourth and toughest chapter forms in that westernmost province. Yves (Le Boss) Buteau is responsible for establishing the Hell's Angels from coast to coast and keeping the club together.

Buteau's killer instinct is in his brain, not his eyes. With a haircut, the clean-shaven Angel passes for a college football player turned stockbroker. Buteau is quiet and thoughtful. He's raised enough hell with the Popeyes. He's seriously taking care of business in the early 1980s. He wants a wealthy club and avoids hassles. He roars over to pick up the tab when 10 Angels eat and run at a Sorel restaurant. No use alienating your neighbors. The men who replace Buteau—Michel (Sky) Langlois as Hell's Angels national president in Canada, and Réjean (Zig-Zag) Lessard as president of the Montreal, Quebec, chapter—are dynamic and charismatic leaders. But neither is farsighted enough to foresee the disastrous consequences to the club of taking care of business by eliminating the violent, cocaine snorting North chapter. Many Angels end up in jail after the slaughter. Others are still on the run.

Zig-Zag Lessard must bear the brunt of the responsibility for the hard times that befall the Hell's Angels in Quebec and Nova Scotia after the North chapter is eliminated. He has the power in 1985 to prevent the killings. Instead, he acts as master of ceremonies at a party where five untameable North chapter Angels are shot.

Zig-Zag is pained by sore gums and a burr up his ass on Friday afternoon, March 15, 1985. Dentist Pièrre Chicoine adjusts the biker's new false teeth to appease his gums. Only bullets can rectify his ass.

The heavily tattooed chapter leader of the world's most fearsome outlaw motorcycle gang agonizes for two months over his problem: the dreaded North chapter in Laval has to be eliminated. The deadliest Hell's Angels chapter in the world —the only chapter whose members, except for two, are killers—is too wild for the good of the club.

He rants against the bastard North Angels as he drives his Jaguar from Sorel to Chicoine's office in Beloeil. Gerry (Le Chat) Coulombe, a 30-year-old prospect with Lessard's Montreal chapter in Sorel, listens respectfully to the man he calls Z.

North chapter Angels are coke addicts—unpredictably violent, undependable in business and a disgrace to the club, Lessard says. They steal $98,000 from the newly chartered Halifax chapter. And fuckface, bonehead runt Apache Trudeau slaughters people on impulse. Lessard fears he's next. The North Angels are too strong and uncontrollable. They're too much like the Angels of old. They're too wild to live.

Coulombe agrees there's no place in the club for brawling, hardass party animals like the North Angels.

"Because of all their sniffing, they're not doing anything useful for the Hells. They forgot about everything else—the war with the Outlaws and other business."

The North chapter is not taking care of business. The rest of the club is. Zig-Zag Lessard, whose brainwaves parallel his street name, is not a man you fuck around with. He's a member of the Hell's Angels Filthy Few—those who have killed for the club. A revolver cylinder is tattooed on his right arm. Six skulls, instead of bullets, stare out the holes. Lessard has a back pack—the Hell's Angels colors tattooed on his skin—to deny rival bikers the honor of stealing his colors. A vicious enemy, especially an Outlaw, would slice it off like a scalp.

Lessard passes sentence. The North Angels are to die on

Saturday, March 23, he tells Coulombe. Laurent (L'Anglais)
Viau, chapter president, Jean-Guy (Brutus) Geoffrion, the
chemist, Guy-Louis (Chop) Adam, the secretary, Michel
(Willie or Jambe de Bois) Mayrand, Régis (Lucky) Asselin
and Yves (Apache) Trudeau, the club's most feared hit man,
must die. Yvon (Le Père) Bilodeau and Jean-Pierre (Matt le
Crosseur) Mathieu will be retired. Michel (Jinx) Genest and
Gilles (Le Nez) Lachance will join the Montreal chapter.

Hits are nothing new to Coulombe. Even Angels have to be
killed. But to wipe out an entire chapter? The Hell's Angels
have not liquidated a chapter in the club's 38-year history.
Lessard's diatribe gives Coulombe a new perspective on tension he notices among club members. The prospect is not
privy to Angel meetings and discussions of club business. He
realizes, as he sits in Zig-Zag Lessard's Jaguar, that the plot to
kill North Angels is months old. A conversation he overhears
between members in the Sorel clubhouse garage a few weeks
earlier now makes sense. Zig-Zag Lessard, Luc (Sam) Michaud, Jean-Yves (Boule) Tremblay and Denis Houle discuss
important business in hushed voices that allow Coulombe to
pick up only snatches of conversation.

"I can't wait until it's over. I can't wait to get rid of them. I
don't sleep anymore at night," Sam Michaud says.

Coulombe likes to give the impression he can't think his
way out of a wet dream. It's saved his ass more than once, as
it will in coming months. He starts his career, like many
Hell's Angels, as a gutter terrorist with smaller, but no less
tame, motorcycle gangs in the Quebec boonies.

"Beer cost nothing, chicks cost nothing. It was like home.
There was always a bed for you."

Coulombe is an avid reader and history buff who collects
Nazi and US Civil War memorabilia. His proudest possession
in 1979 is a genuine Nazi flag that covers the wall of the
Missiles clubhouse in the picturesque Saguenay-Lac-Saint-
Jean region north of Quebec City—an area that produces the
world's most beautiful women. Coulombe later becomes minister of war for the SS and a 30-year-old prospect with the
Hell's Angels Montreal chapter in Sorel, north of the metropo-
lis, in 1985.

Coulombe brings quite a resumé to the gang: convictions
for drug trafficking (speed), contempt of court, breaking pa-

role (when he carries a box of bullets), theft of car batteries (for his Cadillac) and assault (he knifes someone during a strip joint brawl and smashes the mayor's car windows in Baie Comeau). He denies holding down a woman in a blind pig while a friend tries to rape her. And he denies trying to piss on her.

"I beat her up. She was bugging me, saying: 'I'm not afraid of you, I'm not afraid of you.'"

Coulombe, like most drug dealers, is an aggressive businessman. His Doberman pinscher crunches one reluctant debtor's gonads. He takes two other debtors into the woods around Baie Comeau and slaps them across the mouth a few times. He says he doesn't force them to dig their graves. He doesn't have to. He has a network of heavies to collect his debts. Coulombe also denies firing the shot into a Sûreté du Québec police officer's house that causes his wife to go into false labor. And there's no way he tries to get another biker to kill two Ottawa men with his .25-calibre pistol.

"I wouldn't be stupid enough to try to attack anyone with the .25. It's not powerful enough."

Not all Hell's Angels are good businessmen. That is the root of the tension that festers between the North and Montreal chapters from 1981 to 1985. The Sherbrooke and Halifax chapters become involved in the killing late in its planning stages, since they become Hell's Angels in December 1984.

Greed drives Angels to sell drugs. Some become wealthy, others make enough to own three cars and a two-car garage, and a few stumble along. Denis (Le Curé) Kennedy, one of the few North chapter Angels to occasionally shave, bears an uncanny resemblance to Peter Fonda in *Easy Rider*. He's eloquent, charming and witty. He's also deadly. His inner left forearm bears the Filthy Few tattoo of Angels who have killed for the club. Only two North Angels aren't Filthy Few: the chapter can't afford to let Brutus Geoffrion, the chapter's chemist, get involved in risky business; and Yvon (Le Père) Bilodeau is a responsible family man with a wife and three children.

Kennedy's business sense isn't as finely honed as his killer instinct. He has a knack for spending money and less ability to earn it. Kennedy and fellow Angel Charles (Charlie) Hachez owe Canadian drug kingpin Peter Frank (Dunie) Ryan

$305,000 late in 1981. Both men have acquired a taste for cocaine that drains their pocketbooks and makes their colleagues see red. More business-minded members believe addicts and fuckups give the Hell's Angels a bad name.

Kennedy and Hachez dream up a desperate scheme to save their asses. They enlist the aid of Robert (Steve) Grenier, a 23-year-old prospect with the North chapter, and Hachez's girlfriend, Marjolaine Poirier, a 25-year-old brunette whose looks can make the staunchest fundamentalist cream his lizard-sheen polyesters. They plan to kidnap one of Ryan's children from the family duplex in Lasalle—his seven-year-old daughter Tricia, or his three-year-old son Troy. Dunie Ryan, the Hell's Angels' main hash and coke supplier, is so wealthy he can get his hands on $5 million with a few hours' notice. The wayward Angels don't want a large ransom, just enough to cover their debt and a little extra to party.

Dunie Ryan meets the Hell's Angels earlier in 1981 through his friend Jackie (Jake the Snake) McLaughlin, who becomes the kingpin's bodyguard after being released from jail in January. McLaughlin brings Angels from the North chapter to the basement bar of the Cavalier Motel on rue Saint-Jacques where Ryan's gang hangs out. Their presence earns the bar a nickname: The Zoo. Ryan supplies the Angels with drugs. He also exploits their homicidal penchant.

Patrick Hugh McGurnaghan, a 44-year-old West End gangster, rips Ryan off for drugs and cash later in 1981. Ryan hires Apache Trudeau to do him in. McGurnaghan's Mercedes explodes as he drives along Metcalfe Avenue in Montreal's wealthy Westmount district on October 27. Only a male passenger survives the blast.

Ryan sits at the top of a large pyramid. Many ears hear for him and he quickly gets wind of the plot to abduct his children. He gives the Angels an ultimatum in January 1982. They act quickly. The North chapter meets at its Laval, Quebec, clubhouse and members decide unanimously by show of hands to discharge Kennedy and Hachez for dishonorable conduct. They shoot them on the spot. Laurent (L'Anglais) Viau, Michel (Willie) Mayrand and Jean-Guy (Brutus) Geoffrion, who eventually suffer the same fate, are among those who vote to execute. Grenier and Poirier are found and shot.

"They were thrown into the St. Lawrence Seaway in the

usual way," Apache Trudeau says. "With concrete blocks, chains and a sleeping bag. . . . The ferry crossing dock at Berthierville was my personal cemetery."

Grenier's body floats to the surface on May 16. Hachez is fished out on June 26. Poirier is pulled out on July 22. Kennedy is still fish food.

Yves (Le Boss) Buteau convenes a meeting of the two Quebec Angels chapters later in the spring of 1982. The president's message is simple: The Angels are in the business of making and selling drugs, not using them. Addicts are undependable. The Hell's Angels can't afford members who cost the club money and face through fuckups. The only international Hell's Angels law that deals with drugs prohibits the use of needle-injected chemicals, such as methamphetamine or heroin. Buteau wants to ban snorting coke. The Montreal Angels outnumber the North chapter and pass a bylaw that punishes coke use with expulsion or death.

"At Laval, we were against this rule," Gilles (Le Nez) Lachance says. "We favored liberty."

The North chapter votes later in the year to allow its members to use cocaine. Viau snorts daily and becomes aggressive if deprived.

"Geoffrion took a lot, but less than Viau," Lachance says. "Adam was somewhere between the two in his consumption. I was way down at the end of the line."

Lachance snorts coke two or three times a week and smokes two or three hash cigarettes a day. The North Angels contravene Buteau's will and a democratically passed bylaw. They are drunk and stoned more often than not. They are known by Hell's Angels around the world as the club's sex, drugs and rock-and-roll chapter. They are the Angels of death.

14

TCB: LE COUP DE GRÂCE

TENSION grows between the chapters over North's use of cocaine, but Montreal doesn't dare enforce the bylaw. Time and fate ensure discipline.

Zig-Zag Lessard suffers repeated epileptic seizures in 1983 and swears off cocaine. Lessard is a hardnosed businessman and a hardassed Angel. He isn't happy with the chapter's operation. The Angels have an agreement to split profits. But North keeps poor books and Montreal can't audit to find out if it's being cheated. It is. North has two secret clandestine laboratories that produce $50,000 of methamphetamine each week.

Zig-Zag Lessard isn't the only disgruntled North Angel. Luc (Sam) Michaud and the humungous Robert (Ti-Maigre) Richard feel their fellow members taint the club's colors and cause the Hell's Angels to lose the respect of gangs they want to assimilate. The three Angels quit the North chapter and join the Montreal chapter by mid-year. Ironically, a punk drug pusher shoots Montreal chapter president Yves (Le Boss) Buteau in September 1983 and Lessard assumes command. He bides his time as North chapter Angels grow wilder and alienate an increasing number of brothers. Both chapters prey on each others' weaknesses.

North Angels are irritable. Jean-Yves (Boule) Tremblay, a prospect with the chapter, argues with full-color members in

March 1984. The Angels deem him undesirable and kick him out. They strip Tremblay of his Hell's Angels jewelry, his Harley, even his woman. Zig-Zag Lessard, Sam Michaud and Ti-Maigre Richard think Tremblay is fine Angel material. They break an international club rule and take him into their chapter as a prospect, which adds to the tension between chapters. Michaud fuels club resentment against North throughout 1984.

"We'll fix them," he tells Coulombe.

The series of events that converts tension into action and prompts the massacre of the North chapter begins with an underworld assassination in Montreal.

Dunie Ryan is worth between $50 and $100 million on Tuesday, November 13, 1984. Canada's top cocaine importer has a near monopoly on the white crystal, especially in Quebec. The 42-year-old leader of Montreal's West End Gang is not without enemies. Paul April, a drug trafficker in exile from the gang, is one of them.

Ryan drinks with a Montreal lawyer and an Ottawa couple at Rube's restaurant in Hudson on the evening of November 13. He leaves with his driver at 7:25 and returns to Nittolo's Jardin Motel at 6580 rue Saint-Jacques in West Montreal. The motel-bar becomes Ryan's business office when the Cavalier shuts down. April approaches Ryan at 8:30 and they wander into the bar for a private talk. The French-Canadian hood tells Ryan he has a hot piece of ass lined up for him in room 40. Ryan doesn't need a pimp. His animal magnetism—as well as his money—keeps broads humping. But tonight Ryan lets his guard down. His ego is being hustled. She's young, she's gorgeous, and she appeals to the man in his pants.

Robert Lelièvre walks out of the bathroom and aims a shotgun at Ryan as he walks into the room. Paul April pulls out a submachine gun. They order Ryan to sit. Their plan: tape him, find out where he hides his drugs and money, then kill him. (Ryan fears police will rip off bank accounts and safety deposit boxes. He buries most of his cash and keeps up to $500,000 in a briefcase.) Ryan grabs the chair, wheels around and hurls it at Paul April. He ducks and it smashes into a window. April's submachine gun jams. Shotguns rarely do. Instead of getting a blowjob, Ryan gets blown away—a 12-

gauge SSG shotgun shell slams 12 .22-calibre-size lead slugs through his chest. For safe measure he gets a .45-calibre bullet in the face. April boasts about the hit in a Montreal bar later in the week.

"I killed the king and now I'm the king."

Hit men Michael Blass and Hell's Angel Yves (Apache) Trudeau attend Ryan's funeral at St. Augustine of Canterbury Church in Notre Dame de Grâce on Saturday, November 17. Blass is co-owner of 108733 Canada Ltée., which owns the Hell's Angels North chapter clubhouse. He is on the Angel payroll and visits the clubhouse twice a week. Allan (The Weasel) Ross gives them a contract on the church steps to wipe out his boss's killer, they say. The contract's terms: $200,000 cash to Blass and Trudeau, Ross erases a $300,000 debt owed Ryan by three North chapter Angels, and Ross contributes $100,000 to the chapter.

Michael Blass is one of those unfortunate turds squeezed through the asshole of life who has to live up to an infamous older brother. The balding baddie tries to look mean. He wears sunglasses on cloudy days and sports a caterpillar moustache. He kills easily. But he can't shake his brother's shadow.

Richard (Le Chat) Blass, the Houdini of crime, walks away from underworld hits, evades police dragnets and breaks out of Quebec's most secure prisons in the late 1960s and early 1970s. Both sides of the law label him unkillable. Police protect Blass in hospital after he takes two bullets in the head. He jumps out a window to escape. Two underworld friends get Blass drunk one night and put him to bed in his room at the Manoir de Plaisance Hôtel, near Saint-Hippolyte, 45 miles north of Montreal. They set fire to the hotel. Four people die in the gutted building. Blass escapes. The 23-year-old hood drives into a garage in Saint-Michel with Claude Ménard one Thursday in October 1968. Someone riddles the car with bullets. Blass takes a slug in the back of the head and two between the shoulder blades. Policemen crowd around as he bleeds profusely. They ask him to name the hit men before he dies.

"Take a walk dogs. I don't know nothing. They missed me this time, but I won't miss them."

Richard Blass doesn't die and decides at 23 to become a

killer, a profession that keeps him in notorious company. He escapes from Saint-Vincent de Paul Penitentiary in Laval with French gangster Jacques Mesrine in August 1972. The pathological Mesrine kills two game wardens one month later in the woods outside Saint-Louis de Blandford, 60 miles east of Quebec City. Mesrine's only contribution to society before 18 bullets stop his killing spree in Paris on Friday, November 2, 1979, is a message he records days before his death in which he asks not to be remembered as a hero:

> I'll become an example, perhaps a bad example. But what is terrible is that there are those who will want to make me a hero. There are no heroes in crime, only men on the margin of society who don't accept the law.

Such are the Hell's Angels; such is Richard Blass.

Blass makes the last of his many prison breaks on October 23, 1974, from Saint-Vincent de Paul Penitentiary, where he serves 15 years for attempted murder, armed robbery, assaulting a policeman and car theft. Blass smashes a glass window between visitors and prisoners and a woman tosses him a paper bag full of handguns. Five prisoners break out.

Blass kills two men in the Gargantua Bar Salon at 1369 Beaubien Street East in Montreal on October 30. The victims, Raymond Laurin, 30, and Roger Lévesque, 28, are his partners in a 1970 attempted bank robbery in Sherbrooke. Blass vents his anger at the men he feels should have been jailed with him and invites fellow escaper Edgar Roussel to pump two more bullets into their heads before they walk out of the club.

Richard Blass and Edgar Roussel mail a four-page, handwritten letter to Blass's lawyer Frank Shoofey, who makes public on November 6 their demand that Solicitor-General Warren Allmand allow reporters to inspect the inhumane conditions in the penitentiary's maximum security Cell-Block No. 1.

> After having had to endure these tortures for months, nothing would please us more than to shoot some people's brains out. How many we do not know, but if we take a liking to sending those dirty torturers to another world let us tell you that the number of victims will be high. We will surely become the two biggest killers that Montreal has ever known.

A Montreal newspaper announces it doesn't have a recent photograph of Richard Blass. He sends one of himself lying on a couch with a pistol in each hand. Two men walk into an East Montreal bar in early January 1975 in search of "two dirty dogs." They don't find them, so they kill the doorman. Police raid an apartment in Longueuil on Montreal's South Shore one week later. They find a burning cigaret, empty mailbags from a robbery and empty take-out food containers. Blass slips away again.

Blass returns to the Gargantua Bar Salon at midnight on January 21, 1975 to kill witnesses to the October murders there. The topless dance bar is a hangout for small-time underworld punks. Blass lines up 10 men and three women against the wall. He herds them into a six-by-ten-foot storage closet stacked with beer and pop cases. Réjean Fortin, the club's 43-year-old manager, shoves against the door as it closes. Blass puts a bullet in his back through the door, which he padlocks and blocks with a jukebox. He sets a fire behind the bar and another 30 feet from the storage closet. Firemen find the bodies at 2:30 a.m.

"I've been on the force for more than 20 years and I have never seen expressions as I did on the faces of those bodies they took to the morgue," one detective says.

Fernand Beaudet, 28, helps Blass torch the Gargantua. He tells his sister Jacqueline about it over the telephone.

"You're kidding," she says. "Don't tell mom, eh. She's nervous enough as it is."

Richard Blass rents a chalet in Val David in the Laurentians 60 miles north of Montreal on January 23. He fends off the cold with 28-year-old Lucienne (Lucette) Smith, a shapely bleached blonde. Blass surrounds the bed with a sawed-off shotgun, a sawed-off .30-calibre rifle, four pistols and gas masks. Wiretaps tip police to the hideout.

"The place is surrounded—give yourself up," they advise through a bullhorn at 4:30 a.m. on January 24.

A man and woman walk out. Sergeant Marcel Lacoste of the Sûreté du Québec is the first policeman to reach the door.

I tried to kick down the front door, but I couldn't, so I broke the glass beside the door and reached in and unlocked it. I saw this woman in night clothes on the stairs. So I told her to come over or I would shoot her.

Lucette Smith begs to be let out. Sergeant Lacoste lets her go after she points to Blass's room. Sergeant Lacoste and Sergeant Jacques Durocher kick open the door.

"I saw a man on the bed no more than five feet away whom I recognized as Blass because we had been hunting him," Sergeant Durocher says. "I saw he was armed and I fired because at a time like that you don't hesitate. You don't take time to talk about it."

Both policemen fire their 9mm submachine guns. Lacoste's gun jams after firing four bullets. Durocher slams 23 slugs into Blass in two seconds. The body bounces around the bed, jerks onto the floor and slumps in a closet. Only seven bullets stay in the body. The rest tear through, leaving 52 holes from the left thigh to the brain. One bullet pierces Blass's right eye. The legend dies at 28.

His brother, hitman Michael Blass, outlines to Apache Trudeau after Dunie Ryan's funeral a plan to kill Robert Lelièvre and Paul April. Paul April is Apache Trudeau's occasional murder partner. April, a 42-year-old drug dealer, lives in Lelièvre's posh ninth-floor apartment in a 22-story apartment building at 1645 boulevard Maisonneuve Ouest in Montreal. Guns are out of the question. There's a police station across the street and the men in apartment 917 have submachine guns. Blass recruits greed as an ally. The 63-year-old Lelièvre is a sports fan who, despite his wealth, does not have a television set. Why not give him one—packed with plastic explosives.

Allan (The Weasel) Ross tells Trudeau on Sunday to wait at an avenue Papineau address that evening for a courier. The man delivers a $25,000 advance and 35 pounds of plastic explosives. Apache Trudeau visits Paul April on Monday, November 19, and notices he doesn't have a television set. He offers a television, a video-cassette recorder and a tape of *Hell's Angels Forever*, a feature-length movie co-produced by Sandy Frazier Alexander, president of the Hell's Angels Manhattan chapter in New York City.

"I told him I wanted him to have it so he could see how the

Hell's Angels operate, what they're all about," Trudeau says.

Apache Trudeau drives Michael Blass to the apartment building at 3:30 a.m. Sunday, November 25. Blass takes up the video-cassette recorder, which contains the timing device for the bomb in the television. Two other men beside Paul April and Robert Lelièvre are in the apartment: Louis Charles, 54, and Gilles Paquette, 27. Blass sets the five-minute timer in the recorder and dashes out to move his illegally-parked car.

"April found out exactly how the Hell's Angels work," Apache Trudeau says.

So does the rest of Montreal at 4:15 a.m. The explosion flattens the walls in eight apartments, sends elevators to the basement and blows the windows out of 13 units in a building 75 feet away.

Allan (The Weasel) Ross tells Trudeau later in the week he can't come up with the remaining $175,000 for the hit. He tells him to collect $195,000 owed to Dunie Ryan by Montreal Angels and the 13th Tribe in Halifax, which is slated to become a Hell's Angels chapter on December 5, 1984, along with the Gitans in Sherbrooke.

Montreal Angels tell Trudeau to fuck off. He visits the Halifax chapter on February 24, 1985, and collects $46,000. Grub MacDonald, Halifax president, later delivers another $52,000 to the North chapter. Then Halifax complains to Montreal. The four chapters are supposed to split profits. How come they have to pay out? Zig-Zag Lessard decides that the addition of two chapters to the club in December 1984 makes North expendable.

Apache Trudeau is a survivor. He senses in the spring of 1985 that something is amiss. There's too much hatred between the North and Montreal chapters. He's also concerned about his health. He snorts so much cocaine he can't get above 135 pounds. A hit man needs strength. He's also worried about his bank account. He spends $60,000 on coke in three weeks. Trudeau enrolls in the detoxification program in Oka, Quebec, on Sunday, March 17, 1985.

"I saw what was coming. I'd seen it myself in the past, what happened to members who drank or sniffed too much."

Robert (Ti-Maigre) Richard, who sports a Filthy Few tattoo, calls Randall (Blondie) Mersereau, vice-president of the

Halifax Hell's Angels, at the clubhouse on 2675 Agricola Street on Monday, March 18. He tells him the "party" for all four Hell's Angels chapters in eastern Canada is scheduled for Saturday, March 23.

Daniel Raby's sporting goods store in Sherbrooke receives a shipment of sleeping bags on Monday. Georges (Bo-Boy) Beaulieu, president of the Sherbrooke Hell's Angels chapter, pays $34.95 each for three of them later in the week. He's in a hurry and won't take a receipt.

Jean-Pierre (Matt le Crosseur) Mathieu wakes up feeling apprehensive on Saturday, March 23. He doesn't want to attend the afternoon meeting. The Montreal boys are angry at his North chapter and he feels something heavy is going down. Mathieu stays in his Fabreville apartment all day with his 31-year-old girlfriend, Ginette Henri, with whom he has been living seven years. He tells her he doesn't want to be disturbed.

Fellow North member Guy-Louis (Chop) Adam knocks at the door at 5:30 to take Mathieu to the meeting. Henri lies and tells him her man's asleep. He calls later and gets the same answer.

"Why doesn't he put his glasses on and go alone if he wants to jerk off," Mathieu says. "I'm not going to sit around in a car waiting."

Jean-Yves (Boule) Tremblay tells Gerry (Le Chat) Coulombe early in the morning to pick up a van rented under the name of Claude Lavigne at Paul Gamelin et Fils in Saint-Pièrre-de-Sorel. Tremblay gives him a cardboard box to put in the van. It contains a bottle of bleach, a bottle of Mr. Clean, a pair of gloves, a parka and a knife.

"He told me there was nothing to sign, nothing to pay. All I had to do was pick it up. He told me to wear gloves and make sure I didn't touch anything."

Coulombe returns to the clubhouse with the truck. He is told to drive to Ti-Maigre Richard's house, where the Angel gives him two revolvers wrapped in rags to take to Lennoxville. Denis Houle and Jacques (La Pelle) Pelletier give him pistols and revolvers at the clubhouse. He slips them under his car seat. He arrives at the Sherbrooke clubhouse in Lennoxville at 1 p.m. He is given a .22-calibre rifle and stands guard with two other prospects: David Rouleau and Claude (Coco) Roy. Coulombe is happy to have a gun. Anything can happen. He once stands guard in a loft with a shotgun during the expulsion of another Angel. They move members' cars to a downtown parking lot throughout the afternoon and return to the clubhouse by taxi. Zig-Zag Lessard walks out in the evening and tells Coulombe the meeting is postponed until Sunday because some North members aren't there. Zig-Zag returns to the clubhouse and throws a temper tantrum. Coulombe books motel rooms for the visitors. Most Angels stay at the 44-unit La Marquise, about 1,500 feet from the clubhouse. The No Vacancy sign lights up by evening's end. Some Angels stay at the Lennoxville motel downtown. Not one Angel takes a woman to his room.

Coulombe wakes up Sunday morning, March 24, in the La Marquise motel room he shares with Claude (Coco) Roy. He calls home in Sorel and finds out his cat has given birth to five kittens. They eat and return to the clubhouse. Michel (Willie) Mayrand of the doomed North chapter is already there. Coulombe is immediately assigned guard duty and sits in his car with a loaded 12-gauge shotgun.

Robert (Rockin' Robert) Milton calls Ti-Maigre Richard from Halifax. They talk about the sunny, balmy weather in both cities.

Laurent (L'Anglais) Viau wakes up to a sunny Sunday. The North chapter president is in a good mood. He calls Gilles (Le Nez) Lachance at the North clubhouse in Laval at 10 a.m. to ensure his members show up for the meeting.

"Ya, we're all going there," Viau says. "It takes about an hour and a half to get up there. . . . O.K., I'll see you there . . . .We have to go, it's mandatory."

Matt le Crosseur Mathieu calls the clubhouse.

"I went to your place," Lachance tells him. "You were sleeping. I wasn't able to wake you up." He tells Mathieu that Viau will pick him up.

Viau shows up at Mathieu's house shortly after noon.

"Are you bringing your piece?" Mathieu asks.

"No. Everything will work out fine."

Matt le Crosseur Mathieu leaves his .357 Magnum and .45-calibre revolvers behind. They walk out to the street at 12:30, decked out in their Hell's Angels finest: jeans, colors and jewelry. Ginette Henri drives to Mathieu's mother's house in Sherbrooke for a christening. She expects her boyfriend home for dinner.

Gerry (Le Chat) Coulombe watches Guy-Louis (Chop) Adam drive in, followed by Gilles (Le Nez) Lachance and Jean-Guy (Brutus) Geoffrion, all North members. Coulombe has to back up to let Lachance's car into the drive. Viau's black sports car tears along rue Queen and turns up the hill away from the Saint-Francois river and toward the historic red brick building and its mountain backdrop. Angels mill around the 13-acre property. No one mentions the problems to be discussed.

Church starts in mid-afternoon with a shout to enter the clubhouse. Only full-fledged Angels are allowed into meetings. Prospects have to wait outside. Gerry Coulombe, Coco Roy and three others sit in their cars. Jean-Yves (Boule) Tremblay, who receives his colors two weeks earlier, greets the North chapter Angels in the enclosed front porch. It's his first church. The North Angels aren't happy to see their rejected prospect.

Gilles (Le Nez) Lachance sits at the clubhouse bar drinking a beer when the slaughter of the North chapter begins.

"They arrived a few minutes apart," Lachance says. "As each entered, he was announced individually in a loud voice. Then there were sounds of a scuffle. I was sitting at the bar and drinking a beer at the time. Gun shots rang out."

Someone yells: "Watch out, it's the Outlaws."

Jacques (La Pelle) Pelletier, a convicted rapist and armed robber, lifts a .32-calibre submachine gun from behind the bar and aims it at Lachance.

"Don't move, nothing will happen to you."

Lachance puts his hands on the counter. Pelletier tells him to keep them up. Patrick (Frenchy) Guernier, from the Halifax chapter, moves in and trains his gun on Lachance.

"Hey, no guns in here," Viau yells in the front porch.

"You, never mind the guns."

Someone shoots Viau and pushes him against the wall. He slips to the floor.

"Then I saw Viau trying to protect himself, waving his fist in front of his face, and then he was on his back on the ground and another person was standing over him," Lachance says.

An arm reaches down toward Viau but he moves too much.

The gun sways with the body and pumps a shot into his head. Sam Michaud shoots Brutus Geoffrion in the right cheek and upper left side of the head. One bullet goes out the back of the skull. The other lodges at the base near the spine.

"You bunch of dirty dogs," Willie Mayrand yells as he falls to the floor.

Chop Adam runs out the front door to the lawn with Robert (Snake) Tremblay at his heels. Gerry Coulombe jumps out of the car and flattens himself against the clubhouse wall.

"Adam was getting closer to me and Tremblay was shooting at him," he says.

Adam falls dead on the grass. He is shot seven times with .22-calibre and .45-calibre slugs; two are exploding bullets that shatter inside his skull and lungs. He is hit once in the head, once in the forearm and five times in the back.

Snake Tremblay yells for someone to open the garage door. He drags Chop Adam to a pile of bodies. Someone tells Coulombe to keep his gun trained on prospects Normand (Biff) Hamel and Claude (Coco) Roy. He marches the prospects to the parking lot and frisks them.

Gilles (Le Nez) Lachance, Yvon (Le Père) Bilodeau and Richard (Bert) Mayrand, who has just seen his brother murdered, are ordered into a corner while members wash the floors and drag bodies into the garage.

"I told Robert Richard that he had blood on his boots and he cleaned it off," Lachance says.

The Angels gather in a circle around Zig-Zag Lessard. He explains that the five brothers are dead because they snorted too much coke and Trudeau collected the money from the Halifax chapter after Ross told him to.

"You can go," Zig-Zag tells Lachance. "We don't have anything against you." He tells him he can retire or join the Montreal chapter in Sorel. Lachance looks around. He joins.

The Angels burn their dead brothers' possessions in a steel drum outside the clubhouse. Lachance, Pelletier and Snake Tremblay drive to Laval later Sunday night to explain the killings to Michel (Jinx) Genest, a North chapter member who must now join the Montreal chapter. Lachance returns to the Sherbrooke clubhouse and drinks beer with Frenchy Guernier.

Boule Tremblay rolls the blue van out of the garage and Gerry Coulombe hops into a car driven by Hell's Angel Gaétan Proulx. They cruise through the Lafontaine tunnel-bridge in Montreal on their way to Berthierville.

"It was still bright. We couldn't throw the bodies in the water," Coulombe says.

They park the truck and have dinner in a restaurant. Coulombe has spaghetti and beer.

"I didn't eat everything, I remember that."

Boule Tremblay complains about his salad but doesn't send it back. They return to the parking lot. Blood drips from under the back door and forms a large red patch in the snow. The three Angels kick ice and sand on the spot and drive around until dusk. The van's back doors swing open when the road changes from gravel to asphalt to expose a pile of stuffed sleeping bags and a concrete block. Chains wrapped around legs and waists fasten a block to each body. The sleeping bags are stuffed with corpses. Proulx blinks his headlights until Tremblay stops.

The van shorts out minutes later and coasts to the side of the road. Boule Tremblay sends Coulombe to buy gas and fuses to replace those that have blown. He brings back a flashlight too, but has to return to the garage because the fuses don't fit. The truck and car drive up to the dock at Saint-Ignace-de-Loyola as the sun sets. They wait in the distance until the ferry leaves for Sorel. Tremblay backs the van up to the dock as the boat draws near the opposite shore. Proulx shields the van with the car and joins Tremblay at the back doors. Coulombe, in the car, hears five heavy plops. Boule Tremblay and Gaétan Proulx wash the bloody van floor. Coulombe is told to go home when he gets back to the clubhouse and to return in a couple of days.

Zig-Zag Lessard calls a meeting of all Hell's Angels in the province, including visiting Halifax Angels, at the Montreal chapter clubhouse in Sorel on Monday, March 25, to determine how to reimburse the $98,000 to the Halifax boys. The Angels agree to send someone to Vancouver to explain the liquidation to BC Angels. They also vote to steal everything in the Laval clubhouse and the homes of the five dead Angels during the next few days.

Ginette Henri waits all day Monday for Matt le Crosseur Mathieu at his mother's house. She returns home in the evening to find someone has stolen the Hell's Angels photographs from the walls, Mathieu's belongings and jewelry, her coffer of old coins, four of her antique pistols and a gas mask. She calls Jacqueline Dionne, Brutus Geoffrion's girlfriend. Her apartment has been burglarized too. They go to Willie Mayrand's apartment—same thing. Henri returns home then walks to the nearby clubhouse. It is empty. Hell's Angels clubhouses are never empty. They are guarded 24 hours a day. Henri spends the night with L'Anglais Viau's girlfriend. They don't know their men are dead.

Zig-Zag Lessard orders Coulombe Tuesday morning to rent two large trucks with Normand (Biff) Hamel to empty the North clubhouse and dead Angels' apartments. Gerry Coulombe, Gaetan Proulx, Biff Hamel, Louis (Ti-Oui) Lapièrre and Sam Michaud each drive a truck.

Lachance, Sam Michaud and Ti-Oui Lapièrre arrive at Viau's apartment shortly before noon. They walk around the rooms, pick up everything he owns and throw it into a truck. Ginette Henri, Viau's girlfriend, and two other strippers want to know what's happening. Gilles Lachance, Henri's live-in lover in the 1970s, tells them the club has expelled five North Angels. Henri runs to the bedroom and cries. She still doesn't know her man is dead.

Sylvie Thibeault, secretary in the H.A. Enr. de Laval garage owned by the North chapter, watches members clean out the North clubhouse at 8000 rue Arthur-Sauve in Laval. They fill three trucks with motorcycles, guns, tools and photographs taken off the walls. Jinx Genest and Sam Michaud empty the safe. Thibeault, whose job includes paying the garage's three employees with checks signed by L'Anglais Viau, is told her job ends on April 1. Jinx Genest tells her to take her pay out of the till.

Zig-Zag Lessard orders Lachance to fly to Vancouver on Wednesday with Sam Michaud from the Laval chapter, Sherbrooke chapter president Bo-Boy Beaulieu and Halifax chapter president Ronald Lauchlan (Grub) MacDonald to explain the killings to two of the province's four Hell's Angels chapters. It won't look so bad if a member of the North chapter explains the deaths, he says.

Coulombe and Gaetan Proulx show up at Matt le Crosseur

Mathieu's apartment to take what the first looters miss. A police patrol car stops as they start to load the truck. Ginette Henri—known to the boys as "La Jument"—explains it's a planned move, not a theft. They park a block away and the Angels leave with only a table.

Willie Mayrand's apartment is a shambles. The Angels poke around and leave with motorcycle parts. A woman puts a gun to Gerry Coulombe's head as he walks into Brutus Geoffrion's apartment. He bows out with a shit-eating grin and races back to the clubhouse.

An apprehensive Gilles Lachance returns from Vancouver on Thursday, March 28. He feels he doesn't have much of a choice when Zig-Zag Lessard says he can retire or join the Montreal chapter in front of the entire East Coast club membership while the blood of his fellow North members is still wet on the Lennoxville clubhouse floor. He is asked to explain the killings to Trudeau when he arrives from the airport. His nerves shrivel. He goes home and bundles up his colors, T-shirts, jewelry—everything with a Hell's Angels insignia on it. He drives to Yvon (Le Pere) Bilodeau's house and turns in his colors to the club's oldest member.

"I quit."

"Why?"

"Why? I saw the reason on the 24th."

Lachance goes to his girlfriend's house and takes her .38-calibre police special revolver. He leaves her a 12-gauge shotgun she bought him and hides out in a chalet near Piedmont. The Hell's Angels have frightened a member into taking the first step toward turning against the club.

The Angels want to finish the job of eliminating the North chapter and put $50,000 contracts on Régis (Lucky) Asselin and Apache Trudeau, who miss the Lennoxville meeting. Denis Houle and Jacques (La Pelle) Pelletier get the contract on Asselin. Gilles (Le Nez) Lachance and Normand (Biff) Hamel are to hit Trudeau. Hamel tells Apache Trudeau at the Oka detoxification center he's been ruled dishonorable. He orders him to remove his Hell's Angels tattoos. He doesn't say anything about the contract. Trudeau blacks out his tattoos.

"I understood very quickly what it meant."

* * *

Sam Michaud calls Halifax on Sunday, March 31, and tells Grub MacDonald, David Francis (Gyrator) Giles and Rockin' Robert Milton that the North chapter motorcycle parts have been split three ways and their share is being shipped by truck.

"Everything is perfect. Everybody is in good health," Sam Michaud says. Grub MacDonald laughs.

Yves (Apache) Trudeau leaves the Oka detoxification center in early April. He can't find his chopper and $46,000 he left in the North clubhouse safe. He calls Normand (Biff) Hamel on Saturday, April 6. Hamel tells him he'll never see the money, but can win back the motorcycle if he kills two persons the Angels fear might squeal: Jean-Marc Deniger, an Angel hang-around and former clubmate to Trudeau in the Popeyes, and Ginette (La Jument) Henri, Matt le Crosseur Mathieu's girlfriend and accountant for the North chapter.

Halifax calls Sherbrooke on Sunday, April 7, 1985. They wonder why the truck hasn't arrived. Ti-Maigre Richard tells Gyrator Giles not to worry, it's on its way.

"Don't make no plans for your bike now," Ti-Maigre Richard says. "There's a surprise for you in the truck. You'll flip out."

Gyrator Giles tells him not to send a red gas tank airbrushed with a skull and crossbones because it doesn't fit on a Halifax Angel's bike. Rockin' Robert, Gyrator and Ti-Maigre wish each other Happy Easter.

"I love you," they say before hanging up.

Claude (Coco) Roy is badly shaken by the killings. He returns to his apartment on rue Joliet in Saint-Hilaire on Monday, March 25 and gets stoned. He keeps his .38-calibre revolver within reach. He does more coke. He doesn't cross the room without his gun. The 31-year-old prospects for the North chapter in Laval for six months. Now, the most powerful men in his world are gone, including Chop Adam, his Hell's Angels godfather. What's a prospect worth to the Hell's Angels if they can murder full-color members?

Coco Roy is worth money to the Angels. Only he and Ginette Henri—Matt le Crosseur Mathieu's girlfriend and the

North chapter accountant—know where the chapter's drugs are stashed. Henri won't talk until she finds out where her old man is. Then she's sure not to say anything. So the Angels let Coco Roy cool off before they ask him for the drugs. But he gets more upset and more wasted every day. Linda Lord, his 26-year-old girlfriend, watches the man she loves disintegrate emotionally.

Lord, a wisp of a stripper on the Quebec club circuit, meets Coco Roy at La Lanterne Rouge on Montreal's South Shore in 1983. They run into each other again at the same club in the fall of 1984. She is taken by his sad eyes and accepts his offer to shack up in Beloeil, where they share a house with Chop Adam, his girlfriend Sylvie Forbes, and his six- and twelve-year-old children. Chop Adam becomes Coco Roy's godfather in the club and sponsors him as a prospect for the North chapter. Coco Roy has to obey all Angels, 24 hours a day.

Coco Roy buys a motorcycle repair shop in Saint-Charles-sur-Richelieu and rents a house there. His ties with the Angels help his shop prosper and also bring in customers for the hash and coke he sells. Linda Lord babysits the children, keeps an eye on the garage and starts snorting coke heavily. The house burns to the ground early in 1985 and they move in with Chop Adam in March. By this time he lives on rue Joliet in Saint-Hilaire. Chop Adam turns to Lord and asks her to take good care of his children as he walks out of the house to attend a meeting of all chapters on Sunday, March 24. Adam never returns. Coco Roy pounces from window to window for two weeks. Linda Lord has no idea what's happening.

The telephone rings on the evening of April 7, Easter Sunday. Jinx Genest, a stocky, 27-year-old Angel with the now-defunct North chapter wants Coco Roy to meet him in unit 103 of the Ideal Motel on Highway 116 in Saint-Basile-le-Grand. Motel meetings are not unusual for Angels. A major drug deal can be negotiated away from prying eyes and ears for $20. Jinx Genest wants Coco Roy to bring the drug stash. Lord overhears Roy mouthing the address and jots it down.

Coco Roy picks up the coke, stuffs five bags in his underwear, and walks into the motel room where Jinx Genest smashes the left side of his head in, splattering blood from the bed to the bathroom door. He calls Linda Lord after an hour and invites her over to share a whirlpool bath, champagne and cocaine. She tells him to fuck off. Lord slips out the back door and hides when Genest knocks at her door later in the evening.

Jinx Genest drives to the ferry dock at Saint-Ignace-de-Loyola. He rolls Roy's body onto an unzipped sleeping bag in the back of the pickup truck, ties 80 pounds of iron weight-lifting plates to the waist and legs with steel cable and chains, zips up the package and dumps it into the water where the other bodies are slowly decomposing.

Lionel (Figg) Deschamps, a 33-year-old Angel prospect, arrives at the Halifax clubhouse on Wednesday, April 10, in a rented truck filled with motorcycles. Five black Harley-Davidsons with gas tank and fender inscriptions and insignia that read "Filthy Few North," "Crazy Crew" and "Hell's Angels North" are taken to the Eastern Bike Parts shop run by the Halifax Angels. Four bikes have Quebec licence plates: NBE-883, MCW-850, MDM-763 and MZ-5258. Mayrand's vehicle registration is attached to the Harley with the NBE-883 plate.

The Sûreté du Québec launches operation Chant du Coq that day. More than 400 policemen raid 100 Hell's Angels hangouts across the province over two days. The heat is on. The police track the Angels since October 1983 with their secret, $5-million Opération Haro. They've got nothing on the club despite money and time spent on investigations. They scramble after a wiretap on the Sherbrooke clubhouse tips them off in the last week of March that five Angels are missing.

The police finally have something to pin on the Angels—murder. They can wipe out the club in Quebec if they can jail the 40 Angels present at the Lennoxville killing. Chant du Coq is a fishing expedition for bodies. A front-end loader smashes down the Sherbrooke clubhouse door. Police tear walls apart, smash headlights and scour the grounds with metal detectors while a helicopter with heat sensors hovers overhead. They dig holes and find a shirt with an alleged bullet hole. They net a pinch of drugs, money they can't prove as being illegally earned, and legal weapons.

The Angels fight back. They sue the police for damage to property. Their lawyers hold a press conference to condemn the raids and portray their clients as victims of persecution.

"The Hell's Angels of Lennoxville also want to condemn their harassment by the Sûreté du Québec during the past few years in the Saint-Francois district," reads the statement by Angel lawyers Michel Dussault and Jean-Pierre Rancourt.

When grocer Stanley Binette was murdered in Sherbrooke, the SQ insinuated it was the result of a Hell's Angel initiation: however, an individual has just been sentenced to life for this crime and he was in no way linked with the Hell's Angels club. The SQ never retracted its statement.

Similar examples of harassment have been often repeated during the last few years in this region and Justice has often shown that the Angels were not involved. . . .

They also accuse the police of laying needless charges against the Angels.

The SQ announced it seized an arsenal of weapons during its many raids last week: but most of those weapons carried official seals of approval since they'd already been seized many times (and returned to the bikers) during previous raids. As for the other weapons, the police didn't even bother to ask whether permits had been issued for them.

The Hell's Angels don't want to hinder police in their duties: they have work to do, but could easily do it without breaking everything during raids. . . . The Hell's Angels of Lennoxville ask that SQ police officers in the Saint-Francois district respect the . . . Canadian Charter of Rights and Freedoms which require them to respect the laws of Canada.

The police continue their search for the bodies. They launch Opération Zancle. The name is arbitrarily assigned by headquarters from a prepared list. Zancle is a type of fish. The irony waits to be uncovered. Their greatest catch during the mid-April raids also doesn't prove its worth until months later. Yves (Apache) Trudeau is arrested and charged with illegal possession of a firearm. He stays on the streets until sentenced to one year in jail.

Six Sherbrooke chapter Angels leave for Paris on an evening flight out of Mirabel International Airport north of Montreal on Tuesday, April 16. Charles (Cash) Filteau, Yvan (Bagosse) Tanguay, Guy (Mouski) Rodrigue, Georges (Bo-Boy) Beaulieu, Louis (Bidou) Brochu and Gerry (Le Chat)

Coulombe are off to explain to European chapters why North no longer exists and to celebrate the fourth anniversary of the Paris chapter on April 18. The Hell's Angels are the only outlaw motorcycle gang in France. Their clubhouse is in Paris' 19ième arrondissement. The streetwise identify Paris Angels who aren't wearing colors by their footwear: they fancy square-toed boots.

Bo-Boy Beaulieu, president of the Sherbrooke chapter, describes as "bullshit" the police attempt to prove the Angels killed five of their own.

> The police are on a fishing expedition. They don't even have proof there are bodies. It's nice to say there are bodies, but where are they, tabernacle. The police have searched everywhere and they haven't found any bodies. Nothing happened [in Lennoxville]. I don't know where those damn stories came from.

Meanwhile, Apache Trudeau is about to add to the stories.

Jean-Marc (La Grande Gueule) Deniger is a close friend of Coco Roy and Chop Adam. The Angels don't trust him now that his buddies are dead. Deniger, as secretary of the Popeyes in the mid-1970s, parties with US Angels who visit Quebec. He lobbies for his club to become their first chapter in Canada. The Americans like this wild-haired drug dealer who is proven biker material—Deniger stabs another biker to death during a knife fight in 1968. But Deniger doesn't join the club when the Popeyes form the Hell's Angels Montreal chapter on December 5, 1977. He never does. He just hangs around and deals in drugs.

Trudeau wants to kill Deniger quickly to fulfil his deal with the club and get his chopper back from the Montreal Angels. The 35-year-old Deniger says goodbye to his girlfriend and goes out to his car on Wednesday, May 1, 1985. He meets Trudeau, who wastes no time. He ties Deniger up, strangles him and wraps the body in a sleeping bag. Trudeau stuffs the body on the floor of Deniger's car between the front and back seats. Then he goes home and waits. Trudeau loses patience after five days and calls a reporter at the *Journal de Montreal* to tell him where he can find a body. The international Hell's Angels policy on hits is that they have to be verified through the media. He picks up his motorcycle at a Longueil garage.

* * *

Although the Hell's Angels seem to have dropped the contract on Apache Trudeau, they still want North member Régis
(Lucky) Asselin dead because he is too wild. Lucky Asselin, a
runt in a world of beer guts and brawn, leaves his girlfriend's
house on rue Blondin in Bellefeuille in the late evening on
Thursday, May 2, 1985. A silenced submachine gun flashes
from the shadows and six of 30 bullets fired tear through him.
The hitman is either blind or the target too small: Asselin is
five feet, five inches tall and weighs 125 pounds. He stumbles
to his van and speeds away before the gunman can shove
another clip into his grease gun. Blood pours out of Lucky's
chest onto the seat as he leans on the steering wheel. He races
toward the emergency ambulance entrance of the Hotel-Dieu
hospital and crashes through the door. The doctors save him.

The 27-year-old Angel whose original nickname when he
joins the club is Agaçe, lives up to his second monicker once
again. Only close friends know where Lucky Asselin hides
from the Angels. Nicole Desjardins, his girlfriend, has just
moved to Bellefeuille, near Saint-Jerome. Yet, the resourceful
Angels find him, only to lose out to luck.

The bodies rot slowly from the inside out for 69 days at the
bottom of the murky St. Lawrence River. The dead Angels,
like hairy, tattooed wineskins, bloat with methane gas. The
swift current jostles the corpses as they lighten, then slides
them along the muddy seaway bottom through clinging
weeds. The 30-pound blocks they are chained to resist and the
Angels tug gently at their anchors. The more they rot, the
more they swell. The bodies float suspended beneath the surface like grotesque circus balloons above a field of undulating
slimy green arms. The current that rolls Canadian and American excrement to the Atlantic Ocean tugs Matt le Crosseur
Mathieu's stiff along the shoreline for miles. His wooden leg
makes him more buoyant than the other dead Angels. The
bodies stretch closer to sunlight every day.

Brutus Geoffrion, the biggest of the murdered Angels,
breaks surface first. A fat, soggy sleeping bag bobs in the
waves near the Bertheirville ferry crossing between Sorel and
Saint-Ignace Island at 1:30 Saturday afternoon on June 1. The
40-year-old mechanic's body is smothered with mushrooms

and other fungi that feed on his flesh and help it decay. A padlock fastens 18 feet of chain wrapped around his body to a cement block. The watch on his wrist has stopped. Unlike Timex commercials, this Angel stops ticking after the beating.

Three Sûreté du Québec scuba divers, who work out of a rubber dinghy, grope along the seaway bottom and fondle anything that looks remotely human.

"On the bottom, you don't see more than a foot ahead of you, even with a spotlight," diver Harold Sheppard says. "It's more of an outline than a body that you see."

A police joke in Quebec in June 1985: When fishing in the St. Lawrence your limit is five Hell's Angels.

They pull out the bodies of Brutus Geoffrion, L'Anglais Viau, Chop Adams, Willie Mayrand and Coco Roy between June 1 and June 5. A diver puts his hand through a skeleton clad with shreds of rotting cloth on Thursday, June 6. A rope ties it to a concrete block. The once-buxomy Berthe Desjardins is the missing piece in a five-year-old kidnapping-murder.

André Desjardins, 35, and his 33-year-old wife Berthe deal in drugs in the late 1970s. He is an ex-Hell's Angel and travels a lot to the US. The Angels suspect Desjardins squeals to the cops early in 1980. They dispatch Apache Trudeau to plug the leak. Trudeau walks into their rue Drolet apartment during the evening of February 11 and abducts the couple at gunpoint. Jeanne Desjardins, André's 50-year-old mother, confronts Trudeau as he ushers man and wife down the hallway. Trudeau beats the mother to death with the gun and rolls her down the stairs. He leaves her there and takes her son and daughter-in-law for their last ride. Apache Trudeau ties a rope around Berthe's body, fastens it to a concrete block, then wraps her in a sleeping bag before he rolls her off his favorite dock. He zips the sleeping bag around André and hooks the chain tied to the concrete block to the zipper. The weight of the block rips off the zipper when the body hits the water. Andre's skeleton washes up on shore on August 4. Something eats the flesh off the bones during the six months it is in the water.

Divers continue the search for Matt le Crosseur Mathieu's body. Fifty-five-year-old Lucien Turgeon, a farmer from Neuville just south of Quebec City, finds two sleeping bags on the beach on June 9. The shit-filled St. Lawrence spits out another Angel.

The Hell's Angels Motorcycle Club orders members to treat the six murdered bikers as outcasts and forbids their attendance at the funerals. Three men who bring the Hell's Angels to Quebec are buried without colors and motorcycle escorts. Hell's Angel Richard (Bert) Mayrand does not show up at his older brother Willie's hour-long funeral service in Asbestos, Quebec.

The Hell's Angels can't stop killing. Good news turns into a nightmare on Friday, June 26, after a curious Gerry (Le Chat) Coulombe makes a few inquiries. The prospect is told during an evening telephone conversation his initiation into the club is slated for the next day. He calls his friends Gaétan Proulx and Donat Ramsay. They don't know anything about it. Coulombe fears he's being set up for a hit.

The Sûreté du Québec SWAT team crashes into Coulombe's apartment the next day. They drag him out of bed and throw him to the floor while they keep submachine guns aimed at his back. They take Coulombe to the police station in Sorel. Police question him later at the rue Parthenais detention center in Montreal. He tries to call the Hell's Angels lawyer Léo-René Maranda, but the line is busy. He decides to rat.

"I was scared. . . . Sometimes you're better off inside a prison than at the bottom of a river."

The Quebec police have bodies, know where they are killed, yet still can't charge anyone after a four-month investigation. They need more dirt on the Angels. They need another rat. Detective Louis de Francisco, prompted by the Crown attorney's office, uses the media to flush one out.

The Quebec press has a love affair with crime. Quebeckers gobble up murder stories, especially those where a husband finds his nympho wife in the bathtub with the endowed 71-year-old janitor and tosses a plugged-in Cuisinart into the suds. Two Montreal tabloids—*Allô Police* and *Phôto Police* —bring the most minute crime details, in words and pictures, to their readers. Detectives continually visit the newspapers' libraries for background information. The tabloids' reporters can get anyone to talk. Florent Cantin fiddles with his new Bick lighter at a New Year's dance in the community center of the northern mining town of Chapais shortly after midnight on January 1, 1980. A spruce bough catches fire and 48 people die, leaving numerous orphans. One tabloid runs a three-page spread on 19-year-old Cantin three months later in which he brags about the love letters he gets from marriage-minded women across the province. Quebeckers love their criminals as much as their crimes.

Detective de Francisco uses the power of the press against the Angels. He casually mentions at a coroner's inquest on Wednesday, July 31, 1985, that the Hell's Angels have $50,000 contracts on Yves (Apache) Trudeau and Régis (Lucky) Asselin. The tabloids go wild. Sergeant Marcel Lacoste, head of the investigation into the Hell's Angels killing, buys a copy of every newspaper with the story at a corner *tabagie*. He shows them to Apache Trudeau at the Bordeau jail and reminds him he'll be back on the street by the end of August.

"I have killed for them and now they want to kill me. That's gratitude?" an angry Trudeau says.

Sergeant Lacoste asks him to consider rolling over. Apache Trudeau, the most feared Angel in the world, a man dedicated to the outlaw biker lifestyle, listens. He discusses becoming a rat with his common-law wife and pleads guilty to a 1984 motorcycle theft to lengthen his stay in jail. Police move him to the fourth-floor cells of the Parthenais jail. Policemen, not prison guards, patrol this top security floor for informants and child molesters who would be murdered by other inmates.

Apache Trudeau talks.

"I was a dead man, anyways. I had decided to stop doing coke. I thought of my wife and my child."

Police sweep Angels off the streets. René Lamoureux, a 38-year-old former sniper with the US Marine Corps in Vietnam, is arrested on drug charges on Friday, August 30, in Valleyfield, 30 miles southwest of Montreal. Lamoureux is a former Angel and the club's official representative in the US.

Officer Jacques Ghibault cruises Montreal's streets alone on Sunday, September 1, 1985. He chases and stops a stolen chopper that makes an illegal left turn. Ghibault calls for backup before he frisks Zig-Zag Lessard and Bert Mayrand. He finds two stolen revolvers on them and a silencer-equipped submachine gun in a gym bag.

Coroner's inquests are held in Quebec to determine whether there is criminal responsibility in a death. There is little doubt in the case of the floating Angels. But the police need more evidence before they lay charges. The inquest becomes a fishing expedition. Angel lawyer Léo-René Maranda is an experienced defender of underworld figures. The sharp-eyed, 53-year-old lawyer is always on the lookout for flaws in the Crown's case and technicalities that can free his clients. These include Frank Cotroni, the reputed godfather of traditional organized crime in Quebec, and the French-Canadian Mafia of the Dubois brothers of Saint-Henri. Maranda defends the Angels under a shadow—he is charged earlier in the year, after a raid on his Westmount home, with possession of hashish, cocaine and marijuana for the purpose of trafficking.

Maranda stalls the inquest repeatedly with procedural motions and civil suits. He argues that Coroner John D'Arcy Asselin acts illegally when he issues arrest warrants for Angels before being sworn in. Then he forces Asselin to step down when he convinces a Superior Court judge to rule the coroner might be perceived as biased against the bikers who have filed a damage suit against him for ordering them held in jail during the inquest. The inquest continues under Coroner Jean-B. Falardeau on July 31, the day Detective de Francisco manipulates the press. Angel lawyers file a suit in Quebec Superior Court against Falardeau on the first day he hears testimony. They claim he has no authority to sit as coroner because he hasn't resigned his post as sessions court judge. They also say his appointment is illegal because the National Assembly is not in session when Justice Minister Pièrre Marc Johnson assigns him to the case. The inquest gets so bogged down that a citizen calls Liberal party justice critic Herbert Marx and complains that the Hell's Angels appear to be more powerful than the government.

Crown attorney René Domingue decides to end the inquest on Wednesday, October 2, 1985, and has 17 Hell's Angels charged with first-degree murder. Warrants are issued for another 10. Gerry ((Le Chat) Coulombe and Yves (Apache) Trudeau provide police with enough information to make a case

against the Angels. Most of the case is circumstantial, but
police can't wait in hope that more clues surface at the inquest. Angels who testify suffer frustrating memory lapses.
Then coroner Falardeau sets free in the last week of September Angels who have testified. Police want them in jail so
they don't disappear. They lay murder charges rather than
watch more suspected killers go free.

The police take a big risk. They still don't have a witness
to the killings inside the clubhouse. Luck is on their side.
They arrest Gilles (Le Nez) Lachance on Friday, February 21,
1986. He is angry at the club for killing brothers. He also
fears he may be forced to join the gang's diving club. He rolls
over. Three Angels in nine months rat on the club out of fear.
The Hell's Angels are their own worst enemy.

Police consider turning the oldest Angel, Yvon (Le Père)
Bilodeau. A few conversations convince them his mind is too
fucked up by cocaine to be a convincing witness.

Claude (Burger) Berger registers with the Quebec Superior
Court in Sherbrooke for a $15 fee on April 3, 1986, a Hell's
Angels defence fund—#457-15-000883-863. Berger is the
hardest working Hell's Angel in the province. He plays trumpet with the Quebec Symphony and teaches music for 10 years
at the CEGEP de Sherbrooke, a community college. The defence fund supplements the club's own money to pay lawyers
defending members on charges of murdering the five North
Angels. The fund solicits donations in return for T-shirts and
posters through advertisements in motorcycle magazines such
as *Easyriders*. The items read: "Free East Coast Canada," and
show a pair of hands shattering manacles. Supporters across
the continent send money to 375 rue Queen, Lennoxville,
Quebec, JIM 1K8—the clubhouse where the five Angels are
murdered. The Canadian Hell's Angels defence fund address
later changes to P. O. Box 1388, Place Bonaventure, Montreal, Canada, H5A 1H3.

Berger owns the Sherbrooke chapter clubhouse until he
sells it to the Hell's Angels de Sherbrooke Inc. after the Gitans
motorcycle club buries its colors and dons the Hell's Angels
death's head. Georges (Bo-Boy) Beaulieu is corporation president, Robert (Snake) Tremblay is vice-president, Charles
(Cash) Filteau is secretary-treasurer and Berger is administrator.

* * *

The raids and arrests that start in April 1985 shatter the Hell's Angels' expansionist dreams in Canada and cripple their East Coast operations. The entire Halifax chapter is jailed. Prospects man the clubhouse. Angels from British Columbia chapters fly out for two-week stints to keep the drug and prostitution business going. Halifax Angels Randall (Blondie) Mersereau, Frenchy Guernier and David (Wolf) Carroll are convicted of conspiring to live off the proceeds of prostitution on May 30, 1986 and receive one-year jail sentences.

Quebec Angels who aren't in jail work overtime to bolster the club's image and fend off a possible attack by the rival Outlaws. Friendly gangs stand guard at the Sherbrooke chapter clubhouse in Lennoxville. Angels outnumber Outlaws two to one before the arrests. Both clubs make sport of killing the other's members. But the Outlaws are less aggressive than the Angels. They run solid drug, prostitution and enforcement businesses in Montreal, Danville and Joliette. Most of the 31 Outlaws have steady jobs. They know an extended war will cripple the club and their income. Only a handful of Angels work. They'd rather party.

The Outlaws change tactics while the Angels are tied up fighting police. Outlaws with their colors sell drugs at a Verchères concert on Montreal's South Shore in the heart of Angel turf three weeks after the April 10 raids. No one bothers them. Outlaws colors are seen more frequently around the province. The gang recruits actively and stakes out new ground. They lay heavies on small-time drug dealers and force them to sell Outlaw coke, hash and speed. Members set up shop in the Arthabaska region and the local motorcycle gang —the Evil Ones, a Hell's Angel affiliate—stops wearing colors out of fear. Outlaws members even threaten an Evil One in court. Outlaws also gather intelligence on the Angels for a hit they hope will wipe out the gang in Quebec. The Outlaws are tired of living in fear. The club's arsenal is hidden on a member's farm. It includes 200 9mm and .45-calibre handguns, 30 grenades and a case of dynamite. The Quebec Outlaws also prepare to host their first international club run in Dundee, near the Quebec-Ontario-US borders in the summer of 1987. They spend more than a year securing the area against possible enemy attacks.

The Angels try their best to retain control of the province. They lay heavies on smaller gangs. Michel (Sky) Langlois, Hell's Angels national president in Canada, strips Evil Ones president Marc Bourassa of his colors and tells the club to get its shit together or all members will lose their colors and become fish food in the St. Lawrence River. The gang pays $200 a month to hang around with the Angels and gives part of the money from hold-ups in Drummondville, Victoriaville and Sherbrooke to the Hell's Angels defence fund. Bourassa gets his colors back on May 1, 1986, and the Evil Ones submit to the control of a fugitive Angel.

The Angels also strip the ZBeers in Saint-Hyacinthe of their colors and board up their clubhouse when they fail to pay a drug debt. The Angels charm other gangs. Berger takes two members of the Vikings from Matane to Paris. They are told at a meeting with the Hell's Angels and the Evil Ones in the Vikings clubhouse they will get their Angel colors and become an official chapter after they kill four Outlaws. A Viking called Flag beats up Gerry (Le Chat) Coulombe's brother-in-law in an attempt to find the informant. And Le Prof reactivates about 100 former gang members in the Shawinigan area.

Many Hell's Angels chapters around the world face membership problems in 1985 and 1986 because of arrests. The Lowell, Massachusetts, chapter reinstates retired members to keep the roster above the six members needed to keep a charter active. They also try to control gangs in the New England states to build an Angel front between Lowell and Quebec.

The Hell's Angels scramble for a while, but one year after the busts, most chapters appear to be stronger than they were before police raids. Some Angels are brazen enough to thank police for ridding them of weak members. Thirteen years of bloody war with the Outlaws have prepared them for the worst. The Hell's Angels are masters in their own house. And theirs is the house of death.

15

WAR: A WALK ON THE WILD SIDE

THE Breed are cocky outlaw bikers out to make a name for themselves in 1970. They recruit anyone on two wheels—Harleys or Hondas—and have chapters across the north-eastern US. They muscle into Hell's Angels' territory in Cleveland. Fights are commonplace between motorcycle gangs from their birth in 1945. Manhood, then profit, rides on fast fists and hard heads.

The Breed are ready to eliminate the Angels by March 7, 1971. More than 200 Breed from Ohio, New York, Pennsylvania and New Jersey arrive in cars, vans and motorcycles during the day at a barn in the Cleveland suburb of Brunswick. They get ready to rumble with the Angels at the Motorcycle Custom and Trade Show at the Hall of Polish Women on Cleveland's East Side. Older gang members encourage the 18- and 19-year-olds and tell them that no one leaves the hall as long as a Hell's Angel stands. Gang officers plan strategy in a downtown apartment. A police officer tips off the Angels, who consider tossing a few grenades through the windows to solve their problems. They reconsider. The Angels figure police guards won't let the Breed into the hall that night.

Twenty-five Angels display bikes at the show to raise money to buy wheelchairs for crippled children. Breed members march into the hall in platoons of 15 and 20 men one

hour after the doors open. Five police officers confiscate
clubs, chains and knives that some bikers brandish. The Breed
congregate around three Angel motorcycles. Someone yells:
"Now."

"When the fight got off, I started punching people," says
Clarence (Addie) Crouch, vice-president and founding
member of the Hell's Angels Cleveland chapter.

> I kept hitting this one kid. I hit him once, and I went to somebody
> else, and out of the corner of my eye I could see he didn't go
> down, and I turned around and hit him again, and I noticed his
> eyes were rolling back, and I looked over his head and there was
> an arm coming down with a knife in it and he stuck me in the
> chest.
>
> And he dropped the kid. And it was this guy about 35, bald,
> and he was grinning, and he grabbed me by the shoulder with his
> left hand and he had a knife pulling down in my chest over my
> heart, and his feet were almost off the floor, and he was pulling up
> on me, he was grinning at me. So, I pulled my knife and I hit him,
> and I killed him and that is the first person I ever killed. Then the
> fight went on, and I got stabbed again. And I went on and got
> stabbed again, and I got stabbed in the back and I woke up on the
> floor with my knife sticking in some guy.

About 150 policemen clear the hall within two minutes
with tear gas. The outcome of the fight, in which the Hell's
Angels are outnumbered eight to one, illustrates why they are
considered the meanest and most powerful outlaw motorcycle
gang in the world. Four Breed and one Angel are stabbed to
death. Twenty-eight Breed nurse stab wounds. Three policemen are injured. It is the beginning of a long, frightening
battle for the Breed. The Angels declare war on the club. The
Angels never do anything half-assed. They set up intelligence
teams to gather information on the Breed. They appoint security officers to protect the club. They equip hit men.

It is the Angels' first all-out war and they quickly learn
something the American military can't fathom in Vietnam—
guerrilla warfare is the only way to wear down a mobile
enemy. Breed members are ambushed, run off the road and
beaten when they least expect it. Ten Hell's Angels roar
through Staten Island behind two Breed bikers later in 1971.
An Angel shoots. One Breed tumbles and is run over by the

pack. The other Breed loses control and falls. The Angels beat him.

War with the Breed introduces the Angels to a new kind of violence and cements their reputation for taking care of business. The skills and taste for blood they acquire in the early 1970s prepare them for the bloodiest and most sophisticated confrontation between two outlaw motorcycle gangs—war with the Outlaws.

The pressure of war takes its toll on the Breed by the mid-1970s. Resignations and defections hurt the club. James (Gorilla) Harwood, a 300-pound dog killer and drug dealer, joins the Breed on July 4, 1971. He fights the Hell's Angels for six years until he finds a bomb stuck to the side of his house early in 1977. He calls the police, then the Angels, whose number he gets from a recruitment poster in a motorcycle shop. Harwood and four other Breed become Angel prospects on July 4, 1977. They kill a Breed member to prove their loyalty. They become New York state's fourth Angel chapter in Troy on August 23, 1978. Harwood is excellent Angel material. He gets pissed off at a neighbor's dog and beats it to death with a hammer in his basement. He freezes the pet and stands it upside down by the neighbor's door.

The war between the Hell's Angels and the Outlaws starts with Peter (Greased Lightning) Rogers' visit to old haunts in 1974. Two Satan's Soldiers who cruise the Bronx spot Greased Lightning in a shop. Bikers have long memories. They recall that Sandy Alexander put the word out after his wife's rape in 1969 that he wants Rogers alive. Greased Lightning, when he returns to New York in 1974, is national enforcer for the Chicago-based Outlaws. That means fuck all to the Hell's Angels.

The Satan's Soldiers call Vincent (Big Vinnie) Girolamo, a charter member and sergeant-at-arms of the Hell's Angels Manhattan chapter. Girolamo is the quintessential Hell's Angel: tall, massive and mean. His body is covered with tattoos and he sports rings on all fingers. He also wears chains and leather wrist bands studded with hooks he uses to rip out eyes. Big Vinnie Girolamo holds Greased Lightning until Sandy Alexander arrives.

Sandy Alexander is no punk. The pro boxer guarantees

Greased Lightning a fair fight then takes him into the street
and beats him for 20 minutes. The Angels leave him for dead.
Greased Lightning crawls back to Outlaw territory and cries to
the gang that a dozen Angels beat him. The face-saving lie by
the man who becomes Outlaws national enforcer and president
of the club's central region leads to a massacre a few months
later that triggers the war. The Outlaws must avenge the beating of Greased Lightning to save face.

The opportunity comes in April 1974. Albert (Oskie) Simmons skips out of the Hell's Angels Lowell, Massachusetts,
chapter in the early 1970s with club money. He drifts to Florida where he hangs around a motorcycle shop near Orlando.
He complies with a standing club order from Sonny Barger,
president of the Hell's Angels Oakland chapter, that a member
who quits in bad standing must remove the death's head tattoo
and lettering from his arm. He sits around the motorcycle shop
and blanks the letters out with a needle and ink. He covers the
H, the *E*, and starts on the *S*. Two Angels from Simmons' old
chapter track him down at the motorcycle shop to check out
his tattoo in mid-April 1974. Edward Thomas (Riverboat)
Riley, 34, and George F. (Whiskey George) Hartman, 28, are
not the type of men you want on your tail. They're both
wanted for murder.

Big Jim Nolan, president of the Outlaws tough South Florida chapter, hears that the Angels are in town. He calls a
meeting on Friday, April 26, to discuss what the club should
do about the presence in their territory of the maggots who
beat brother Greased Lightning. (Nolan has twice been acquitted of ordering their murder. He is currently indicted in the
killings.) The Outlaws hang out at the Pastime Bar the next
day and wait for the Angels to show up at the nearby motorcycle shop to talk to Simmons. The smiling Outlaws befriend
the three Angels and invite them to a piss-up at their clubhouse. The two visiting Angels explain they aren't wearing
colors out of respect for Outlaw territory. When enough wine
and beer is put back, an Outlaw argues that they shouldn't
drink with scum. Everyone agrees.

The Angels are tied up and loaded into a van by four Outlaws: William (Gatemouth) Edson; Norman (Spider) Riesinger, a visitor from the Chicago chapter; (Funky) Tim Amis,
who is stabbed to death by a prison turd burglar in 1980 for
refusing to be corn holed, drives the van; and Ralph (Lucifer)

Yanotta, who carries a sawed-off shotgun. They stop at a flooded rockpit near Andytown. The three Angels are lined up facing the water, arms tied behind their backs with pink clothesline and eight concrete blocks tied to their legs. Riesinger literally blows their brains out with a 12-gauge shotgun. The killers sit around for a while to smoke and drink beer. A man spots a foot with a blue sock bobbing in the water on Wednesday, May 1. A diver pulls out the bearded, tattooed bodies.

Clarence (Addie) Crouch from Cleveland and Howie Weisbrod from the Manhattan chapter investigate the murder at the request of Sandy Alexander, who fears police killed the Angels to set the club against the Outlaws. They return to Cleveland and blame the killings on the Outlaws. The Hell's Angels East Coast officers and representatives from all chapters meet in Cleveland in 1974 to declare all-out war on the Outlaws.

Both clubs build up their arsenals and plan hits. The Outlaws get jittery. The South Florida chapter kidnaps from bars and homes 10 people they suspect of gathering addresses for Brand X—their codeword for Angels. They also call Angels maggots because they eat their own kind. Gatemouth Edson sits his bound victims in tubs of water into which he dips an electrical cord to make them talk. He takes the silent ones into the Everglades and makes them dig their graves. He realizes he's got the wrong people when they still don't talk.

Harry (Stairway) Henderson, Outlaws national president, orders all Florida clubhouses surrounded with a cinderblock wall equipped with gunports. Guards must be posted 24 hours a day and clubhouses have to be stocked with enough weapons to fight off enemies. Every Outlaws clubhouse has at least two signs: "GFOD" (God Forgives, Outlaws Don't) and "AHAMD" (All Hell's Angels Must Die). This sign hangs upside down. Stairway Harry orders that one gang member only will pick up old ladies and mamas from their jobs rather than have each Outlaw pick up his woman. This ensures enough members are in the clubhouse to fend off an attack. It also minimizes the chance of Outlaws being caught alone on the street. Outlaws from northern chapters are transferred south, where they don't don colors, to gather intelligence. Stairway Harry orders members to ditch stolen motorcycles and buy legitimate wheels to reduce the chances of being arrested and locked up.

Five members of the Jacksonville chapter head for the nearest motorcycle shop. Stairway Harry bans drugs in clubhouses and bars entry to all but color-wearing members. All members must contribute to the club's war fund to buy weapons, dynamite and grenades.

The precautions pay off. The Angels machine-gun Outlaw clubhouses in Atlanta, Jacksonville, South Florida and Ohio in 1975. No members are shot. Outlaw (Horrible) Harry Ross, a Vietnam veteran, teaches members from every chapter how to use explosives at a training camp in the Everglades that year. The former US navy commando gets plastic explosives, guns and grenades from his friends in military bases. He rigs booby traps and remote-control bombs in his spare time. One of his pet projects is figuring out how to insert a 12-guage shotgun shell in a motorcycle frame center post with a trip wire to the rear wheel. The discharge will tear the ass and spine off the person who starts the bike.

Three Satan's Choice chapters in Ontario and one in Quebec don Outlaws colors in the spring of 1977. Ross arms the Windsor and Montreal chapters later in the year with six cases of grenades from Florida and machine guns for the impending conflict with the Hell's Angels. Chapters in Youngstown, Ohio, and Detroit also supply weapons to Canadian Outlaw chapters. Quebec is the largest red zone—where both clubs kill each other for drug turf—in North America.

The Windsor Outlaws' clubhouse is a farm outside the city until April 1978. They move into a concrete-block building on Crawford Street for better protection against an Angel attack. They also inform the local police they are at war with the Angels and ask them to be alert for the bikers in their neighborhood. They give police licence numbers of suspicious cars. When police seize their guns they say they'll get more—not to shoot lawmen or to commit crimes, but for protection.

The Outlaws in Charlotte, North Carolina—another red zone—move their clubhouse from West Boulevard in March 1981 to 5420 Howard Street in North Mecklenburg, near the black section of Hunter Acres.

"Anybody white that comes around here and we don't know 'em, we know they don't belong," chapter president (Larry Mack) McDaniel says. McDaniel, a deadly knife fighter who shaves his head and sports a handlebar moustache, is former president of the Outlaws Atlanta chapter before he moves to Charlotte.

The two Outlaws chapters in North Carolina—the other is in Lexington—face tremendous pressure from three Hell's Angels chapters in Charlotte, Durham and Winston-Salem. These Angels chapters are among the most heavily armed in the club. Charlotte Angels are ready to die to maintain their charter. Members from other chapters visit to help set up security and gather intelligence on Outlaws. North Carolina is the halfway point in the Miami–New York drug pipeline and three of the Big Four outlaw motorcycle gangs maintain chapters in the state. Loss of a foothold there would hurt the clubs financially.

The Outlaws' white frame clubhouse 50 miles northeast of Charlotte is called Fort Lexington. It is surrounded by a 12-foot wooden fence reinforced with concrete blocks on two sides. The Angels' clubhouse in Charlotte until 1980 is a one-story building off Rozzelle's Ferry Road called the Alamo. It has gun slits for windows.

The Durham Hell's Angels chapter is formed on July 24, 1973, from the ruthless Storm Troopers motorcycle club. The Storm Troopers attack a van that carries six Pagans and an old lady on their way north from Florida on I-85 outside Durham on June 30, 1972. Two Pagans are killed and the five other passengers are wounded as 34 bullets rip through the van. Six Storm Troopers are charged with murder, but the Pagans don't return to testify. Outlaw bikers don't trust the police and the courts. They mete out their own justice.

"Every dog has his day," one Pagan leader, Mike (White Bear) Grayson, says in Pilot Mountain, North Carolina.

The Pagans whip the Outlaws in a bloody rumble during bike week at Daytona, Florida, in the spring of 1976. They have a special patch made to commemorate the event. The baby blue, red-rimmed patch features an upside down Charlie —the ultimate insult among bikers.

The Outlaws miss bike week for the first time 10 years later in 1986 when corrupt leaders and mass arrests throw Florida chapters into disarray. The South Florida chapter is reduced to two members. Veteran Outlaw Wayne Hicks is sent to Florida from Toledo to rebuild the club. He is helped by old-line Outlaws from around the country. The Hell's Angels

take advantage of the Outlaws' weakness in 1986. They show
up at bike week and hire a plane to fly a banner that reads:
Support Your Local Hell's Angels. The Outlaws show up in
full force at bike week in 1987, where the most common cry
uttered by bikers at women is "Show your tits." Many comply.

The Angels, who are more practiced at intelligence gathering and warfare, spook the Outlaws. Angels in colors walk
into Outlaws motorcycle shops and browse. They discreetly
leave miniature bugs with long wire aerials near the main
counter. They sit in their cars and listen to conversations in the
shop through radios tuned to FM 93. They photograph Outlaws called in by the clerk to discuss the visit.

The Outlaws use the guise of war to clean house. Three
Outlaws and two associates are shot in the two-room, green
frame clubhouse in Charlotte, North Carolina, on July 4,
1979. William (Mouse) Dronenburg, 31, Randall Feazell, 28,
Leonard (Terrible Terry) Henderson, 29, William Allen, 22,
and Bridgette Benfield, 22, are riddled with bullets. The club
blames the Angels. But a member on guard duty is shot while
he sits on a side porch with a gun on his lap. The others are
shot as they sleep. There is no struggle. The Outlaws are a
cautious lot by 1979, especially in the Carolinas. No one gets
near the clubhouse unless he is well known. Curiously, the
killing comes a day after a nearby meeting of the club's national executive.

The Charlotte clubhouse is heavily secured after the killings. The Outlaws post a 24-hour guard outside and install an
alarm system that rings when a car comes down the street.
Guard dogs patrol the walled-in yard. Outlaw leaders in Charlotte and Lexington are so worried the murders are committed
by their own members they conduct lie-detector tests. They
put a 9mm gun barrel in members' mouths and ask them to tell
the truth.

Marked men don't last long in the world of outlaw motorcycle gangs. Outlaw Tommy Stroud takes five .45-caliber
slugs in the head while he uses a pay phone outside a Belha-
ven Boulevard florist shop in Charlotte on February 23, 1981.
His father, police captain Wade Stroud, investigates the killing.

The Hell's Angels are as nervous as the Outlaws. The president and intelligence officer in Cleveland get on Clarence

(Addie) Crouch's case for not having killed an Outlaw. They order him to cut down a shotgun and they set up a hit at an Outlaw meeting. Another Angel has a machine gun. The driver has a .45-calibre pistol.

"There was a bunch of people standing outside and it was dark and we pulled up an' stopped, and the machine gun opened up, and I started shooting," says Crouch. "I shot a window out. I shot a bike. I shot up the driveway and I hit somebody. . . . It turned out to be a 17-year-old kid."

Crouch takes time out from business in Memphis to have his appearance upgraded in 1976 and seizes an opportunity to take care of business.

> I was in a tattoo shop getting a tattoo on my arm, and a lot of Outlaws walked in and one of the Outlaws had "Outlaws, Memphis" on his back with their center logo, and I put 80 stitches in his back with a big X through it. . . . I made him an X member. Ha ha.

The war between the Hell's Angels and the Outlaws is not only a vendetta, but a desperate grab for the North American drug market. The Outlaws are happy to sell enough drugs to make them filthy rich; the Angels are expansionists. They want it all. The battle for the veins and pleasure centers of Canada best exemplifies the Angel philosophy. Quebec Angels are the most vicious and conscienceless bikers in the world. They have no qualms about killing and compete with each other to prove their bloodlust. Two months and 10 days after Quebec's scuzzy Popeyes become Hell's Angels, the first shots are fired in the battle with the Outlaws. Many Charlies die before an Angel is felled.

Although violence among Quebec bikers escalates with the arrival of the Angels and the Outlaws in 1977, murder is nothing new to the long-haired Neanderthals who terrorize the province. The Popeyes, the Satan's Choice and the Devil's Disciples shoot, bomb and knife each other to control drug trafficking in Montreal. Some bikers weary of the pace. It's one thing to party and fight for the hell of it, but the struggle for the drug market is too heavy for them.

A hefty biker called Gunner quits the Satan's Choice in Montreal in the early 1970s. His friends strip him of his colors and beat him unconscious. Gunner enrolls in a film studies course at the University of Ottawa. He keeps a reminder of his wilder days in the closet of his university residence room: rifles, spiked brass knuckles and his favorite weapon, a shortened baseball bat thickly wrapped with electrician's tape melted together with a torch. Gunner goes on periodic fag-bashing sprees with the bat, and kicks the shit out of a car and its driver who honks at him for crossing the road too slowly. He shares his residence room one year with another outlaw biker from Winnipeg. A horny brunette spends a semester in the room hoping back and forth from bed to bed greasing their dicks.

University life is like retirement for the biker. His silent, blonde girlfriend, whom he brags can accommodate a Mack truck, photographs the stern biker as he poses with his baseball bat against the pristine white tiles in the men's washroom. Every once in a while, he merges his photographic skills with his penchant for violence. When another student smashes a prowler's face in the stairwell at 3 a.m., Gunner follows and photographs the trail of blood four floors down to a basement sink.

"Shit, man, all I have is black-and-white film."

Canada's second largest city supports three heavy-duty bike gangs, a Calabrian and a French-Canadian Mafia, the West End Gang of safecrackers and truck hijackers, top-notch bank robbers and festering cells of terrorist separatists in the 1960s and 1970s. Montreal police director Jean-Paul Gilbert forms special squads to combat "wild hippies" and bikers in June 1968.

"We must have peace on our streets, and my department will do everything in its power to see that every citizen be free to go about his business without fear or hindrance."

Even separatist demonstrations are "less of a problem than those uncouth motorcycle gangs and those dirty, pot-smoking hippies."

Montreal, like all major cities across North America in the late 1960s, is in the throws of the pharmaceutical revolution. Underground chemists produce cheap highs for a rebellious generation and bikers are the go-betweens. Widespread political corruption, bordellos and gambling dens earn Montreal the nickname Sodom on the St. Lawrence in the 1940s and 1950s. The body count from the war to control drug trafficking in the 1970s makes it Canada's murder capital.

* * *

Although the bikers fight among themselves, they don't fuck with the mob. Claude Dubois, drug mogul of the nine-brother French-Canadian Mafia, controls drug trafficking in downtown Montreal in the early 1970s. He takes over Saint-Louis Square—the nerve-center of the city's drug trade—from the Devil's Disciples in 1975. Fifteen Disciples die during the 1974–75 speed war between two rival factions of the gang fighting for control of methamphetamine production and distribution. They later regroup as the Huns in 1977. No one complains when Dubois takes over their downtown turf. Claude Ellefsen, alias Johnny Halliday, leader of the Disciples faction that sells drugs in the square, talks about the takeover in a telephone conversation with mobster Jean-Guy Giguère:

Halliday: "Another thing . . . Dubois, the big one. . . ."

Giguère: "Hm . . . hm. . . ."

Halliday: "He knows I was makin' money out of dope you know. . . ."

Giguère: "Oh! yeah."

Halliday: "Like, he wanted to take over my business."

Giguère: "Oh! Maybe."

Halliday: "Like, you know, I didn't bug him, man, I just got the hell out."

Giguère: "Yeah."

Halliday: "I started business somewhere else."

Giguère comes from a meeting with Dubois. He tells Halliday that Dubois wants to kill the biker and Pierre McDuff, his right-hand man. McDuff is murdered in his car a few days later. Halliday sets up a methamphetamine laboratory in Quebec City.

The Satan's Choice in Quebec smuggle drugs from Asia and Europe to peddle all over North America from 1971 to 1975. They discover the joys of home chemistry in 1974 and set up clandestine methamphetamine laboratories with the Devil's Disciples. The Choice, under the presidency of Joseph (Sonny) Lacombe, manufacture their speed under the guise of legitimate chemical distributors, wax, soap and laboratory equipment manufacturers by 1977. The Choice are as professional as any outlaw motorcycle gang in the spring of 1977 when the Outlaws want the club to sport their colors. The

Outlaws meet little resistance absorbing Montreal's Rockers in February 1978, two months after the Hell's Angels take over the Popeyes.

The Popeyes are Quebec's most powerful club in 1977, with chapters in Gatineau, Montreal, Sorel, Trois-Rivieres and Drummondville, where they absorb the Mongols. These rapists, thieves, killers, bombers and drug traffickers are allied with dozens of rural gangs across the province. They also have strong ties to gangs in Alberta, Manitoba, Nova Scotia and Ontario, which they visit regularly. This network, and its potential for expansion, attracts the Hell's Angels. So do the Popeyes' violent inclinations. Gilbert Groleau and Richard Bertrand are pissed off at the way prisoners are disciplined at Archambault penitentiary. They blow up a car in the prison disciplinary officer's driveway on June 28, 1975. They sympathize with punk on the lam, Richard (Le Chat) Blass, and his letter campaign for better treatment of inmates before he is killed in January 1975. The two bikers decide to blow up a subway station to support prisoners' rights. The bomb goes off prematurely.

The Angels and the Outlaws party heavily for years with the clubs they want to take over in Quebec. The Hell's Angels party harder and travel more than the Outlaws. They befriend more clubs and establish a larger drug network. While they build bridges, they watch the gangs slowly destroy each other in a war over turf. When the Satan's Choice are scared enough, and when the Popeyes are greedy enough, the American clubs move in. Now that they have a foothold, the Angels are poised to expand. But they can't do that until they prove to outlaw bikers across the country they mean business. The Quebec Hell's Angels travel to Boston and New York early in 1978 to talk business with their US brothers.

The slaughter begins on February 15, 1978. Robert Côté, 22, and a friend sit in the Brasserie Joey at the corner of Saint-Hubert and Castelnau drinking beer. Both former rockers have recently joined the Outlaws in the working class district of St. Henri. Joey's is a Hell's Angels hangout and the bikers start arguing. The Outlaws are thrown out. Shots from a passing car hit Côté in the head and graze the other Outlaw. Côté dies in hospital on February 20. Hell's Angel hit man

Yves (Apache) Trudeau draws first blood in the club's feud
with the Outlaws.

Outraged Outlaws show their strength at Côté's funeral.
Three hundred Outlaws from across the US and Ontario attend
to intimidate the Hell's Angels. Three are known hit men
whom police escort to the border. Harold D. (Old Man) Scog-
gan, a 72-year-old resident of Tampa under whose name the
local Outlaws clubhouse is registered, is among the mourners.
The world's oldest biker dies in 1985.

Gilles Cadorette, the 27-year-old leader of the Montreal
Outlaws, walks out of a Bordeaux Street bar with Donald
McLean at 8 p.m. on Tuesday, March 21. They climb into
Cadorette's custom-painted Camaro parked at the curb. A
bomb under the car explodes to kill Cadorette and seriously
injure McLean.

Two Hell's Angels knock on the door on the Outlaws clubhouse at 144 rue Saint-Ferdinand on Tuesday, April 25. Denis
(Le Curé) Kennedy and Grosse Plotte want a sitdown to discuss ending the killings. The outlaws let them in. The Angels
pull out automatic pistols after a few minutes and start firing.
One pistol jams. The other nervous gunman sprays everything
but his many targets before they escape.

Athanase (Tom Thumb) Markopoulos walks 50 feet from
the Outlaws clubhouse to the Dépanneur Paul corner store to
buy cigarettes at 11 p.m. the following night. The 21-year-old
Outlaw bangs on the locked glass door until the frightened
woman who runs the store slowly approaches in the darkness.
She watches as someone in the shadows pumps six .45-calibre
slugs into Markopoulos. He spins and falls on his back near
the curb where he dies with crossed legs. Two hit men flee in
a green car. The Outlaws clubhouse empties at the sound of
gunshots. The members, expecting a police raid, pile into one
car and speed away with their stash of guns and drugs.

It is well known in Montreal early in 1978 that one is likely
to get shot hanging out in a biker bar. A hooded gunman
walks into the Brasserie Industriel on rue Notre Dame and
wounds Outlaw François Poliseno, 25, and his 19-year-old
girlfriend Suzanne Harvey on Thursday, April 27. Police stop
a green car near the Hell's Angels' clubhouse 10 minutes later.
They find Le Curé and Grosse Plotte in the car, along with a
hood, a toy pistol, binoculars and a bullet-proof vest. Ballis-

tics tests show the bullets that hit Poliseno are fired from the same gun that missed hitting everyone in the Outlaws clubhouse two nights earlier.

The Outlaws blow their first hit attempt on May 12. Rene Hébert is grazed by a bullet as he walks out of the Angels' clubhouse.

The war between the two clubs forces street people to take sides. The smart ones don't. Jean Gonthier, a 22-year-old inmate in the Saint-Vincent-de-Paul penitentiary argues with Paul Ringuette on May 26 that the Outlaws are the better club. Ringuette, a Hell's Angels associate, beats the man to death. The official notice says the men argued over a hockey game.

Ringuette escapes from prison on a day pass in the spring of 1984. He runs to Orlando, Florida, with his girlfriend, Brigitte McCurdy. They meet Robert (Squirrel) Barrett by the swimming pool in early June. They do drugs and sightsee together. Barrett is looking for someone to kill the wife of Helmuth Buxbaum, a millionaire nursing-home owner in Kokoma, Ontario. Buxbaum goes middle-age crazy and wants to get rid of his wife so he can indulge in prostitutes without guilt. Barrett learns of Ringuette's Angel connection and offers him $10,000 to kill Hanna Buxbaum. Barrett gives Ringuette Polaroid pictures of the woman, a map of the London-Kokoma area and a $500 advance. He tells Ringuette to return to Florida with the woman's ring to collect the rest of the money. Ringuette never kills Hanna Buxbaum. Someone else does. Ringuette is arrested shoplifting in Calgary, Alberta, and returned to prison in Laval, Quebec, where he is serving 17 years for manslaughter and robbery.

René (Baloune) Francoeur, a member of Trois-Rivières club affiliated with the Hell's Angels is beaten to death. He might be a victim of the war or of greed. He pays a pusher with counterfeit money.

Angel Adrien (Pistache) Fleury is blown away with a 12-gauge shotgun in a Sorel hotel on July 25 after he steals a Harley. The death has nothing to do with the war, but gives the Angels a chance to show their strength. Angels from all North American chapters and affiliated clubs show up to ooze power. They turf out the undertaker on the last night of the wake, get stoned and screw all over the funeral home—any excuse to party.

Another Outlaw death might be accidental. François Ouellette's car rolls over near Chateauguay after a wheel falls off.

The Outlaws pull off their first successful hit seven months after the Hell's Angels fire the first shot in the battle for Quebec. Guy (Gator) Davies, a member of the Wild Ones Motorcycle Club in Hamilton, Ontario, sits in Montreal's Le Café Tourbillon on rue Beaubien with a group of Hell's Angels on October 12. His club wants to become the first Hell's Angels chapter in Canada's largest and wealthiest province. The go-go girls finish their show and start walking off the stage. Two well-dressed men, who patrons believe are off-duty policemen, finish their drinks and walk by the Angels. They cooly pull out guns and shoot everyone at the table. Jean Brochu and Georges (Chico) Mousseau die on the spot. Davies dies in hospital two days later. Angels Louis (Ti-Oui) Lapièrre and Bruno Coulombe are wounded. The hit men, one from Detroit, one from Miami, stalk the Angels for days and hit them in a bar they rarely frequent. The Angels know all the Outlaws in Montreal. The smaller gang doesn't hesitate to use outside talent for jobs it can't pull off discreetly.

The Angels retaliate on Saturday, November 10. Apache Trudeau pumps nine .45-calibre slugs into the head of Brian Powers, former Outlaws president, as he opens the door of his west Montreal home. Once again, the Outlaws turn out in force for the funeral. This time, though, two Ontario clubs join them—an indication clubs in the province have joined forces to keep the Hell's Angels out. The Vagabonds and Para-Dice Riders from Toronto have lucrative drug and prostitution businesses they don't want to share with the Angels.

Two Hell's Angels approach William Weichold on December 8, 1978, as he walks up to a house he rents from an Outlaw in west Montreal's Greenfield Park neighborhood. "Are you Roxy?" asks Apache Trudeau. He shoots before Weichold can answer no. The most prolific hit man in Angeldom pulls a boner. He doesn't care.

He gets the right man on Thursday, March 29, 1979, when he blows up Roland Dutemple and his car in Longueuil. Dutemple fingers the Angels and Gator Davies for the Outlaws at Le Café Tourbillon in 1978.

Apache Trudeau shoots 25-year-old Robert Labelle twice in the face as he answers the door of his Faberville home on Tuesday, April 3. Labelle, a clothing importer and drug trafficker, is former president of the Huns, who are merging with the Outlaws. Trudeau doesn't like competition.

It is Donald McLean's fate to die violently. The 30-year-old Outlaw and his 22-year-old girlfriend Carmen Piché mount his 1963 Harley in the laneway behind their apartment building at 193 4ième avenue in Verdun on Tuesday, May 9, 1979. The thick-set, bearded McLean kick starts the bike and triggers a bomb planted by Apache Trudeau, Yves (Le Boss) Buteau and Jean-Pierre (Matt le Crosseur) Mathieu. Someone marks the spot with a *Playboy* magazine after the ambulances take the corpses away.

The Angels rent an apartment near the Outlaws' clubhouse in Joliette to spy on their rivals. They keep a submachine gun and two revolvers handy.

Four Outlaws out for a Sunday drive on northern Ontario's Highway 17 on Sunday, July 17, 1983, go slackjawed as they pass a Greyhound bus—a winged skull grins at them from a window. The almighty Hell's Angels are travelling on the cheap. The driver eases off the accelerator and follows the bus to the middle-of-nowhere town of Wawa. Inside the bus, Michel (Jinx) Genest and Jean-Marc Nadeau, of the redoubted North chapter, sit stoned on PCP with a 17-year-old girl. They are going to British Columbia to celebrate the Satan's Angels' conversion to Hell's Angels one month earlier. Genest and Nadeau buy hamburgers while passengers embark in Wawa. A car races by and bullets pierce the windows as the Angels board the bus. All they see is Charlie smiling through the car's back window. No one is hurt, but the trip is ruined. Police find 56 grams of PCP inside a cigarette package in the depot and two handguns in a trash container outside. Angels travel light.

Nadeau gets his revenge on April 4, 1984. The thick-necked, 29-year-old Angel walks into the Domino bar in Montreal's east end and fires his .357 Magnum at Outlaw Normand Labbe. The member of the Angels Filthy Few is nervous. His best shot severs Labbe's spine. The injury confines the biker to a wheelchair for life.

Daniel Savoie, 33-year-old Outlaws president, and member John Galipeau, 30, drive along the highway near St. Norbert one month later, on Monday, May 21. A motorcycle pulls up beside the car. Two Angels rake the car with a submachine gun and a pistol. They return to the stopped car and finish the job. The Savois are unlucky. Thirty-year-old Bernard blows up with his car on March 22. Robert, 23, ends up in hospital full of bullet holes in April.

The skirmish spills over to the Canadian capital of Ottawa, an Outlaw stronghold on the Ontario-Quebec border. The Bad News and the Satan's Choice, who become Outlaws in 1977, fight continually during the 1970s for control of the speed market. Bad News president Gordon Martin tries to bomb the car of Choice president Frank Shaw in 1973. Choice cars are bombed in 1973 and 1976. A Windsor Outlaw is shot while driving on Ottawa's Queensway in July 1976.

Martin's car blows up on Prince Albert Street in January 1977, shredding his girlfriend Nancy Larose's right arm at the shoulder and her left leg at the knee. He lives. Two gunmen break up a poker game in a ground-floor apartment on Iris Street in November by shooting three of seven players through a window.

Quebec Angels cross the border to Ottawa regularly to chat up local bike gangs and to size up the Bad News. This gang is so rattled by warfare with the Outlaws in 1978 it offers the Angels $100,000 in speed for help. The Angels back off. The News don't have enough jam for the big leagues.

Two Montreal Angels who live in Hamilton make life tough for local Outlaws. Richard Williams, the 37-year-old Outlaws president in the steel city, is sentenced to 16 months in jail on November 9, 1984, for possession of eight handguns and four sticks of dynamite found near the gang's east-end clubhouse in 1983. Crown attorney Laverne Urban tells County Court Judge Walter Stayshyn that Williams should not be prohibited from carrying a gun after his release because he fears being attacked by Hell's Angels. The judge agrees. Prohibition is mandatory only if a gun is used to commit an offence.

War between the Hell's Angels and the Outlaws leaves bodies in gutters across the continent.

Ronald Edward Brown drops in to the Tom Thumb Grill on Rozzelle's Ferry Road in Charlotte, North Carolina, just before midnight on June 8, 1981. The 20-year-old Brown usually doesn't frequent the Hell's Angels' hangout, but his favorite club is closed. He never makes it inside. An Outlaw plugs him in the head from a passing car. He dies eight hours later, an innocent victim of the war.

The Charlotte Hell's Angels take their joyride in Outlaw territory on June 27. Angels in a green van and a dark pickup truck speed through a parking lot behind Live Models, a Wilkinson Boulevard massage parlor run by Outlaws, and fire shotguns at six men who eat watermelon. Mark Gilbert, a 23-year-old Outlaw associate, dies. Mitch Hoover, the 24-year-old bouncer, is wounded. The Outlaw the Angels want to kill walks into the building seconds before the shooting.

"They were in the wrong place at the wrong time," Outlaws president (Larry Mack) McDaniel says.

The war with the Angels does not temper the Outlaws' badass streak. Like good bikers, they continue to terrorize the meek. A young woman surprises four Outlaws breaking into her Pointe-aux-Trembles, Quebec, apartment on October 12, 1978. They beat her, rape her and make her suck their cocks. Outlaws shoot two uniformed apprentice firemen—one in the head, one in the leg—during a discussion about bikers in a rue Sherbrooke restaurant on November 13. Both live. Two Outlaws approach Detective-Sergeant Normand Ostiguy as he sips his coffee in an east Montreal restaurant on November 25. They tell him they don't like cops and beat him senseless with ashtrays and sugar dispensers. Policemen who come to Ostiguy's aid kill Outlaw Jean-Marc Patenaude during a shootout. The biker is the heavy and right-hand man for Ziggy Wiseman, Montreal's massage parlor king. The Outlaws take over a ferry on the Ottawa River in June 1979 and run circles for two hours. The operator is too scared to complain to police.

Both clubs are edgy. The Hell's Angels warn police officers to wear uniforms when they approach the clubhouse or members on the street so they aren't mistaken for enemy bikers or hit men and shot. The Angels, even as they fight an enemy at home, explore the country for gangs they can take over. Many smaller gangs buckle under their pressure. Frightened old-time weekend bikers hang up their colors. They won't risk their lives for the gang. Natural selection in the world of outlaw motorcycle gangs: the toughest, cruellest and greediest hog the road, the broads and the business.

The aggressive Hell's Angels spread their wings from coast to coast and control nine of Canada's 10 provinces by 1984. The Outlaws control the largest and most lucrative province, Ontario. The Angels have four chapters and about 72 members in British Columbia, three chapters with 69 members in Quebec, and an eight-man chapter in Halifax, Nova Scotia. They are affiliated to major clubs in Alberta, Saskatchewan, Manitoba, New Brunswick and Newfoundland. The Rebels in Edmonton, Alberta, and the Vikings in Matane, Quebec, are the two clubs most likely to become Hell's Angels chapters next. The Outlaws control the largest and most lucrative province, Ontario, where they have 85 members in eight chapters. Their 38 members in Quebec chapters are boxed in by Angels.

The Hell's Angels do to themselves in March 1985 what the Outlaws fail to achieve during eight years of war—they liquidate Quebec's North chapter after killing five longtime members during a party at the Lennoxville clubhouse, and draw police heat that paralyzes the club. The Outlaws mock the maggots. They drop anti-Angel leaflets on the streets from Montreal to Joliette and staple photocopied derogatory posters to telephone poles during the July 1985 funeral of Outlaw Carl (Carlos) Hannan, who dies from a heroin overdose. The leaflets and posters show five Hell's Angels wrapped in sleeping bags floating in the St. Lawrence River. Sharks spit out the shit-tasting Angels after they take a bite.

Police allow the mourning Outlaws, as they do all bikers at funerals, to ride their motorcycles bareheaded. It is not a compassionate gesture. Police want photographs of the bikers without their helmets for their intelligence records. But they won't let them fire a last salute with their guns as Outlaws in the US do after every member shovels a clod of dirt on the coffin—no one but an Outlaw throws dirt on an Outlaw. The first six mourning shots fired at the funeral of an Ontario biker thunder in a rain-soaked Burlington cemetery in April 1987 at the burial of Para-Dice Rider Sean (Pigpen) McCabe. Someone slits the biker's throat and torches the body in the back of his father's station wagon parked on the shoulder of the Queen Elizabeth Way near St. Catharines, Ontario.

Police raid the Outlaws Montreal clubhouse on Tuesday, March 17, 1987. They find hundreds of photographs of Hell's Angels clipped from newspapers during trials pasted to the walls. The Outlaws want to make sure they recognize Angels, their associates and women, on the street.

The war consumes the Hell's Angels, who spend their time and money figuring out ways to protect their asses and kill

Outlaws. Members are reemed out at church for not gathering enough intelligence or rolling bones. The shooting is indiscriminate.

"The killings just kind of got out of hand," says Clarence (Addie) Crouch, of the Cleveland chapter. "There was women and children killed."

No one is innocent in the world of outlaw motorcycle gangs. Just unlucky. Angels and Outlaws shoot and bomb each other in cities across Canada and the US. The Outlaws have a plan they hope to implement some day. They want to hit hundreds of Angels during an annual run. The war exacts a heavy toll not only in bodies, but in lifestyle.

> They are down to only about one or two runs a year now [Addie Crouch says]. Because of the war—the war stopped a lot of their freedom of moving around on bikes and everything, which contributed to a lot of them cleaning up. They are not the same as they used to be—greasy, dirty, long hair and everything else. It is not uncommon to see somebody with a three-piece suit now.

The war also toughens up the clubs and forces them to refine their operations. The benefits carry over to all club business. Strong intelligence and security networks set up during the war foil police attempts to stop drug and prostitution operations.

16

BOOBS, BOOBY TRAPS & BOMBS: THE HELL'S ANGELS INTELLIGENCE & SECURITY OPERATIONS

THE Hell's Angels—vagabonds of vice—forsake true freedom in 1973 and chain themselves to their fears: of death, of arrest, of losing their freedom. The Angels protect themselves from the world in 1948 by locking it out. Today, they lock themselves in their clubhouses. You can draw a white line across the living-room floor, but it sure ain't the open road.

Nothing exists outside an Angel's field of vision before 1973. Today, Angels see an enemy behind every friend. The ritual hugs they so often engage in when cameras are around reflect more than brotherly love. An Angel hugs to pat parts of the body where electronic devices can be hidden, usually the small of the back. Paranoid? You'd be paranoid too if everyone was out to get you.

Two years after they declare war on the Breed in Cleveland, and one year before they engage the Outlaws in mortal combat, the Angels add a security/intelligence officer to the club hierarchy. This spy answers to the president. The security officer is responsible for taking care of business: he collects and analyzes information; he devises ways to protect the organization and sets up hits; he gives club executioners, including prospects who try to prove themselves, detailed dossiers on victims with times and places to kill them. Albert Anastasia would be proud of today's Murder Inc.

The crude intelligence and security teams set up during the war with the Breed are refined during the ongoing war with the Outlaws. Clarence (Addie) Crouch, former vice-president of the Hell's Angels Cleveland chapter and participant in the fight that starts the Breed war, boasts of his club: "They have perfected their killing skills. They have perfected their intelligence. They have perfected everything."

The security/intelligence officer becomes crucial to the club's existence as the Angels evolve into a highly sophisticated criminal organization. He travels incognito under a variety of names, doesn't wear colors and is never seen near a clubhouse. He compiles photographs, descriptions, addresses, phone numbers, personal and financial information, and vehicle descriptions of rival club members, police officers, reporters, lawyers, judges, public officials and witnesses—anyone seen as a threat to the club. Dossiers include names and addresses of relatives, girlfriends and boyfriends. He even infiltrates rival clubs and sets up surveillance teams for Angel chapters that don't have their own intelligence officer. Many Hell's Angels learn intelligence gathering in the military, where they also are taught how to use weapons and make bombs.

A Cleveland Angel who owns a motorcycle shop computerizes the information kept on scraps of paper in 1980. He even keeps files on where Angels have done their mandatory hit.

The Hell's Angels know a lot of people [says Addie Crouch]. They call them spies. They bring them information on this or that, and they collect all their addresses and everything. And they have a saying in the Hell's Angels that came out in the paper a long time ago, about 1971 or so, that "A Hell's Angel has a memory like an elephant. He never forgets." So if they have a grievance with somebody, it never ends. Someday—they keep a record of everyone. They keep a record of a person, of families, the whole smear, addresses, types of cars, what girls they used to go with or whatever, bike clubs.

[The security/intelligence officer] is supplied with money from
the treasury for that specific reason from a TCB fund, which is
taking care of business. Everyone is assessed so much money for
this TCB fund [from $200 to $500, on top of weekly dues of $20].
The intelligence officer goes to different towns with another
member of the club, either his assistant—or he will send two
people from security or whatever, but he is in charge of all the
information gathering. They will rent cars, fly on planes, whatever, motel rooms, whatever, to watch specific clubs in towns like
Chicago, Detroit, Dayton, Florida, whatever, and gather information on them for a hit in the future.

James Ezekiel (Jim-Jim) Brandes, security officer of the
mother chapter in Oakland in the mid-1970s, has a file at
home that contains photographs of informants, undercover officers and special agents. It includes physical descriptions,
where they work and their schedules. He also has boxes of
documents obtained with the aid of the Freedom of Information Act. Bikers are no fools. *Easyriders*, one of the magazines that caters to them, runs a two-part story in 1979 on the
FOI Act. It describes how the law works, how to get copies of
the legislation and how to request government records.

Brandes is an amateur interior decorator. He snuffs an
eagle with a pellet gun, stuffs it with the insides of a Volks-
wagen seat and perches it on a rafter in his living room high
above the dark hardwood floor. He cruises the streets in his
dark Lincoln Continental doing business at 5 p.m., November
14, 1977. The car is equipped with a police radio with frequencies from Reno to Fresno, a radio-band directory, a radio
transmitter smaller than a cigarette pack, a bug detector, a
pocket-size tape recorder, a homemade police siren and a blue
flasher, a 233-page photocopy of a military book on booby
traps, and an address book that includes the address, telephone
number and licence-plate number of William Zerby, a police
inspector who dogs him.

William (Wild Bill) Medeiros, security officer of the Manhattan chapter in New York City until 1985, has a printed
membership application form that prospects fill out. He photographs them and finds out where their parents and family live.
The club wants leverage to prevent members from ratting—
and victims in case they do. Medeiros keeps files on prospects
in cardboard boxes at home. Files on members are kept in a

bank safety-deposit box. He also has maps that pinpoint Outlaw, Pagan and other rival motorcycle gang clubhouses as well as members' homes. A Florida map shows all Outlaw clubhouses, homes and bars club members frequent or own. The files contain detailed drawings of the inside of houses for hits.

The Hell's Angels try to get their information first hand—through theft, extortion or carnal bribes. The FOI lets them find out about investigations. Their old ladies work in prisons, welfare offices, public utilities, government offices and as telephone operators. They infiltrate police-department records offices, communications centers and criminal-investigation bureaus. They gather sensitive information through these jobs and collect personal information on anyone, including prospective members, who sometimes undergo lie-detector tests before they can join the club. You can't hide anything from the Angels.

Old ladies steal blank birth certificates, drivers licences and vehicle registration papers that are used to provide false identities for fugitive club members. Angel women who work in motor vehicle registration offices help process the paperwork to alter vehicle identification numbers of cars and motorcycles stolen by the gang. Those who work for telephone companies and in courthouses warn the gang about wiretaps. Old ladies hang out in bars where police officers drink and use their wiles to compromise them. One biker takes criminal justice college courses to cultivate police contacts. He dates the secretary for a state attorney general to find out about police activities.

Three Hell's Angels old ladies work for the telephone company in Rochester, New York, in 1980 and get home addresses of people the gang wants.

Angels photograph police officers and law enforcement agents outside their offices and homes. One biker calls law enforcement agencies around the country and says he is a police officer riding undercover with an outlaw motorcycle gang. He asks for the name of the officer working on area gangs, saying he would like to share information when he arrives in town. Sometimes he gets the name, sometimes he doesn't.

A New York State Police officer tries to find out in April 1987 how Brendan Manning, president of the Hell's Angels

Manhattan chapter, got a classified US Department of Treasury training manual on outlaw motorcycle gangs. The 1981 manual—*Dangerous MC Gangs*—is distributed only to law enforcement officials attending special agent courses at the Federal Law Enforcement Training Center in Georgia. An occasional copy is sometimes sent to law enforcement agencies after a request is made in writing on official letterhead.

An Angel old lady in Winston-Salem, North Carolina, complains to a police officer of being forced to fuck a bulldog. She offers to help him update his files on the club in revenge. He plays the game, but offers little information as she asks more and more questions. She goes straight to the clubhouse when she leaves the station.

The Hell's Angels hire a private investigator in Boston to do background checks on police officers and special agents involved in the arrest of more than 100 Hell's Angels and associates by the FBI on May 2, 1985. The former Israeli intelligence officer tries to uncover personal information to blackmail investigators to keep them from testifying or to discredit their testimony.

The Angels infiltrate conferences of motorcycle gang investigators. They get their women jobs in hotels as registration clerks or chamber maids, who can go through conference and personal papers left in rooms. Angels pose as tourists to photograph people at conferences. An intelligence bulletin warns motorcycle gang investigators who plan to attend a Toronto conference in the fall of 1985:

"Due to recent court decisions in Canada, prostitution is virtually legal, and many of these women may be biker old ladies."

The Hell's Angels stay in close contact with their brothers through a complex telephone tree. East and West Coast chapter presidents call their faction president between 7 and 8 p.m. weekly on a given night to update him on club business: who's in jail, who's a new member, problems with rival gangs and police, parties and other concerns. The day for the weekly phone call changes periodically. East Coast calls are made every Wednesday in 1985 and 1986. They are made on Mondays in 1980 and 1981. Chapter secretaries or treasurers call pre-designated chapters an hour later to exchange the information. All chapters know what their brothers are up to or up against within two hours.

Each chapter is also required to send a monthly letter to its regional office, which relays the information to chapters around the world in a newsletter. Here is an excerpt from the March 1985 newsletter that compiles messages from chapters around the world. Chapters that don't send the required monthly letter are penalized:

South Coast, England
... Harry got three years, his address is: H. Weir J91858, H.M.Prison, Ramsey Road, Winchester, Hampshire. That's all for now. South Coast.

London, England
Greetings all, Crazy Charlie has been sentenced to 18 months jail, so he's off the street for a year. We did a welcome to Englands new charter Lea Valley, and wish them the best of everything. Our Congrats to Oakland, Monterey, Paris and Brekshire Co. on their anniversaries this month. Also this month two officer changes a new Sec. as Snob has moved a little to the north, a new V.P. Mickey as Goatis [sic] in prison. Finally thanks to Wessex for their hospitality when we arrived with the mofo's. Respect Paul.

Goat: D. Price 258809, H.M.P. Wandsworth, P.O. Box 757 Heatfield Road, London SW 18 3H8. C. Charlie: C. Batten L33044, H.M.P. Highpoiont, Stradishall, Bury St. Edmonds, Newmarket Suffolk CB8 9YG.

Kent, England
No correspondence. $50 fine 28 days.

Wessex, England
DITO

Winsor, England
DITO

Tyne and Wear, England
DITO Arrived late, in next Newsletter.

Lea Valley, England
DITO Arrived late. Dear bro's, please about charter, everyone on road. Love and Respect Jim Sec.
Mail address: H A Jim, 145 Lea bank, Luton, Beds., England

Each chapter also sends out letters emblazoned with its personalized death angel's head. The Melbourne, Australia chapter sends this handwritten note to Quebec chapters on April 16, 1985, under the stamp of the club's Australian secretary. To the right of the letterhead is a feathered, toothed death's head over the initials A.F.F.A. —Angels Forever Forever Angels:

Hells Angels
Motorcycle Club
Melbourne
Australia
633 Heidelberg Road*
Fairfield, 3078,
Victoria,
Australia.
tel. 497-3104

Gooday Brothers,
    On behalf of all Melbourne members thank all chapters for their condolences at the death of our brother Lindsay. I've had requests for a photo of Lindsay which I am now working on which will be sent to all chapters A.S.A.P.
                                                            Love Jack:
    I would also like to inform everybody of the change of postal address for Australian sect. As of 16th April '85 it is as above address* which is Melbourne club house.
    Hello Bob.
    Just received your letter in regards to North. Thank you.
                                                            Love Jack

The reference to North means the chapter liquidated on March 24, 1985. Hell's Angels chapters around the world are quickly informed the chapter no longer exists, although the grisly details are kept secret for months. Club members know each other by name and exchange Christmas cards with group photographs and club insignia. The cards are functional as well as social—the photographs ensure police officers and rival bikers can't pass themselves off as Hell's Angels visiting from other chapters. The Angels place such a priority on intelligence gathering the club pays the telephone bills of five smaller outlaw motorcycle gangs to keep the information flowing. All Angel clubhouses are equipped with shortwave radios and top-quality aerials. They relay messages around the world at all times of day and night.

The clubhouse is the center of gang activity. Church, drug deals, motorcycle maintenance, parties, gang bangs, murders —if it's going to happen, it will happen in the clubhouse. These vary from chapter to chapter, with the Hell's Angels' clubhouses in Quebec being most fortified. Some are on city blocks, like that of the New York City Hell's Angels at 77 East Third Street. The Sherbrooke, Quebec, chapter in Len-

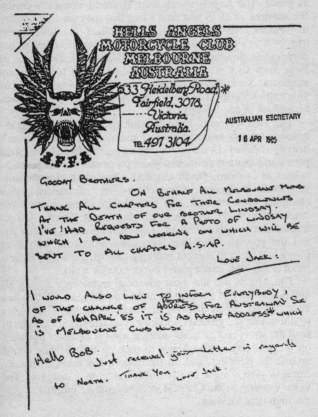

HELLS ANGELS
MOTORCYCLE CLUB
MELBOURNE
AUSTRALIA

633 Heidelberg Road *
Fairfield, 3078,
Victoria,
Australia.
TEL. 497 3104

AUSTRALIAN SECRETARY

1 6 APR 1985

J.F.F.B

GOODAY BROTHERS.

            ON BEHALF ALL MELBOURNE MEMB
THANK ALL CHAPTERS FOR THEIR CONDOLENCES
AT THE DEATH OF OUR BROTHER LINDSAY.
I'VE ! HAD REQUESTS FOR A PHOTO OF LINDSAY
WHICH I AM NOW WORKING ON WHICH WILL BE
SENT TO ALL CHAPTERS A.S.A.P.

                    LOVE JACK :

I WOULD ALSO LIKE TO INFORM EVERYBODY
OF THE CHANGE OF POSTAL ADDRESS FOR AUSTRALIAN. SO
AS OF 16th APRIL '85 IT IS AS ABOVE ADDRESS WHICH
IS MELBOURNE CLUB HOUSE

Hello BOB.
        Just received your letter in regards
to NORTH. THANK YOU   LOVE JACK.

noxville sits atop a knoll across from a river on the outskirts of town. Rural police are less equipped than city cops to gather intelligence on bikers, who get away with more in smaller towns.

Most Hell's Angels' clubhouses have signs that identify them as such. Their walls are adorned with Angel memorabilia, club photographs and pictures of funerals and dead members. Members, strikers or old ladies occupy the building 24 hours a day to prevent police from planting listening devices. Every member, regardless of status, must work his shift as guard. The Angels sweep their Montreal clubhouse during the summer of 1978 and find a bug that they proudly display to visitors. No one shows up to collect it. While most members live elsewhere, some clubhouses are designed to accommodate dozens of people. The Manhattan clubhouse in New York City is a tenement building which houses many members. Some Angels buy homes near the clubhouse to provide extra security. The Angels are trying to buy all the houses on a block in one US city.

The Hell's Angels learn through experience that a clubhouse is useless against police or enemy biker raids if it isn't heavily fortified. Doors and windows are reinforced with steel plates and shutters or mesh. Many properties—like the clubhouses in Durham, North Carolina, Charleston, South Carolina, and Bridgeport, Connecticut—are surrounded by a chainlink fence topped with barbed wire. Some clubs have cinderblock walls with gunports inside the fence. Attacktrained German shepherds or Doberman pinschers usually patrol the grounds. Building frames are reinforced with steel plates and mesh to prevent breaking through the walls. Bulletproof waist-high armor plates cover exterior walls.

The Angels use the most advanced technology among all outlaw motorcycle gangs at home and on the road. Clubhouses have burglar alarms that ring at members' homes, flood lights to illuminate the grounds, closed-circuit television cameras to scan the street and grounds, motion sensors to detect intruders on the property, microphones to pick up the slightest sound around the building, and, in Bridgeport, Connecticut, remote cameras give a view of the clubhouse from a distance. The video cameras in the Charleston clubhouse are infrared to permit nighttime viewing.

To stay one step ahead of the law, clubhouses are equipped with telephone scramblers, wiretaps, police radio frequency scanners, lists of police radio frequencies, tracking devices, radio jamming equipment, bugging and de-bugging equipment and sensors to detect body transmitters. Bearcat scanners not only allow them to monitor police frequencies, but alert Angels when someone around them wears a bug. Angels have their houses and clubhouses swept for bugs regularly. Albert Perryman and Howard Weisbrod, members of the Oakland chapter, have their houses swept on April 17, 1985.

Business conducted over the telephone is done with codes to foil wiretaps. The Angels use the RATS system—receiver adds, transmitter subtracts—to confuse listeners. The word *rats*, when used in conversation, is paired with a number. One Angel may describe how five Angels hang rats while the club's newest twat blows them in succession. One of the Angels gives the number of a safe phone later in the conversation. He subtracts five from each digit to protect the unbugged phone's number and the receiver adds five.

Important matters are dealt with eye to eye. A Montreal Angel flies across the continent to Vancouver in 1986 to deliver a message and returns on the next flight. The Hell's Angels spare no costs. When they have a problem, they send someone to deal with it—hands on TCB.

Angels learn how to use their high tech security toys in the military and in jail. As an added precaution, they post neighborhood sentries, including children, to watch for policemen and other bikers.

Despite these safeguards, the Angels (and other clubs) have an affinity for booby traps. The most archaic, yet revealing, trap is a poisonous snake, hidden in a drawer, on a shelf or in a box. Police seize 18 venomous snakes and a boa constrictor during a raid of five buildings that house Hell's Angels in Rochester, New York, on August 16, 1980. One Toronto man—not an Angel—illustrates the dink mentality among more Neanderthal bikers. He thinks a rattlesnake that slithers around the clubhouse is great protection. But the snake can't differentiate between members and intruders and one biker is bitten. A popular shelf trap is a pen, modified to fire a .22-calibre bullet, attached to a mousetrap. It fires when the trap is moved.

One of the most desperate traps is an incendiary bomb. A two-litre plastic bottle, one-third full of concentrated sulfuric acid mixed with two cups of gasoline, is leaned against a door. A tea bag filled with potassium chlorate granules hangs from a string above the solution. The tea bag touches the liquid and ignites the mixture when the bottle is knocked over.

Although Hell's Angels' clubhouses differ, what happens inside them is consistent from chapter to chapter. Here are glimpses inside Hell's Angels' clubhouses across North America:

President Ronald (Big Cheese) Cheeseman collects $7,000 from another Angel for a methamphethamine deal in the Binghamton, New York, clubhouse on February 8, 1984. The Angels keep a 3.5-inch rocket launcher, better known as a bazooka, in a steel safe at the back of the clubhouse.

Cheeseman and another Angel load three riot guns, 20 12-gauge shotguns, a large canvas bag full of .45-calibre automatic pistols, a box of four to six grenades, and 10 Uzi submachine guns from the Troy, New York, clubhouse on June 27, 1983, into a van going to a run.

Surveillance cameras are being installed to monitor activity outside the Durham, North Carolina, clubhouse on March 27, 1984. (By May 8, a surveillance television above the regular television shows what happens outside.) The club's arsenal included a semi-automatic sawed-off shotgun with infrared scope and an eight-round magazine, an Uzi submachine gun, four .45-calibre automatic handguns, three riot shotguns, one MAC-10 submachine gun, one Soviet-made AK-47 assault rifle, and rounds of hollow-point ammunition. James (Gorilla) Harwood, vice-president of the Troy, New York, chapter, is trying to get a LAW rocket for the Durham chapter. The thin metal, shoulder-mount firing tube and rocket is three-and-a-half feet long and costs the military about $75. It sells for $1,000 on the black market. A variety of weapons, including an M-60 machine gun on tripod, shotguns, and two cases of dynamite are stashed in a closet over the stairs, the sliding door of which is covered with an American flag. An M-79 grenade launcher sits on the living-room floor and automatic rifles and a nightscope are mounted on the wall on December 15.

The Charleston, South Carolina, clubhouse has five Uzi

submachine guns and two shotguns mounted on a rack in the bedroom of the main building on February 9, 1985. There's a shotgun behind the bar in the auxiliary building. Both buildings have burglar alarms and two fences around them. Two Doberman pinschers patrol the area between the fences. There are trip wires near the fences. Surveillance cameras feed a view of the grounds to monitors in many rooms, which have intercom systems. The doors are made of steel and concrete walls are reinforced with steel bars.

The Berkshire chapter clubhouse in Pittsfield-Lee, Massachusetts, has a trap door next to the steps that conceals the club's weapons cache on July 30, 1984.

Martin Pulver, former president of the Troy chapter, tells a man in the Bridgeport, Connecticut, clubhouse on February 19, 1984, he can automatically get his colors if he obtains a LAW rocket for the club or kills an Outlaw. Either incident should be verifiable through newspaper coverage. He says the club has a warehouse half full of automatic weapons. The one-story clubhouse in the middle of the block is surrounded by a chainlink fence and guarded by a dog. The home of Roger Mariani, chapter president, is protected by an alarm that rings at the clubhouse.

The San Francisco chapter clubhouse on May 1, 1982, is above Frisco Choppers, Inc., owned by chapter president Gary Kautzman. A wall switch near the counter on the first floor activates microphones that pick up conversations outside the building. There's a similar microphone in the second-floor meeting room.

A 3.5-inch rocket launcher hangs on the wall in a fourth-floor room of the six-story Manhattan chapter clubhouse in New York City on February 4, 1982.

The Cleveland, Ohio, clubhouse holds an anti-tank rocket, hand grenades, dynamite, an M-16 assault rifle, two submachine guns, shotguns and an automatic pistol on November 23, 1980. An Angel sells several hundred dollars worth of T-shirts in September 1983. The profits go into the club's defence fund to pay for legal expenses.

The San Diego clubhouse is stocked with machine guns, shotguns, more than 50 handguns, explosives, bomb manuals, torture kits, electronic eavesdropping equipment, police radio scanners and drugs in November 1980.

The Omaha chapter keeps 57 weapons, drugs, a human finger and a skull in its clubhouse in 1981.

The Hell's Angels Montreal chapter clubhouse in Sorel, Quebec, has signs warning "Enter at your own risk" and "No bozos allowed." Three video cameras mounted on the roof of the three-story building feed a view of the streets to a command center that is manned 24 hours a day. A 35-millimeter camera photographs the streets at regular intervals. Hidden microphones detect the slightest sounds and visitors are allowed through an electronically locked steel door once identified. Bull terriers roam the grounds and tinted bullet-proof glass covers all ground-floor windows. Sorel Police Chief Jean Lalonde says he is jealous. "See our old police station? They're equipped to the hilt. From their clubhouse, they can count at all times the number of cars in our parking lot."

The Sherbrooke chapter clubhouse in Lennoxville, Quebec, is surrounded with bear traps that can snap a man's leg off. Like other clubhouses, it is protected with sensor wires under the driveway, floodlights, burglar alarms, six guard dogs and closed-circuit television cameras mounted on posts. The building has secret rooms entered through electronically controlled panels. A front-end loader is needed to smash through the fortified steel doors during a dawn raid on April 11, 1985.

The workaholic Hell's Angels take their business home:

A pit bull terrier called Springs protects the Port Crane house of Ronald (Big Cheese) Cheeseman, president of the Binghamton, New York, chapter on July 14, 1983. Inside, Cheeseman shows the surgical gloves he wears to prevent leaving fingerprints on packages of drugs he weighs on a digital scale.

An Angel is given a list of FBI agents, a description of their cars and licence plate numbers, the channels they use and a schedule of their working hours in the Johnson City house of Kim DiLuzio, member of the Binghamton chapter, on February 9, 1984. A man who lives on the first floor of the building brings up an M-60 machine gun, a .357-calibre revolver, a .44 Magnum revolver, a silencer and a riot shotgun stamped with the emblem of the New York State Police.

James (Gorilla) Harwood shows off between 50 to 100 knives and swords and a new 9mm Smith and Wesson model

459 handgun in his Troy, New York, house on November 30, 1983. He keeps methamphetamine in the kitchen ceiling and a loaded semi-automatic AR-15 with bayonet nearby on August 29, 1984. He has a 3.5-inch rocket launcher hidden in the ceiling in an upstairs bedroom on January 17, 1985. A visiting Angel from Montreal is asked in Harwood's house on February 15, 1985, how his chapter avenges the killing of an Angel by the Outlaws. "We hit two."

The two-story single family home of Glenn (Hoppy) Main, president of the Lynn-Salem, Massachusetts, chapter is bullet-proofed with sheet metal placed inside the front walls on November 27, 1984. The chapter's computer is on the second floor.

The rural house of Phillip Utley, vice-president of the Durham, North Carolina, chapter is protected by several pit bulls on December 15, 1984. A gunrack near the front door holds five Uzi submachine guns and shotguns. Flashlights in the basement are stuffed with methamphetamine.

The house of Roger Mariani, president of the Bridgeport, Connecticut, chapter is protected by an alarm system that rings at the clubhouse on September 24, 1984. Plexiglass is mounted behind the regular glass windows. The house contains Hell's Angels memorabilia and a loaded M-16 rifle near the front door. One telephone has only one button labelled N.Y. City. He monitors the inside of the clubhouse through a five-inch television set.

The Hell's Angels worry about personal safety not only around the clubhouse, but also when they are on the road, especially in packs. Runs, more than any other biker activity, have engraved the Hell's Angels in the public imagination. Two hundred grinning Angels thundering down the highway will loosen anyone's sphincter and roll last night's snack down the tightest pant leg.

But scaring the masses ain't what it used to be. Business and war have taken the fun out of Angels outings. The foot-loose and fancy free bikers of yesterday plan runs for months to prevent ambushes. The Angels have to know they are secure before they can let loose. One or two members of each chapter's security team sits on the committee that prepares the run.

Some runs are mandatory and each chapter must ensure a

certain percentage of its members participate. Most long weekend runs in May, July, August and September, as well as world runs in which members from around the globe participate, are well attended and well protected.

Columns of motorcycles have always been accompanied by a crash truck or war wagon that contains drugs, weapons and beer—a two-four is tough to carry on a chopper. The van is driven by an Angel, an old lady or a striker, who keeps in touch with the club's road captain at the front of the pack through a CB radio.

Former Hell's Angel Clarence (Addie) Crouch, who has organized runs near Cody and Yankton, Wyoming, describes how the job is done.

Security sends out two people. They take all the electronic equipment out. They take booby traps—they have had booby traps around the camp. They have had shotgun mikes. Like, you just point it at a car that is sitting way away and listen to whatever somebody was saying, point it at their face.

They have twilight scopes, where they can see in the dark by starlight. They have FM radios that—they have their own crystals installed in them. In fact, they sent to Washington and got a chart of all the FM frequencies and then from that chart they could figure out which Government agency is on which frequency, and they got frequencies that would fit in between where no one is using these different frequencies so they are all on their own channel.

The run committee and the security people set up and secure the whole area for a good mile all the way around it, from the highest point or whatever. They set up different command posts all the way around it, which may be six or seven that are manned by prospects when they get there. It is manned by a member and a prospect all the way around.

They are all equipped with guns, silencers and they are all in touch with each other through radios. They use CBs around from those command posts, and they have a car running up and down the road. Then when each pack leaves from their home place or whatever—sometimes, two or three chapters will get together . . . whoever is up front will have one of the FM radios. Somebody in the back will have a mobil FM. And then there will be a chase car. And the chase car will have automatic weapons in it, and it will be a fast car following the pack. And there is usually a van.

Usually up under the van or the chase car they will have plates welded up under it for boxes to be installed to carry plastics, to carry grenades, to carry any kind of weaponry, and they set up the whole secure area there. And they guard the packs going out.

The Hell's Angels have a run in upstate New York in June 1984. Three Angels carry M-60 machine guns on slings and are prepared to mount them on tripods. One Angel has two shotguns and a duffel bag full of pistols in his truck. Another Angel carries an Uzi submachine gun and one biker walks around the grounds with a 9mm handgun. Two Angels kick the shit out of a car they wrongly believe to be an unmarked police car when the gang stops for refreshments on the way home. The car gives chase and an Angel shoots at it.

An Angel climbs a telephone pole during a June 1983 run and fixes a device to the wires that allows him to monitor, through equipment in a van, all calls from pay phones in the area. He also monitors frequencies of police agencies that conduct surveillance of the run, including those in helicopters.

Members of the Manhattan chapter on a May 1984 run to Myrtle Beach, South Carolina, are armed. The Quebec Hell's Angels on a run through Nova Scotia in August that year carry shotguns with fold-away stocks.

The public rarely gets a glimpse of the security precautions taken by the Hell's Angels during runs. The club holds its August 1982 10-day National Run in the Officers Gulch campground in the Arapaho National Forest, four miles west of Frisco, Colorado. Police close airspace for a two-mile radius over the campground. They distribute an advisory to local newspapers that warns residents not to worry. It also alerts them not to pick up hitchhikers and to stay away from the Hell's Angels' camp—many members have been arrested for murder and rape.

Remember, there will be no one to protect an outsider from this gang. . . . People who have a problem with any of the bikers [should] call police immediately. DO NOT TRY TO HANDLE THE SITUATION YOURSELF.

The Angels arrive with their saintly image.
"We're here on vacation," Al Abono, president of the Richmond, California, chapter says. "A lot of us are married

and have kids. We just want to have a good time and ride our bikes."

An Angel called Indian, who has been with the Richmond chapter for 10 years, adds:

> Once a year we try and all get together. There are some brothers from the East Coast—I've seen their kids grow up at these and I'm looking forward to seeing them again. I've gotten older, a little more mellow, do a lot more fishing. I've been talking to fishermen here and I've got some real good spots located. Hey, I'm not going to tell you we're Boy Scouts. If somebody pushes on my chest, I'm going to push back.

The Angels schedule a softball game with local firemen. The Rotary Club makes it known it will approach members to donate blood. The Angels don't fuss even when someone shoots Big John Strasser in the back with a shotgun as he rides along a side road.

The bravest residents are those who make money from the run.

"Hey, I'm not really worried," Bill Dickson, owner of Smokin' Willy's Restaurant, says. "I've met some of these guys and they're real gentlemen. I think these guys are different than they were 13 or 14 years ago. They're a lot older, for one."

Dickson feeds 100 Angels twice a day—$10 a meal.

Ben Fogle, president of the Frisco Chamber of Commerce, illustrates the power of money and its ability to sway feelings toward the Hell's Angels.

> A few people always get bent out of shape. But if everybody keeps an open mind, things will be OK. These people have to buy food and fuel and pay cash. Any time you can get cash over the counter, you can't beat that.

The Hell's Angels pay the best lawyers to keep them out of court and jail. When legal recourses fail, they protect themselves from prosecution by intimidating police investigators, potential witnesses, judges, lawyers and reporters. Scaring people is a fine art that the Angels, in all their crassness, have mastered. Judge David Dowd orders Hell's Angels attending the trial of two club members charged with 12 counts of possessing grenades, automatic weapons and an anti-tank rocket to wear ties and suits or jackets in US District Court in Cleveland on November 1, 1983. Old ladies must also dress properly to avoid intimidating jurors. A woman juror is excused during the 1982 murder trial in Toledo of Hell's Angel Jack Gentry after her son is approached in a bar and told his mother knows "how to vote" on the case. Gentry is acquitted of murdering an Outlaw.

The lawyer who defends Hell's Angel Douglas (Sluggo) Fellows on a charge of involuntary manslaughter in the March 1978 slashing of another biker's throat doesn't like the local newspaper reporter's accounts of the trial. David Weiner complains to Yolo County Superior Court Judge James C. McDermott while the jury is out to lunch on August 30 that a story by George Thurlow in the Woodland, California, *Daily Democrat* is erroneous and biased in favor of the prosecution. The tall, thin Thurlow covers the story since the discovery of the victim's body. The judge says he'll instruct the jury not to read newspapers. When the trial resumes, he orders all potential witnesses out of the courtroom—a normal practice that ensures witnesses are not influenced by the testimony of others. Wiener surprises the court. He announces he plans to call Thurlow as a witness, forcing the reporter out of the courtroom for the rest of the trial. Thurlow is never called to the stand.

The US Hell's Angels are scared shitless of the Racketeer-Influenced and Corrupt Organizations (RICO) statute, although they are organized to prevent prosecutions under the act. (There is no similar law in Canada.) Justice officials use the law in attacks on the club, to show members don't commit crimes independently, but operate as a gang. Although major RICO cases against the Angels have failed, the club fears a solid investigation can wipe out entire chapters. Angels have been ordered, as a precaution, to get their act together: pay taxes and get phony papers to prove they have jobs. The Angels pay companies to "deduct" income taxes from their "salaries." Lawyers advise the club how to prevent prosecution under the RICO statute, how to prevent police from linking criminal activities to the gang.

Every Hell's Angel in the US is assessed a $250 defence fund fee when the lawyer who defends the Hell's Angels at the

RICO trials in California in 1979 and the early 1980s is sent to Nebraska to defend the Omaha chapter on similar charges. Angels from all chapters travel to Omaha on a rotational basis to ensure the lawyer has two bodyguards 24 hours a day. The club is worried that Outlaws from Minnesota will hit the lawyer and cause the Angels to lose the case.

If intimidation doesn't work, death does. The Hell's Angels code of retribution knows no mercy. Angels kill witnesses and suspected informants. They also murder each other. Disagreements end in death rather than beatings when big business supplants brotherhood in the Hell's Angels. Because the club's vast criminal empire is built on fear, the only way out of the Hell's Angels is death. A member can't quit; he knows too much. The Hell's Angels, like traditional organized crime, is a job from which you don't retire. The Angels don't trust anyone out of gun range. The occasional member who is allowed to walk away is closely watched for flagging allegiance to the organization. George (Baby Huey) Wethern, vice-president of the Oakland chapter and best friend to Sonny Barger who recruits him in 1958, tires of the pace in 1969. The club's top psychedelics distributor, who makes as much as $200,000 a year selling acid made by LSD King Augustus Owsley Stanley III, retires with his wife to a farm. The Angels drop in and ask a favor. Sure, he says. And two bodies are buried in a well near his house. A third body is found in the same well when police raid the farm on a tip.

No one can count the Angels killed by Angels. The 1965 murder of Gary Kefauver is the first recorded killing of a Hell's Angel by the club. Fellow members in the Oakland chapter accuse Kefauver of ratting to police in a case that doesn't involve the club. There's no place for weakness in a man's world. They trick Kefauver into putting on thumb cuffs, kill him, and dump his body in the countryside.

Paul (German) Ingalls, a 21-year-old member of the Oakland chapter who transfered from Omaha, Nebraska, is accused by the club on February 1, 1968, of stealing Sonny Barger's coin collection. He is forced to swallow barbiturates and taken home where he dies.

The Nomad chapter in Vallejo, California, goes through a succession of presidents more quickly than shit through a junkie in the mid-1970s. One president dies in a shoot-out during which he murders drug dealer Gail English, who allegedly encroaches on Angel Kenny Owen's territory in 1973. Members fear his successor, Tom DeWilde, has fried his brain with methamphetamine. He can feed police damning information on the club's operations if he panics and rolls over after a bust. They weld him inside a 55-gallon drum and dump him into Oakland Bay. Dennis Mehyre also doesn't last long. No one outside a few club members knows where to plant his tombstone. The bad luck streak ends at three. Kenny Owen, the next president, is still alive.

Members of the Hell's Angels San Francisco chapter further south also exercise their outlaw democratic right and oust an anachronistic president. Harold (Harry the Horse) Flamburis is accustomed to having things his way after living most of his 37 years as an Angel. The hardworking night longshoreman even shoots at neighbors who disturb his daytime naps. Flamburis is an old-time Angel, a fighter and boozer who sees no need for the club to get involved in peddling drugs and pussy. Flamburis and his 21-year-old girlfriend Dannette Barrett are shot in the head with a .22-calibre pistol fired through a pillow on January 6, 1977. His motorcycle is lowered into the grave a month after he is buried. (Flash) Gordon Grow, a marketer of meat, takes over the chapter.

Morris A. Womble, a 28-year-old Angel in line to become president of the Durham, North Carolina, chapter, disappears in 1980. The Angels say he's in Alaska.

James (J.J.) Johnson, a 27-year-old member of the Hell's Angels Manhattan chapter, helps hijack a gun shipment in the Carolinas in 1981. Agents of the US Bureau of Alcohol, Tobacco and Firearms seize the weapons near his Staten Island home and figure the Angels are involved in the heist. An ATF agent interviews Johnson and tries to get him to roll over. The club hears about it. Members ride up to Johnson's house and see him talking to the agent in the kitchen. Johnson tells them he's just bullshitting to keep the ATF off his back. One Angel who doesn't like Johnson brands him a weak link in the club and gets on his case at church.

The opportunities to abuse Johnson quickly run out. New York City police find him floating in Battery Park in Sep-

tember 1981. His head, arms and legs are sliced off with a
chain saw. His back pack—the club colors tattooed on his
back—is carved off. Police search for the missing body parts.
They find the head with a deep rip in the forehead.

Michael Franklin (Thunder) Finazzo, 40-year-old president
of the Hell's Angels Charlotte, North Carolina, chapter, is a
national powerhouse in 1981. Finazzo, a member of the Filthy
Few, is a charter member of the Omaha, Nebraska, chapter on
November 27, 1966. He travels to North Carolina with two
other Angels and forms the Charlotte chapter on October 19,
1978, when he takes over the Tar Heel Stompers and turfs out
president Johnny Edsel High. Finazzo tightens up security and
controls club prostitution.
   Someone in the hierarchy thinks Finazzo is too powerful.
A hit team is dispatched. Finazzo refuses to kneel before his
executioners in September 1981. Someone lashes out and
breaks both bones in his lower left leg. Finazzo crumples and
takes a 9mm bullet in the back of the head. Tyler Duris (Yank)
Frndak dies at his boss's side with three bullets in the brain.
The bodies are stuffed in the trunk of a new blue Oldsmobile
88. Their heads are wrapped in plastic to prevent blood from
dripping. More than 100 Angels fly the colors down Main
Street in Marshville, North Carolina, when they escort the
hearses to the cemetery on October 1.

William Ivan Grondalski quits the Hell's Angels in northern California in June 1986 to keep his family together when
his wife files for divorce. He regrets the pain he causes his
family during his two years in the club. Grondalski loads the
tow truck and drives north to Fort Bragg with his 34-year-old
wife Patricia, their five-year old daughter Dallas and his 17-
year-old stepson Jeremy. They live in a trailer at Westport-
Union Landing state beach, 19 miles north of Fort Bragg.
Bikers harass them. He rents a house on September 24 that
local woodsman Juan Gonzales has just bought at an estate
auction. Neighbors hear a popping sound and see flames lick
out the windows on Monday, October 6. The coroner finds
bullet holes in all bodies but the 33-year-old Grondalski's—
he's too charred. An X-ray finds the bullets. The Angels
found him.

(Hippie) Richard Asbury, an Angel hanger-on, pisses off four Oakland members, including 280-pound Thomas (Big Red) Bryant and Richard Robles in 1975. Bryant's nerves are frayed after three years as an Angel. He answers the door armed with a pistol and shoots spiders off the wall. The Angels beat Asbury so badly they think he is dead. They load him into the trunk of a car and drive to a rural area to dump the body. Asbury pleads for his life on his knees in the middle of a dirt road when Robles pumps four bullets into him.

Donald Krosky, the 48-year-old manager of the Village Cafe in the Sandy Hook section of Newtown, Connecticut, shoots and kills Frank D'Amato, 23, and Salvatore Saffioti, 34, of the Hell's Angels Bridgeport chapter as they break into the bar on July 31, 1975. He wounds a third Angel, 28-year-old Donald Meredith. The bullet-riddled body of Bruce Meyer of Brewster, New York, is found outside Krosky's apartment on December 14. He receives a letter: "You're next." Krosky gets into his car with a woman in his home town of Trumbull on July 19, 1976. Smeone puts a shotgun to the window and blows him away. Two men walk into the Lakeville Restaurant in Bridgeport at 12:25 a.m. on October 5, 1977. One man calls Meredith, president of the Bridgeport chapter, a name and shoots him in the head. He also shoots Russell Kutzer, 25. The second man stabs both Angels.

W.T. Ferguson sets up a robbery for the Hell's Angels in North Carolina in February 1980. He agrees on February 22 to help the cops nab the Angels after they put pressure on him. He disappears on February 26.

Anyone who crosses the Hell's Angels risks death. Margo Edith Compton is tired of being stomped by her husband at the height of the disco decade. She pleads for help and grabs the first extended hand. Her guardian is Angel Odis (Buck) Garrett of California's Nomad chapter in Vallejo. He tells Compton she's in good hands, pumps her full of drugs and makes her work as a prostitute at The Love Nest massage parlor in San Francisco to pay off her protection fee. Garrett runs the parlor with (Flash) Gordon Grow, president of the San Francisco chapter.

A customer rapes and beats Compton in 1976. She wants out, but Garrett says she owes him $4,000 for protection and amphetamines. Compton violates the Hell's Angels code: she tells the police four women who work The Love Nest have to pay the Angels 40 percent of their earnings. Two vice officers with San Francisco police protect the business for cash and pussy, she says.

Local and state police promise to protect Compton, who testifies against Garrett and his associates on prostitution charges. Compton is relocated in the Oregon village of Laurelwood with her twin six-year-old daughters. The 25-year-old woman avoids neighbors and keeps her daughters in the house as she spends the winter of 1976 writing a book on her life with the Hell's Angels—with names, places and incidents.

Compton and her daughters start a new life with the Oregon spring. The kids make friends and she lets word slip out she's on the run from the Angels. Compton sits in the cottage talking with a 19-year-old member of the US Coast Guard on August 7, 1977, two weeks before she has to testify again. The twins are asleep, face down in their beds. Two men walk in. Compton is shot once behind the ear with a .22-calibre pistol. Three more shots are fired. The men leave four bodies and Compton's .357 Magnum revolver behind.

Compton's mistake: she writes to relatives in Vallejo. The Angels intercept the letter and send hit men from the Oakland chapter to the return address.

The Hell's Angels Motorcycle Club in its early days, before drug trafficking, prostitution and the paranoia big business engenders, has an easy-going relationship with police officers. They bust the punks for drunkenness, rowdyism, hooliganism and whatever else greaseballs do. The punks, in return, respect the authority of the badge and hold no grudge against a man who does his job. Outlaw bikers and cops, after all, are just different sides of the same law. Both groups wear uniforms, speak their own lingo and admire power in man and machine. Neither would be caught dead holding a liberal attitude. And not even God can save the first pinko Commie who tries to change their way of life.

The Hell's Angels take the shit kickings and move on until they acquire material goods the police can deprive them of. They play dirty when the heat threatens their livelihood and the newly found comfort easy money brings.

Inspector William O. Zerby of the Solano County Bureau of Narcotics Enforcement is a pain in the ass for the Hell's Angels from 1976 to 1978. Zerby follows them everywhere. He helps arrest Jim-Jim Brandes, for the Oakland chapter, and Kenny Owen, president of the Vallejo chapter, and other Angels and associates 17 times in two years. Zerby heads to the Fairfield Municipal Court for Brandes' pre-trial hearing on charges of possessing methamphetamine on Monday, January 30, 1978. Zerby is cautious. The car of San Jose Police Sergeant John Kracht blows up in the drive when he backs over a pressure-sensitive bomb the Hell's Angels plant in 1977. Zerby walks around his black and green Mercury Montego, parked by the curb, and looks for bombs. Nothing. He opens the door. A remote-control dynamite bomb explodes in a tangle of ivy two feet behind him. He lives, but loses nearly all his hearing.

An undercover investigator with the San Diego County district attorney's office participates in the arrest of 20 Hell's Angels on October 7, 1977, on charges of attempted murder, false imprisonment, possession of illegal weapons and drugs. Two Hell's Angels prospects are arrested as they watch his Poway house in San Diego County on February 27, 1978. They have binoculars, a description of the man, a machine gun and a silencer-equipped pistol.

Someone leaves a bomb on the porch of Sheriff C.L. Waldrep's Gaston County, North Carolina, house on April 9, 1979. Jeffrey Thompson, of Kings Mountain, identifies the man from police photographs as William (Spook) Sosebee, a 28-year-old Charlotte Angel. Thompson's friend receives a phone call:

"You tell him if he picks Sosebee from a lineup we're going to kill his mother."

Thompson's memory fails during the lineup.

"All patrols should be made aware that Hell's Angels members are said to be armed with various deadly weapons, including firearms, and most are known to carry ball-peen hammers in a sheath at their sides."—New York State police bulletin dated October 21, 1985.

* * *

The Hell's Angels have legitimate, but not legal, reasons to carry guns. They deal with traditional organized crime families, other outlaw motorcycle gangs, Colombian and Cuban cocaine cowboys, pimps, pushers, drug addicts, and victims from all walks of life. Even Nancy Reagan keeps a pearl-handled revolver at her bedside, and the only man she sees in that room is the President.

The Hell's Angels carry drugs and money. They have enemies. Idle threats don't mean anything in a dispute over territory, whether it's to sell drugs or pussy. A biker has to show he's willing to take care of business. And the Angels are nearly always armed. If an Angel doesn't carry a knife or handgun in his pockets, boots or belt, an old lady who stands nearby will hand it to him. Most Angels wear bullet-proof vests of better quality than those worn by police officers.

Military contacts and gun runners provide the Angels with machine guns, such as M-16s and Uzis, pineapple, M-26 and M-27 grenades, C-4 plastic explosives with adhesive backing, TNT demolition blocks, hand-held Light Anti-Tank Weapons (LAW rockets) that can pierce 12 inches of steel, and Claymore mines. They steal dynamite from construction sites. Club gunsmiths convert semi-automatic pistols and rifles to fully-automatic fire. Angels like to fit their guns with silencers they make in their own factories. Sergey (Sir Gay) Walton, former president of the Oakland chapter and one of the five most powerful Angels in California, escapes from a San Francisco jail in March 1981, while he waits to be taken to a federal penitentiary to serve a sentence for firearms violations. He is caught in May armed with a stolen military rifle, two pistols converted to fully automatic fire and a stolen 9mm pistol— bought from two local gun runners.

Robert Leclerc, 39, is charged in Miami on January 29, 1987, with conspiring to buy rockets, rocket launchers, grenades, automatic weapons and plastic explosives for the Montreal Hell's Angels and Columbian buyers. A US Customs agent testifies seeing Leclerc pay $29,000 and a kilo of cocaine for the weapons.

The Hell's Angels Charlotte, North Carolina, chapter hides its weapons in a Rent-a-Space mini warehouse near Interstate

77 in Rock Hill, South Carolina, in July 1982. The booby-trappd stash contains bombs made of C-4 military plastic explosives, grenades, fully automatic and silencer-equipped MAC-10 and AR-15 machine guns, and ammunition.

The Charlotte Angels also have one of two East Coast arsenals in 1981. The "Hotel" on the banks of the Catawba River in Mecklenburg County contains every weapon imaginable, from grenades to LAW rockets in greater quantities than regular club arms stashes. Armed guards protect the white, brick-front Victorian building 24 hours a day. Visiting Angels and prostitutes stay at the house, but motorcycles, colors and anything else that can identify the club are not allowed in the area. Visitors are blindfolded.

The MAC-10 and Uzi grease guns are the Hell's Angels' preferred war weapons. Both guns are compact and combat proven. The Uzi Model B, the world's most respected weapon, is made by Israel Military Industries and sells for $429 to $460. It fires 600 9mm-calibre bullets a minute. The MAC-10, made by S.W.D. Inc., fires 1,100 9mm or .45-calibre bullets a minute. It costs $289. Most Angel MAC-10s are bought legally as the SM-10 semi-automatic version. The difference: a MAC-10 empties a 30-shot magazine in three seconds; it takes the SM-10 five seconds. Semi-automatic guns are easily converted to fully automatic fire with conversion kits. The SM-10 converts in one minute. The AR-15, the civilian semi-automatic version of the military's M-16, is made into a machine gun with a seven-piece mail-order conversion kit and an illegal two-inch Z-shaped piece of metal called a drop-in auto sear. Angels who are Vietnam vets experienced with the M-16 prefer the converted AR-15, made by Colt Industries. It fires 650 .223-calibre bullets a minute. Angels load their guns, when possible, with exploding bullets and Teflon-coated "cop killer" bullets that slide through steel.

The favorite Hell's Angels assassination weapon is a .22-calibre pistol with silencer. The light bullet distorts as it ricochets around the skull or off bones, making ballistics tests impossible and the gun untraceable.

The Angels have homemade weapons that police officers will never find during a search of cars or vans. They make shotguns with the regular lug wrench found in the trunk of any car by adding a hollow extension into which they slip a 410-guage shotgun shell. A firing pin is welded to the tip of the original wrench. The gun is fired when the pieces are fitted and slammed together. Angels also rig modified shotguns in the door panels of vans and cars. The door is opened slightly and aimed at a policeman who stops the vehicle. A tug on a wire blows him away.

The Vietnam War has provided the Angels with experienced demolition experts who make their bombs. Pipe bombs are among the simplest bombs used by the Hell's Angels. They can be sealed tubes filled with matchheads and ignited with a fuse, or they can be powder-filled and detonated electronically. Tubes are scored to produce shrapnel when they explode, or BBs are glued to the outside to increase the chance of injuring someone.

A time bomb is made of dynamite with blasting caps, a clock and a six-volt flashlight battery. Fuses are wired in parallel to the battery and wires are fastened with alligator clips to the clock hands. The circuit is completed when the hands meet and the clips touch. BOOM.

A remote-control bomb is triggered by a servo motor used in remote-controlled planes to manipulate rudder and landing gear from the ground. The transmitter allows someone to detonate a bomb on cue. A former Manhattan chapter Angel, now a member of the New York Nomad chapter, teaches members across the US how to handle explosives.

Electronic gizmos aside, these weapons are the Hell's Angels' security. All Angels can use them, but they are mainly the tools of the club's killers: the Filthy Few.

17

THE FILTHY FEW, THE MAD
BUMPER & POGO

Three can keep a secret if two are dead.
— Hell's Angels motto.

We has met the enemy, and it is us.
— Walt Kelly's Pogo.

THE Filthy Few are born in the throttle, throb, thunder of the gang bang, chain-whip days when Angels party until the beer stash and gonads run dry. The Filthy Few prove themselves to be Hell's Angels above and beyond the rest. They are the club's ultimate party animals: the first to arrive and the last to leave.

The original Filthy Few collect dirt like the inside of a foreskin. They're the boys with furze on their teeth and chunks of shit caked to hair around their assholes. These putrid few prepare campsites for runs before the pack hits the road. They chop wood and haul water. They dig trenches and set up tents. They can make a whore gag at 50 feet.

The requirements to earn a Filthy Few patch or tattoo change when the Angels go to war in the 1970s. The status is now won with a display of courage.

"Let's go out and do some Outlaws," someone suggests in an East Coast clubhouse. A contingent of volunteer Angels

275

takes off for Sturgis, South Dakota, where the enemy Outlaws are expected to party. It's a suicide mission. The odds of getting beaten and killed are great. Although the Outlaws leave before the Angels arrive, every Angel on that run gets a Filthy Few tattoo.

Many chapters—including Bridgeport, Manhattan, Cleveland and those in Quebec—issue the Filthy Few tattoo to members who display courage by killing. The Filthy Few are not a team of hit men, just a grisly group of killers, some who murder for the club, some who don't.

"We don't have a hit team. We're all capable of doing that," William (Wild Bill) Medeiros, charter member and former security officer of the Manhattan chapter, says.

Hell's Angel hit men have double Nazi lightning bolts tattooed underneath the words Filthy Few. Some Angels tattoo skulls around the words Filthy Few for each Outlaw hit.

The Hell's Angels claim to be egalitarian. Any Angel can kill. Any Angel can be chapter president. All Angels are great in bed. But as any old lady knows, some Angels are more equal than others. John (Pirate) Miller, charter member of the Bridgeport, Connecticut, chapter and former sergeant-at-arms of the Manhattan chapter, issues the Filthy Few patches for all East Coast Angels until 1985. The cold-blooded Quebec Angels are his best customers.

I'd keep a stack of Filthy Few patches for the crazy Canadians. They'd come down here and tell us how many Outlaws they killed.—"I killed an Outlaw. Give me a Filthy Few patch."—I didn't ever ask questions. If they said they got the Filthy Few, I gave the patch to them.

Canadians came down for a party and said in broken English: "I don't unerstan. Up dere we do Outlaws. We take care of business. We don't hear you people in de States doing dat."

One Quebec Hell's Angel is recognized worldwide as the most ruthless and formidable hitman in the club: Yves (Apache) Trudeau. The five-foot-six, 135-pound psychopath carves his way into underworld legend with bullets, bombs and a strangler's hands strengthened by a primal lust for death. Trudeau's soul is a relic of pre-moral, pre-social, pre-literate man. How it gets into a 20th-century body is anyone's guess. Trudeau's birth on April 2, 1946, is nature's vicious afterthought and cruel joke.

Yves (Apache) Trudeau is the first Canadian Angel to be recognized as a club killer.

"Sonny Barger himself gave me my Filthy Few," he boasts.

Apache Trudeau is the ultimate Hell's Angel. He takes care of business efficiently and ruthlessly. The police have no proof, until he confesses, that he murders. Yet, there is an old entry in Trudeau's police record in Quebec: *tueur a gages*— hit man.

The dark-haired, square-jawed, handsome biker is the most prolific Canadian killer known. He murders 43 people from September 1970 to July 7, 1985. Twenty-nine victims are shot, 10 are blown up, three are beaten to death and one is strangled. Most of the killings—38—are committed after September 1978. Two are cases of mistaken identity: Biker William Weichold is mistaken for an Outlaw on December 8, 1978 and shot outside a Greenfield Park house. Truck driver Robert Morin borrows a friend's car on Darling Street in Montreal on March 14, 1981. The car is rigged with a bomb crafted with knowledge a younger Trudeau picks up working in a CIL plant.

"I became somewhat of an expert with explosives," he says with a lipless smile.

The scrawny hit man plans each killing meticulously. He often befriends targets to learn their habits and ices them when they least expect it. His cold-blooded professionalism earns him the nickname The Mad Bumper in Montreal's underworld. He takes care of business for the Angels, he takes care of business for Montreal's West End Gang, which pays him in cash and drugs, and he takes care of business for himself.

Many victims are part of Montreal's competitive and treacherous drug enterprises. An associate of three men who make and sell diazepam to US druggies gives Trudeau a contract to kill his partners in 1983. André Forget, 34, is shot on May 7 while he pumps gas at a self-serve station in east end Montreal. Hold-up artist Ronald Bernard, 42, is shot on July 7 in north Montreal. Raymond Filion, 42, is shot outside his sister's house in Laval on October 10.

Paul April, whom Trudeau later kills with a bomb, gives the hit man a contract to ice drug dealer Phillipe Galipeau in 1984. He shoots the 37-year-old man and his 21-year-old girl-friend, Rachelle Francoeur, in their rue Cartier house. Another girlfriend is in the wrong place on Mother's Day, May 9,

1981, when Trudeau wastes drug dealer Donat Lemieux and Lucille Vallières on their porch in Rosemont.

The Hell's Angels kill fearlessly and indiscriminately. They worry Michel Desormiers, son-in-law of reputed Montreal underworld godfather Santos (Frank) Cotroni, will leak information on a quadruple murder by the club for which he drives the getaway car. Trudeau clears the killing with appropriate members of the Cotroni organized crime family. Desormiers, 39, is shot on July 15, 1983, at his home in Deux-Montagnes.

Apache Trudeau epitomizes the success and failure of Hell's Angels. His fearlessness and ability to take care of business are attributes on which the club's power is based. His lack of conscience and willingness to execute brother Angels for violating club rules or hurting club income makes the club vulnerable to defections. Trudeau himself, the most dedicated and exemplary Angel by original standards, falls prey to the club's calculated venture into big business and its savage pursuit of the bottom line.

An uncomfortable feeling gnaws at his gut when he finds out the Montreal chapter marks him for death in 1985 because of his addiction to cocaine, his inclination to kill on impulse and the North chapter's derelict bookkeeping. Apache Trudeau learns the fear of being on the Hell's Angels' hit list. Few escape the wrath of the Angels. Trudeau's status in the club makes him a lucky man. The police offer to protect him in return for information on the club. Quebec police aren't competent enough to nail him for even one of his 43 killings. They tell justice officials that the killings will remain unsolved without Trudeau's cooperation and convince them to reduce the murder charges to manslaughter offences, which means the killings are not intentional. Apache Trudeau, in return, answers questions about the Hell's Angels and Montreal's underworld: a who's who and who done what to who and why. The hit man also fingers 95 other murderers, 34 who are already in the ground.

Trudeau lives in a fourth-floor cell in Montreal's Parathenais jail equipped with bath, shower and color TV. He eats steak and gets $35 a week for cigarettes. The Quebec Government deposits $10,000 a year into his trust fund. Four cops escort him to his common-law wife's three-bedroom house every two weeks for servicing. Apache Trudeau will be a free man in 1991 when his seven-year sentence for 43 manslaughter convictions is served.

Apache Trudeau, with his hair neatly trimmed and his Fu-Manchu moustache shaved off, looks respectable and safe—until you look into his eyes, where the sparkle of life has been supplanted by the dull gleam of death. Trudeau walks by 14 Hell's Angels in a plexiglass booth during the 1985 inquest into the five St. Lawrence River stiffs. He pauses in front of the men who put a contract on his life, extends his gold-banded pinkies, shapes an imaginary submachine gun and sprays them with bullets. Everyone laughs. He is safe from them and they are safe from him.

Apache Trudeau epitomizes the Hell's Angels as they become ruthless killers in the 1970s and 1980s. Death is no longer a form of punishment or business security for the club, but a paranoid end in itself. The taste of blood makes killing easy for many Angels. It even overrides the bond of brotherhood as a suspicious club periodically purges itself of suspect members.

The Hell's Angels wield death out of fear. Killing gives them power, but also weakens the organization. It creates a climate of terror that turns against the club Angels who are true to its decades-old creed. Apache Trudeau, William (Wild Bill) Medeiros, John (Pirate) Miller, James (Gorilla) Harwood and Gilles (Le Nez) Lachance are among dozens of Hell's Angels who flee the butchery for the safety of prison and, later, new lives in the counterfeit world of protected witnesses. The Hell's Angels are their own worst enemy.

Clarence (Addie) Crouch at 43, after 14 years as a Hell's Angel in Cleveland, Ohio:

> I joined because of a brotherhood, and I thought it was a good idea. There are always a lot of theories. Everyone had different theories about it. It was all the same thing—we were all one family, one big brotherhood, we would all stay together. Our kids would be Hell's Angels and this and that.
>
> There are some members that are 60-something years old and their kids are Hell's Angels now. You know, it was something that we would all grow old and be proud of—and our brotherhood—but after we got into the war [with the Outlaws] and then after the senseless killing of women and children, numerous times, women getting killed and everything, it just kind of tore at the whole, and

then people got into drugs really heavy and the dealing of drugs. They accumulated big money.

They had different ideas. After *The Godfather* movie and everything, it kind of evolved all into just one big organization for profit. They got away from the brotherhood, the whole thing of it, and now it is nothing to kill somebody. There is no fist fighting anymore. If you are in a bar, or something like that, and some drunk jumps on you, or something like that, or you get mad at somebody, they do not like, they used to just fist fight with him. They will just wait—push him off or something—and then wait and shoot him.

It is killing now. It is not fist fighting. All the honor, all the dignity has gone out of it, and everyone knows, but everyone just keeps holding on hoping for a better day, which the better day just keeps getting worse and worse and worse.

INDEX

ABOUT THE AUTHOR

Yves Lavigne was a reporter with *The Toronto Globe & Mail* for over a decade. Since 1977, he has delved into many aspects of crime: the Miami riots of 1980, the Asian mafia, and the illicit sale of prescription drugs in Canada, among others.